"Walker's splendid book res
the culture wars and locates
many readers by surprise: the
and eye-opening, *Liberty for All* is essential reading for Americans
seeking to understand the deepest cultural currents of our time—
including those of different creeds, and those with no creed at all."

—Mary Eberstadt, author of *Primal Screams: How
the Sexual Revolution Created Identity Politics*
and *How the West Really Lost God*

"Religious liberty is not, first and foremost, a constitutional right.
The great contribution of Walker's excellent book is to remind us
that religious liberty is a *doctrine* grounded in the Bible—in eschatology, anthropology, and missiology. That means religious liberty's
defense by Christians is an act of biblical obedience, and its observance by governments is a fundamental act of justice. I do not know
of a better explanation and defense of the doctrine of religious
liberty. Walker's book deserves a wide hearing and a long life."

—Paul D. Miller, professor, School of Foreign Service,
Georgetown University

"There may be pragmatic reasons to embrace religious liberty, but
Christians need to be satisfied that this is a *theologically* sound idea.
Liberty for All is thus a timely and important work. Walker invites
readers to reflect on religious liberty in light of some of the most
important Christian doctrines and makes a bold case that honoring
religious liberty is not merely consistent with Christian conviction
but also its necessary corollary. Christians of all sorts should read
this book and digest Walker's case."

—David VanDrunen, professor, Westminster Seminary California;
author of *Politics after Christendom*

"Religious liberty has become surprisingly controversial of late.
Walker's excellent book offers Christians a strong, incisive set of
theological and scriptural arguments in favor of a robust religious
liberty. We would do well to heed his arguments and, even better,
put them into practice."

—Bryan T. McGraw, associate professor, Wheaton College

"Walker shows that the strongest case for religious freedom—
including a freedom from confessional political orders—is the Christian case. In Walker's account, the public square is richly garbed in
the free discourse of all faiths, not stripped bare for the sake of a

desiccated secularism, and the kingdom of God is advanced in a civic friendship of Christians with fellow citizens. Religious liberty, he shows us, is the essential predicate of our reasoning together about ultimate things in our penultimate time together here."

—**Matthew J. Franck**, associate director, James Madison Program in American Ideals and Institutions; lecturer, Princeton University

"In this welcome and timely resource, Walker has brilliantly articulated a thoroughgoing treatment of religious liberty for our secular and pluralistic context. Seeking to retrieve a tradition for the common good while offering his own understanding of Baptist distinctives related to this important subject, Walker makes a convincing case for religious liberty for everyone. One of the most important books on this subject in recent years, *Liberty for All* is a must-read, and I heartily recommend it."

—**David S. Dockery**, president, International Alliance for Christian Education; distinguished professor, Southwestern Baptist Theological Seminary

"Walker has successfully demonstrated that religious liberty, vindicated by history as good public policy, is also demonstrated by Scripture to be good Christian theology. *Liberty for All* aids a new generation in recognizing that religious liberty enthrones Christ as King, respects people as his subjects, and promotes the Christian gospel. This book will quickly find a place on the shelves in seminary libraries. May God also bring it to church libraries and home libraries."

—**Bart Barber**, senior pastor, First Baptist Church, Farmersville, Texas

"Christian public witness—and human flourishing in general—is inseparable from a full-orbed understanding of religious liberty. In this important book, Walker rightly underscores how high the stakes truly are. As he points out, religious liberty hinges on some of the deepest questions of ethics and worship. *Liberty for All* will be essential reading for any thoughtful Christian eager to faithfully navigate a pluralistic and increasingly secular public square."

—**Matthew J. Hall**, provost, The Southern Baptist Theological Seminary

LIBERTY FOR ALL

Defending Everyone's

Religious Freedom in a Pluralistic Age

ANDREW T. WALKER

Foreword by ROBERT P. GEORGE

BrazosPress

a division of Baker Publishing Group
Grand Rapids, Michigan

Published by Brazos Press
a division of Baker Publishing Group
PO Box 6287, Grand Rapids, MI 49516-6287
www.brazospress.com

Printed in the United States of America

Library of Congress Cataloging-in-Publication Data
Names: Walker, Andrew T., 1985– author.
Title: Liberty for all : defending everyone's religious freedom in a pluralistic age / Andrew T. Walker.
Description: Grand Rapids, Michigan : Brazos Press, a division of Baker Publishing Group, [2021] | Includes bibliographical references.
Identifiers: LCCN 2020046462 | ISBN 9781587434495 (paperback) | ISBN 9781587435331 (casebound)
Subjects: LCSH: Freedom of religion.
Classification: LCC BV741 .W35 2021 | DDC 323.44/2—dc23
LC record available at https://lccn.loc.gov/2020046462

Scripture quotations are from The Holy Bible, English Standard Version® (ESV®), copyright © 2001 by Crossway, a publishing ministry of Good News Publishers. Used by permission. All rights reserved. ESV Text Edition: 2016

Some material in chapter 5 is from Andrew T. Walker and Casey Hough, "Toward a Baptist Natural Law Conception of the Common Good," *Southwestern Journal of Theology* 63, no. 1 (Fall 2020): 153–74. Used by permission. Portions of chapter 6 are included in Andrew Walker, "The Gospel and the Natural Law," *First Things*, December 8, 2020, https://www.firstthings.com/web-exclusives/2020/12/the-gospel-and -the-natural-law, and "Holding the Ropes: How Religious Liberty Helps Advance the Gospel," *First Things*, February 20, 2014, https://www.firstthings.com/blogs/first thoughts/2014/02/holding-the-ropes. Used by permission. Some material in the conclusion is from Andrew Walker, "Freedom of Religion and the Christian Ethics of the Nation-State," *Providence: A Journal of Christianity & American Foreign Policy*, January 11, 2019, https://providencemag.com/2019/01/freedom-of-religion-and-the -christian-ethics-of-the-nation-state/. Used by permission.

The author is represented by the literary agency of Wolgemuth & Associates, Inc.

21 22 23 24 25 26 27   7 6 5 4 3 2 1

To my wife, Christian

"AND I WILL WALK AT LIBERTY: FOR I SEEK THY PRECEPTS."
PSALM 119:45 KJV

Contents

Foreword

Robert P. George

ONE OF THE TOWERING FIGURES of contemporary philosophy, Alasdair MacIntyre, has observed that all of us approach moral questions, including questions of justice and political morality, from a perspective—a perspective shaped and, indeed, constituted by a set of background beliefs and understandings. There is no neutral ("Archimedean") point from which someone can begin inquiry and reflection on such questions. On the contrary, what makes inquiry, reflection, deliberation, analysis, and judgment possible are resources provided by what Professor MacIntyre calls traditions. Some traditions are religious; some are secular; some do not fall neatly into either category. But there is no inquiry, reflection, deliberation, and the like apart from traditions that provide us with ideas, concepts, modes, methods and techniques of inquiry and analysis, analytical tools, and other indispensable resources.

What primarily motivated MacIntyre to make his point about the role and importance of traditions was the claim made by leading figures in modern liberal moral and political philosophy to be operating from a position of neutrality on controversial questions of what makes for, or detracts from, a valuable and morally worthy way of life, and to propose such putative neutrality as the standard for law-making in modern pluralistic democratic societies. The dominant forms of liberal political theory of our time have presented themselves as theories of rights (including rights to basic liberties), rights that can, and indeed can only, be identified by "bracketing" questions of what is (and is not) good—what makes for (or detracts from) a worthy life. MacIntyre and other critics of these forms of liberalism—I myself among them—have denied that this "bracketing" is desirable or even possible.

We critics have argued that leading secular liberal theories of justice, such as the one famously proposed by the late John Rawls, quietly smuggle in ideas about human goods, and the overall human good, in violation of their own strictures, in identifying what the proponents of these theories believe to be genuine rights and defending their conceptions of the specific shape and content of these rights. If we are correct, then, as MacIntyre observes, liberalism of the sort we are here talking about, far from being a neutral or "tradition-independent" standpoint, is a tradition like other traditions, and should be regarded as such. It should neither be excluded from the competition for the allegiance of citizens nor privileged in that competition. It should be treated as one among the competing traditions and assessed on its merits.

Characteristically, traditions include, or provide the resources making possible, critiques of competing traditions, and, interestingly, internal critiques of themselves that could in principle, and sometimes do, cause people operating within a certain tradition to lose faith in the tradition and look to other traditions in search of a new home. (That, MacIntrye notes, is how conversions happen.) One of the claims contemporary liberalism makes for itself and against its competitors is that it, and it uniquely, can place on an intellectually secure footing widely accepted basic civil liberties, such as the rights to freedom of speech, religion, and conscience. I have never found this claim to be plausible, and much of my own scholarly work has been dedicated to refuting it.

The book you hold in your hands is a theological and ethical work written by a gifted scholar who writes from the perspective of a Southern Baptist Christian. I am a philosopher of law, rather than a theologian, and a Catholic; so in two respects I'm "looking in from the outside." And yet, I find Andrew Walker's arguments and analyses illuminating and, indeed, instructive. I believe you will too—whether you are Protestant or Catholic, Christian or Jewish, a believer or an unbeliever, and whether you are a theologian, a philosopher, or none of the above.

An impressive aspect of Walker's work is his willingness (and skill) to draw on insights and analytical tools derived from other traditions of thought—secular as well as religious, including the tradition of natural law theory—to understand more thoroughly the moral foundations and practical implications of a properly understood right to religious freedom.

He writes from within a tradition, drawing powerful insights from it, but avoids hermetically sealing himself off from what is to be learned and gained from other traditions. His work is in no way insular or sectarian. It is certainly not exclusively for Southern Baptists (or Protestants, or Christians).

And yet, *Liberty for All* is a work of Christian ethics and—like any work worthy of that description—Christian witness. It explains why, for disciples of Jesus, religious liberty is indeed for all, and not just for Christians ourselves. It shows why Christians must respect and, what is more, be in the forefront of protecting the liberty of non-Christians and even nonbelievers. Further, as Walker makes clear, a sound understanding of religious liberty cannot be narrow or cramped but must be capacious. It is not merely the freedom to worship or to exercise one's religion in the private domain of the home or church, synagogue, mosque, or temple; it is the freedom to give public witness to one's convictions and to bring one's religiously informed judgments regarding justice and the common good into the public square to vie there on terms of equality with those who propose competing ideas. This is a lesson Christians of all traditions and denominations need to take on board, and it is a fact about authentic Christianity that it is important for everyone to understand.

Acknowledgments

THE WRITING OF A BOOK IS ITS OWN STORY, and no less is that true than with this one. An unexpected job transition and move from Franklin, Tennessee, to Louisville, Kentucky, occurred during the writing of this volume, which understandably slowed its progress. Nonetheless, in between moving, settling into a new normal, and adjusting to life in the classroom, life and writing went on. The book's completion happened during the COVID-19 quarantine, which ensures this book will be deeply etched in my memory. One would think that a government-mandated excuse to stay home and write and rewrite would be an author's ideal, but life with three small children proved otherwise, grateful as I am for their joyful mischief.

Many people are owed recognition for the role they played in the development of this book. Alex Ward, as always, was a helpful editor who provided essential feedback. Josh Wester and Casey Hough are two friends for whom the ideas expressed in this book are the source of endless conversations about matters of first principles related to theology, ethics, and political philosophy. I also owe a debt of gratitude to individuals such as Jonathan Leeman and David VanDrunen, whose intellectual influence over me is considerable. Russell D. Moore is owed appreciation for overseeing the initial draft of this book while in its dissertation phase. Many colleagues (past and present)—including Phillip Bethancourt, John Wilsey, and Jonathan Pennington—have proven to be faithful friends and encouragers. Many more individuals deserve credit for sparking the academic interest I have in religious liberty, among them Ryan T. Anderson and Robert P. George.

The academic administration of the Southern Baptist Theological Seminary—R. Albert Mohler Jr., Matthew Hall, and Hershael York—deserves special mention for trusting me with the ideas in this book, which I hope will influence the next generation of Baptist Christians to reflect Christianly on religious liberty.

Some of the material in this book has been worked out in articles written for the Ethics and Religious Liberty Commission of the Southern Baptist Convention, and I appreciate their permission to use it here. I am also grateful to *Southwestern Journal of Theology*, *First Things*, and *Providence: A Journal of Christianity & American Foreign Policy* for permission to reproduce material that originally appeared in those publications.

My agent, Andrew Wolgemuth, is both a friend and a warm encourager. His help in facilitating this project is not without my gratitude. Katelyn Beaty, James Korsmo, and the team at Brazos Press have been consummate professionals, and I am deeply thankful to have worked with them in the acquisition and development of this book.

Lastly, I would be remiss not to acknowledge the role my family played in drafting this book. My wife, Christian, gave me time and encouragement to persevere. Aside from the fact that Jesus is alive, my family is the reason I wake and live each day. My children—Caroline, Catherine, and Charlotte—are the greatest source of joy I have in this world. Children, who are our future, are what matter. To quote Rust Cohle in HBO's *True Detective*, "They're the only reason for this whole man-woman drama."[1]

Introduction

You Get to Decide What to Worship, Not Whether to Worship

SEPTEMBER 12, 2018, marked the tenth anniversary of David Foster Wallace's tragic suicide. Wallace is not typically well known by Christians, but he was one of his generation's most unique and extraordinary writers. He was also a deeply troubled individual, as revealed in portraits of his life. Though not a professing Christian, he seemed respectful at times toward Christianity, especially Catholicism. Some speculate as to whether Wallace was on the verge of converting at one point, but a life wracked by depression and addiction kept him from the altar, as far as we know at least.

When one reads Wallace, one finds someone grappling with existence, someone trying to assemble meaning through the brokenness of addiction and severed relationships. But in some embryonic form, his dalliance with religion and his comments on at least one occasion provide a launching pad for further discussion of the contested issue of religious liberty.

Wallace gave a now-famous 2005 commencement address at Kenyon College titled "This Is Water." For a long time, I had heard how this commencement address had gained cult-like status in underground pop culture. When I listened to it a couple of years ago, I was awestruck at what I heard and instantly became a Wallace fan. On the verge of tears, I sat on my bed and listened to a YouTube recording of the speech given what seemed like a lifetime ago.

By his own admission, Wallace was a man of "faith," even if he did not come to a conclusion about "the faith" (Jude 3). Still, a sincerity that punctuated his comments drew me in, and I heard a man wrestling with the surrealism of his existence. In the address, Wallace says that education is designed to help individuals pursue the examined life.

> Twenty years after my own graduation, I have come gradually to understand that the liberal-arts cliché about "teaching you how to think" is actually shorthand for a much deeper, more serious idea: "Learning how to think" really means learning how to exercise some control over how and what you think. It means being conscious and aware enough to choose what you pay attention to and to choose how you construct meaning from experience. Because if you cannot exercise this kind of choice in adult life, you will be totally hosed.[1]

But further on, Wallace appeals to the purpose of education to go even deeper, to the purpose of life itself.

> But if you've really learned how to think, how to pay attention, then you will know you have other options. It will actually be within your power to experience a crowded, loud, slow, consumer-hell-type situation as not only meaningful but sacred, on fire with the same force that lit the stars—compassion, love, the sub-surface unity of all things. Not that that mystical stuff's necessarily true: The only thing that's capital-T True is that you get to decide how you're going to try to see it. You get to consciously decide what has meaning and what doesn't. You get to decide what to worship.

Because here's something else that's true. In the day-to-day trenches of adult life, there is actually no such thing as atheism. There is no such thing as not worshipping. Everybody worships. The only choice we get is what to worship. . . . Look, the insidious thing about these forms of worship is not that they're evil or sinful; it is that they are unconscious. They are default settings. They're the kind of worship you just gradually slip into, day after day, getting more and more selective about what you see and how you measure value without ever being fully aware that that's what you're doing. And the world will not discourage you from operating on your default settings, because the world of men and money and power hums along quite nicely on the fuel of fear and contempt and frustration and craving and the worship of self.

Wallace is calling people to take hold of their lives, to reject the "default setting" of monotony and spoon-fed distraction. He knows that at the core of every person is a driving force, and for Wallace, true living is being aware of that driving force, being able to evaluate it and harness it toward critical awareness, becoming, and meaning. This is not run-of-the-mill motivational speaking. His argument is given the fullest color when the people he is calling forth to live intentionally understand themselves to be made in God's image, to be creatures of meaning ordering their lives according to the pattern of creation. But this sincerity—this awakening from the "dogmatic slumber," to borrow a phrase from Immanuel Kant—requires a certain freedom. We need space to test the maxims and ideals we want to live by to determine whether they are delivering what they promise.

What Wallace argues for shares the architecture for how Christians ought to understand religious liberty, a not-so-popular and now-misunderstood topic. As I will explain, authority, adoration, and authenticity are at the center of what it means to be human. We are wired to anchor our quest for fulfillment and truth in something that we believe possesses the rightful authority to unlock this journey. We end up adoring what we give authority to in order to design our lives. Beauty, security, sex, money, power—each of these can become a focus of adoration. In the most generic sense, the authority we live by and the worship we give this authority are driving each of us toward the goal of finding our true self, our authentic self. Of course, as Christians, we do not believe that all quests for authenticity are equal. But as beings created in the image of God, we crave authority, adoration, and authenticity. As Wallace says so poignantly that it could have issued from a biblical prophet, "Everybody worships. The only choice we get is what to worship." How true.

What do Wallace's observations have to do with religious liberty and the pursuit of truth in a secular age? As Wallace drives at, we humans are truth-seeking creatures. I argue that these three concepts—authority, adoration, and authenticity—explain why religious liberty matters to Christians, but not just to Christians. We Christians should extend religious liberty to everyone, because everyone is pursuing truth, even if incorrectly. In a secular and increasingly pluralistic age, we need to allow falsehood a space to be wrong in hopes that individuals will "come to the knowledge of the truth" (1 Tim. 2:4). This does not mean we refrain from naming moral wrongs or fall captive to empty-headed relativism. It means we do not seek to criminalize, persecute, or marginalize people whose beliefs are sincere and are animating them toward lives of purpose, meaning, and goodwill (and there are checks and balances to consider when convictions pose risks and harms to civil society). This is not a world where limits and authority are cast off; instead, within properly understood limits, people are allowed to act in accordance with what they believe is choice-worthy and will produce flourishing.

What Wallace describes, Christians can affirm: a sense of agency in our personhood and a humility in our awareness of our need for personal reform. Religious liberty requires both. We humans are often wrong about the things we perceive, because we are fallible. No human is a perfect arbiter of truth. This means we cannot impose truth on others; truth must be discovered after thorough, rigorous examination. We plead and persuade. And this means we need to leave room for people to search for truth, to err, to self-correct, to realize the possibility, as finite beings, that each of us is incapable of possessing absolute truth. We Christians believe the Word of God declares the truth; we have confirmation of the Spirit's work inside us; but we are still imperfect creatures who "see in a mirror dimly" (1 Cor. 13:12). This, in so few words, is why religious liberty is so important. Religious liberty, and liberty itself, exists to allow people to align themselves with truth, even if some align themselves incorrectly. Humans crave the space to make meaning of their existence, rightly and wrongly. Again, in Wallace's words, "The really important kind of freedom involves attention, and awareness, and discipline, and effort, and being able truly to care about other people and to sacrifice for them, over and over, in myriad petty little unsexy ways, every day. That is real freedom."[2]

Religious liberty is not about relativizing truth claims or treating all religions as equals. That, as I will explain, is actually the opposite of true religious liberty. From the perspective of fallible humans, religious liberty is about giving individuals space to figure out for themselves who God is. From a theocentric perspective, religious liberty is about the era of unfolding history—an "in between" age—in which the church lives with anticipation that Jesus will judge every conscience because he and he alone is truth itself (John 14:6).

It is so fascinating to me how a postmodern prophet like Wallace could so beautifully and powerfully articulate echoes of truths so central to Christianity. Christians would certainly disagree with a great deal of what Wallace believed, but I am thankful for a sliver of common grace that shows up in his "This Is Water," which teaches Christians a little bit about how we as humans were made to worship—and why freedom is essential to give breath to what we believe is true.

A Road Map

Liberty for All offers a public theology of religious liberty. Religious liberty, tragically, is now a casualty of culture wars in the West. I will talk some about cultural challenges toward the end of the book, but that is not what this book is primarily about. Rather, this book is about acknowledging a few essential truths: (1) because humanity is made in God's image, each human is religious and truth seeking in nature, regardless of whether they understand themselves as "religious"; (2) we live in a pluralistic era, and the biblical story line expects religious difference to occur in this temporary "secular" age (I will explain what "secular" means later); (3) religious liberty and freedom of conscience promote human and societal flourishing; (4) the Bible does not command any formal, institutional union between a religious body and government; and (5) Christianity is the best arbiter for religious liberty because it has theological resources to help us grapple with some of the most difficult societal challenges. To make this argument, I will show why eschatology (the kingdom of God), anthropology (the image of God), and missiology (the mission of God) all point toward a public theology of religious liberty. An underlying point of this book is to explain why an idea like religious liberty is intelligible and choice-worthy for a society to organize itself around.

A word about the intended audience of this book is necessary. I am writing this as an in-house explanation for how Christians ought to understand religious liberty. I am not writing to persuade the convinced skeptic. I hope Christians will walk away from this book with an appreciation for how religious liberty functions integrally in Christian thought. What I will argue later is that if Western culture cuts itself off from its Christian roots, religious liberty and freedom of conscience will be public goods less recognizable and less valued. If the West hopes to remain politically and religiously free, it must appreciate and retrieve a principled account of religious freedom that owes its most secure foundation to Christian social thought. Secularism does not have the explanatory power within itself to make sense of religious liberty, and, in fact, without the checks and balances offered by a transcendent worldview, will prove to be inimical to religious liberty.

My hope for this book is simple: I want Christians to come away with a greater understanding of the reality of diversity and how we as Christians are expected to confront such diversity in light of the gospel. A key part of the answer is religious liberty.

Last Things First

The intelligible good of religious liberty exists on the grounds of eschatology, anthropology, and missiology. First, the person and work of Christ provide the eschatological orientation for why Christians should promote religious liberty and defend others' freedom of conscience—even the freedom of those with whom we disagree. Second, the fact that we are God's image bearers portends something about our nature and how we are made to flourish. Last, Christians should prioritize religious liberty as a pillar of public theology, because religious liberty gives shape to the church's mission in a secular age while fostering conditions that make the common good attainable.

Religious liberty is not an accident born solely from liberal democracy or Enlightenment rationalism. Religious liberty did not start with John Locke. It originates with Christ's authority over creation. Christianity on the margins of an oppressive empire birthed a revolutionary idea that created the freest civilization the

7

world has known (though abuses of Christianity, tragically, have also been a source of oppression as well).

Jesus Christ is the king and judge over history. The questions then become, What era of history is the church in? and, How do Jesus's kingship and judgment manifest themselves now?

1

Religious Liberty as a Christian Social Ethic

The Importance of Religious Liberty

"A belief in Christian ethics is a belief that certain ethical and moral judgments belong to the gospel itself; a belief, in other words, that the church can be committed to ethics without moderating the tone of its voice as a bearer of glad tidings."[1] So remarks Oliver O'Donovan, who notes in his seminal work on Christian ethics that the gospel of Christ must be tied to any study that purports to be Christian. It follows, then, that every task of Christian ethics should be done within the horizon of redemption and the unfolding of God's kingdom.

Religious liberty is of supreme relevance to Christian social ethics and public theology, but as it is often framed in public discourse—even among professed Christians—it is not clearly tied to the gospel. The present fear is that religious liberty is merely an accident of history, a social construct, or a settlement born of pragmatic need. In a time when religious liberty has been sadly situated as a culture war issue, what religious liberty needs is an apologetic arising from Christian conviction.

How should we define religious liberty? I contend that religious liberty is the principle of social practice wherein every individual, regardless of their religious confession, is equally free to believe, or not to believe, and to live out their understanding of the conscience's duty, individually and communally, that is owed to God in all areas of life without threat of government penalty or social harassment. It is nothing short of grasping truth and ordering one's life in response to it. From this angle, religious liberty is an enterprise of both worship and ethics. As a person submits their whole life to God, religious liberty gives them agency to express their convictions about God through their actions and choices. Nothing less than personhood is at stake. Religious liberty is a juncture where one's duty to God intersects with one's obligation to live out duties and moral commitments for the sake of personal authenticity. It enables individuals, and individuals gathered in communities, to respond to their understanding of divine truth and to manifest the obligations of that divine truth in every dimension of life.

As a topic of immense value to Christians, especially Christian advocacy groups, religious liberty is taken for granted but insufficiently explained on biblical and theological grounds. More often than not, religious liberty is situated as an answer to political controversy.[2] Or religious liberty takes its cues from politics, whether of liberal or conservative varieties. And if not seen as a matter of political philosophy, it is often situated as a sociological paradigm concerned about forging cultural détente.

One important goal of this book is to more clearly connect religious liberty to eschatology, anthropology, and missiology in contemporary Christian discourse. When one reviews Christian literature surrounding religious liberty, one finds few resources that provide systematic Christian accounts of religious liberty. Moreover, when surveying topics within Christian ethics, especially in textbooks, one finds that the literature is replete with books and chapters on abortion, capital punishment, homosexuality, marriage and family, euthanasia, and the like, but religious liberty does not receive proportional emphasis. If treated at all, it is tucked under an umbrella category, such as church-state relations. But religious liberty is much broader than just church-state relations. Religious liberty reveals how temporal authority understands its relationship and jurisdiction in relation to eternal authority. Religious liberty is thus revelatory and presuppositional in deciphering how religion and politics relate to one another in a given context. By my reading, not a single volume by a Christian scholar attempts to offer a systematic or comprehensive account of religious liberty's theological origins and purpose within the biblical story line.[3] This absence is a problem because religious liberty ought to function as a preeminent foundation for Christians' understanding of their entry into the public square as religious individuals embedded within religious communities that exist in particular social contexts.

Consider the manifold ways that religious liberty addresses key aspects of social ethics and public theology. First, religious liberty supplies the justification for religious persons to act freely at the behest of a religiously motivated ethic. Second, religious liberty implies delineating between the church and the world and how the church and the state ought to relate to one another. Third, religious liberty facilitates ethical duties that consciences owe a Creator and how those obligations are discharged. Consider also the implications of religious liberty for theology and ethics: exercising one's conscience is related to moral agency, which demands that there be a horizon for this agency to occur. The conscience responds to truth that demands obedience. Among other ways it is important, religious liberty informs our understanding of the kingdom of God and how the kingdom's mission advances in society: Does it advance through voluntary acts of faith, by proxy, or by coercion?

Religious liberty is thus a pillar of Christian social ethics; every other topic within the public square presumes it. For example, advocating for the unborn—whether praying in front of an abortion clinic or casting one's vote in a referendum on the issue—assumes some framework that makes such activity possible. The collective action of a Christian advocacy organization working to dismantle sex trafficking networks relies on unstated assumptions about the freedom guaranteeing such activity and the public expression of its convictions. We might be tempted to see each of these as a mere right of basic political liberty, but more deeply, political liberty exists to allow the exercise of convictions born of religious foundation. (I would contend that the underdeveloped theological aspects of religious liberty in American Christian social ethics is the result of the fact that the American context focuses almost exclusively on matters related to religious exercise and religious establishment debates found in the First Amendment of the United States Constitution. American Christians often find themselves held captive to a culture that engages in debates on religious liberty more out of pragmatic concerns to negotiate among competing claims of power than out of theological conviction.)

The freedoms Christians ought to enjoy in society and how the church relates to the state are paramount to any Christian public theology. As a result, religious liberty should be a *doctrine*, not just a constitutional device. Moreover, how Christians understand the reality of divergent religious systems occupying the same social space is critical to their mission. Dismissing or overlooking the centrality of religious liberty in Christian public theology demonstrates a failure to establish first principles that are necessary for the church's mission.

Religious liberty helps Christians recognize the era in which the church's mission exists—a time when Christ's kingdom has been inaugurated but awaits consummation. In this intervening period, religious liberty reveals the nature of religious difference, what mission entails, and how people come to saving faith in Jesus Christ. Religious liberty, then, is of deep eschatological concern, as it helps one understand the church's mission and expectations in society. It is also central to a proper understanding of Jesus's kingship over consciences that are to be held accountable to future judgment and the manner in which individuals come to apprehend the gospel (John 5:27; 2 Cor. 5:11; 2 Pet. 3:9–10). Both religion and government are forced to reckon with the authority claims of the other. Religious liberty is a crucial cipher to unlocking the underlying statecraft of the political community. As one scholar has commented, "It is difficult to avoid the conclusion that it is in its posture toward religion that a nation most fully and clearly defines itself."[4] These words capture the gravity of religious liberty, and they are doubtlessly true. How a state understands the nature of its own power and how that power is distributed testify to whether that state is acting biblically (Rom. 13) or as an antichrist (Rev. 13). As Robert H. Mounce writes about the state's self-aggregating power tendencies, "The worship of a Satanically inspired perversion of secular authority is the ultimate offense against the one true God."[5] And indeed, the greatest struggles of Western history take place against a backdrop of conflict over religion and political authority attempting to unite or compete.

A Biblical-Theological Basis for Religious Liberty

How can religious liberty become an issue of Christian preeminence and focus when the phrase "religious liberty" is nowhere in the Bible? As Baptist missionary and scholar John David Hughey notes, "Religious liberty is implicit in Christian theology, and theologians, eager to lay solid foundations for freedom already achieved or still to be won, are giving serious attention to it. Several major Christian doctrines have implications for religious liberty."[6] Hughey's observation begs that an explicit connection be made between religious liberty and basic Christian theology. A. F. Carrillo de Albornoz similarly observes that religious liberty "is not in single passages in the Bible; it is God's whole way of approaching mankind that gives us our lead."[7] Carrillo de Albornoz goes on to state that "our prime question is, therefore, to investigate this 'nexus' or to see exactly how religious liberty is implied in the Christian revelation."[8]

Recent Christian scholarship, in both quantity and quality, has failed to provide a robust account that makes religious liberty intelligibly Christian.[9] Indeed, there is no Christian consensus for developing a framework or conceptual paradigm around religious liberty that incorporates essential elements of Christian theology. Religious liberty is mostly seen as a concern about preserving religious identity and religious exercise in pluralistic societies. Biblical arguments (e.g., the rich young ruler was given a choice to follow Christ) are crafted piecemeal or merely implied. Indeed, in contemporary Christian scholarship, religious liberty is discussed in the context of debates about pluralism and negotiations concerning cultural conflicts rather than being shown to connect to biblical reflection. With religious liberty left almost exclusively to the province of legal theory and political philosophy, Christians lack a key component of Christian social ethics.

A consensus regarding religious liberty is foundational for Christian social ethics because "authentic Christian faith necessarily means, for the Church as well as the individual Christian, involvement within an historical context."[10] The more that Christian leaders develop a concept of religious liberty, the better they will grasp the church's identity and mission at a time when history is replete with competing claims of authority and allegiance. Religious liberty is a form of self-conscious reflection by individuals and organizations to decipher their engagement in society. As long as the church lacks a Christian framework for religious liberty, it will fumble about in its interactions with the world, unable to ground essential truths necessary to its social witness that are integral to its theology and mission.

The remedy to an anemic or underdeveloped biblical-theological basis for religious liberty is to anchor religious liberty to biblical motifs. Indeed, by not doing so, Christians leave a vacuum to be filled by constitutionalism, humanism, or secularism. Carl Emanuel Carlson comments:

> Now if humanism is the fundamental basis of our movement, then we are involved on the horns of a quite different dilemma. . . . The concern for liberty might be disassociated from the redemptive work of Christ. It may have nothing to do with Christology or eschatology or with much more that is traditional Christian theology. . . . If the authority of the lordship of Christ in the church and in the experience of the person contravenes our understanding of the nature of man as expressed in the doctrines of religious liberty, the future of liberty is not bright at the present time.[11]

The quest to connect religious liberty to biblical theology is the central and driving concern of this book, and tethering religious liberty to areas such as eschatology, anthropology, and missiology forms central planks in its overall argument.

To be clear, several academics have shown the connection between Christian ethics and religious liberty, but their approaches are piecemeal and do not consider, generally speaking, key themes in biblical theology. Christian reflection concerning religious liberty is informed more by vague theisms and the United States Constitution than by explicit theology. By contrast, an approach to religious liberty should be centrally concerned with recognizing Jesus's kingship over the conscience and his absolute and exclusive right to execute judgment over it. Religious liberty is best understood when built on the foundational biblical motifs of the kingdom of God, the image of God, and the mission of God. The reality of Christ's already/not-yet kingship is the ground on which religious liberty ought to be intelligible for Christians.

Think of a three-legged stool. We might think of religious liberty resting on the three legs of the kingdom of God (eschatology), the image of God (anthropology), and the mission of God (missiology). Each leg supports the overarching and uniting reality of Jesus's kingship. This threefold strategy is deliberate and based on a schematic framework seen in J. Budziszewski's *Evangelicals in the Public Square: Four Formative Voices on Political Thought and Action*.[12] Budziszewski says that any "adequate political theory" has at least three elements: (1) an orienting doctrine, "or a guide to thought"; (2) a practical doctrine, "or a guide to action"; and (3) a cultural apologetic, "or a guide to persuasion."[13] While this book is not a work of political theory per se, Budziszewski's framework supports the method taken here. The kingdom of God is the orienting doctrine, the image of God is the practical doctrine, and the mission of God is the cultural apologetic.

The kingdom of God functions as the orienting doctrine because it serves as the primary locus for guiding this book's argument concerning religious liberty. Think of the orienting doctrine as the vertical relationship between God and humanity (the "what"). The image of God functions as the practical doctrine because it offers guidance for understanding how religious liberty applies to persons in historical-political contexts (the "how"). Think of the practical doctrine as the horizontal relationship between persons existing in community. Finally, the mission of God functions as the cultural apologetic because every horizon where religious liberty occurs is embedded in cultural matrices that are either hospitable or inhospitable to the claims of religion. Think of the cultural apologetic as the engine of momentum that gives force to religious liberty in society (the "why"). We will look briefly here at these themes before laying them out in turn in the three parts that follow.

The Kingdom of God (Eschatology)

Religious liberty begins not with jurisprudence, legal philosophy, or even questions about state authority over religious affairs but with a central question that the kingdom of God answers: "What must I do to be saved?" (Acts 16:30).[14] Religious liberty is concerned with the means and ends of salvation as it focuses on how one is genuinely converted and the outworking of that conversion. It asks a fundamental question: Who holds ultimate judgment over the sincerity of a person's religious faculties? Is one saved through good works? By proxy? Or through the operations of the individual conscience brought to faith through repentance? And moreover, if salvation is received through an individual's conscience grasping religious truth, the conscience's agency has immense consequences for lesser authorities or mediators who would attempt to disrupt or thwart one's active response to God. If religious liberty is a matter of conscience, who has the ability to execute judgment on redeemed or erring consciences? If salvation is experienced personally and communally through membership in the church, what boundaries distinguish the church from the rest of the world—and the church from the state? And central to these questions is one overarching question: How does inaugurated eschatology play into the current role of the state and the mission of the church in society? This book answers the question by arguing that the kingdom of God is the standard of measurement by which the authority of the state in a secular age of contestability is determined.

The Image of God (Anthropology)

A Christian approach to religious liberty must determine the nature and purpose of the person as made in God's image. The doctrine of the image of God offers the best foundation for questions related to anthropology and the conscience because it securely anchors the inviolability and integrity of the reasoning conscience as ordered to God's moral law and held liable to judgment. The image of God is the best place to locate a doctrine of human rights that makes religious liberty practical and relevant to Western political order.[15] The image of God makes noncoercion and voluntary assent foundational for religious liberty. Understanding the image of God and its meaning for humans as being rational and free creatures confers dignity on the conscience.[16] The conscience is the vehicle by which people are held accountable to Christ and liable to judgment by Christ (Acts 17:31).

The Mission of God (Missiology)

Religious liberty is needed in order to advance the gospel. I offer this cautiously, not wishing to imply that absent religious liberty, God's mission will advance no further. Rather, a Christian account of religious liberty, driven out of concern for a proper understanding of missiology, must determine the relationship between the mission of God, the mission of the state, and the existence of erring belief in light of the current era of redemptive history.[17] A Christian understanding of mission, religious liberty, and the era of history in which the church's mission is located should allow for divergent religious and ideological viewpoints and foster a cultural milieu that prioritizes religious liberty for the sake of the common good and the church's moral witness in society.

Conclusion

Carlson explains why religious liberty is "an integral part of Christian thinking": "If it stems from our religious presuppositions, then we have an obligation to make these relationships clear so that this modern confused world can understand. If there are such relationships, they should become clear in our preaching and teaching."[18] This book takes up Carlson's charge. A tradition aware of its own internal views on religious liberty is obligated out of concern for social witness to see such views publicly articulated for its own good but also because articulating them might lead to society's flourishing.

Carl F. H. Henry wrote that "if the Church fails to apply the central truths of Christian religion to social problems correctly, someone else will do so incorrectly."[19] Henry's message is a call to arms, reminding us that Christianity rejects gnostic religion. It is a religion of the here and now and of the future. Christianity offers a comprehensive critique of secularism and modernity. The Christian religion believes not only that it properly understands humanity's problems but also that it has the message that can restore humanity. A Christian understanding of religious liberty can never be severed from this central truth. From the New Testament onward, Christianity has impacted kings, empires, and modern nation-states with a message of competing kingship (Matt. 2:1–18; Acts 9:15; 17:7; Rev. 2:26–27). How people have reckoned with the claim of Jesus Christ's kingship has been a driving force in world history ever since a once-and-former corpse walked out of a grave and claimed to be a king (Isa. 9:6–7; Acts 13:30; Rev. 15:3).

The proclamation that Jesus is Lord has worked itself out in varying political contexts. Some people have received such news with glad acceptance. Others have sought to distort this message for political gain. Others have rejected the message altogether. Christian teaching on religious liberty demands greater explanation because the gospel impacts people who inhabit particular places at particular times in history with the announcement that the kings and governments of the world do not possess absolute authority.

This book argues for consensus, because a lack of consensus means there has not been a constructive way to understand religious liberty comprehensively. This book aims to synthesize existing arguments into a better conceptual framework, to provide the connective tissue between ideas related to religious liberty that have previously floated independently. It attempts to take existing arguments about religious liberty and unite them into a thematic system more amenable to Christian thought. The argument of this book is not that Christians have failed to reason or argue persuasively about religious liberty; it is, rather, that religious liberty has not been given the sustained reflection, treatment, and prominence it deserves as a crucial foundation for Christian social ethics and public theology.

PART 1

ESCHATOLOGY

2

The Reign of Jesus Christ and Religious Liberty

THE KINGDOM OF GOD is the central theme of Scripture. From Genesis to Revelation, every act of revelation is about God's rule. This narrative advances from creation, through Abraham, through Israel's dynasty, to the climactic dawning of God's final kingly revelation, Jesus Christ. The story of Scripture is the unveiling of God's purpose to install his Son, Jesus Christ, as heir over all things (Eph. 1:8–10; Col. 1:15–20, 26–27; Rev. 11:15). In the arc of Scripture, Christ's rule is the "central message of Jesus" and represents history's ultimate direction and purpose.[1]

The kingdom of God is God's reign in which Jesus is enthroned as the sovereign King with all power, sovereignty, and authority.[2] This is not merely a pious truth to tuck away in our hearts. The announcement of Jesus as Lord of lords and King of kings enacts a rule among his people (Acts 2:36). The news of Jesus's kingship is to go in all directions to all peoples, including even kings (Acts 9:15). The kingdom is present where Jesus reigns. While Jesus reigns cosmically over all, his saving rule is known only in and through the church in the current age. According to George Eldon Ladd, it is a present reality (Matt. 12:28) and also a future blessing (1 Cor. 15:50).[3] The rule of God deals with the inner renewal that follows from experiencing salvation through Christ alone (Rom. 14:17), but it will also impact nations of the world as all powers and principalities are, at the end of history, subsumed under Christ's authority (Matt. 28:18–20; Rev. 11:15).

The kingdom of God also refers to "the people belonging to a given realm."[4] Today, that is the church—the redeemed of the ages from every tribe, tongue, and nation. Thus, the kingdom of God is bearing witness as the church proclaims the gospel and forms consciences within it. Jesus is ruling and currently reigning through his church, and the church serves as an outpost or colony of Christ's kingdom (Eph. 1:20–23).[5] Crucially, nowhere in the New Testament is the kingdom of God identified as directly allied with state power in the postresurrection age to facilitate the gospel's advance, and neither is it identified as universally received in the present. Rather, the kingdom of God confronts the "thrones or powers or rulers or authorities" with the message that their power is penultimate and passing away (Col. 1:16).[6] Thus, the kingdom of God began its final enactment with the unveiling of Jesus's ministry, is borne witness by the testimony of the church, and awaits conclusion until God ushers in the end of history (1 Cor. 15:20–28).

The kingdom came in full with the incarnation and resurrection of Jesus Christ, but it will not be consummated until Jesus reigns over all earthly kingdoms. Yet, Christians believe the end of history has begun. As the battle of Gettysburg paved the way for eventual Union triumph, the dawning of the kingdom of God in the life and ministry of Jesus Christ marked the beginning of the end of history. Carl F. H. Henry argued, "The future is actually already at hand, and is unfolding within man's present earthly existence:

the incarnation of Christ inaugurated God's kingdom, the resurrection of Christ publicly identified him as the future judge of the human race, and the present church has initiated 'the last days' (Heb. 1:3); the final consummation of all things is imminent."[7] But what does the kingdom's inauguration and consummation have to do with religious liberty?

Inaugurated eschatology serves as an essential foundation for religious liberty, because it helps sort out Christians' understanding of where and how God's rule and mission on earth unfold. We do not confuse the government's agenda with the church's mission. Government pertains to what is temporal; the church is oriented to what is eternal. Eschatology clarifies that the Christian mission is about a message of reconciliation and the free response of humans and is distinct from the coercive institutions or political orders that do not hold the keys of the kingdom (Matt. 16:18–19). An "eschatological futurism," argues Baptist theologian and ethicist Russell D. Moore, would ensure that "existing structures were not given the uncritical imprimatur of the kingdom of God, but also that Christianity would not succumb to the Constantinian temptation to Christianize forcibly any political order."[8] The kingdom of God gives shape to religious liberty because its promise of future judgment demands patience toward erring consciences in the present. In the present era, as the church bears witness to the kingdom, it heralds an announcement of Christ's present lordship and the available, unhindered offer of salvation.

This eschatological orientation requires that we clearly separate the kingdom's mission from government jurisdiction. This has been no small controversy in the history of Christian thought, but for our purposes, we should consign to the state temporal affairs those things that attend to making life livable in society. The state orders temporal affairs for the fulfillment of the common good, while the church orders spiritual affairs pertaining to the fulfillment of the eternal good. They overlap insofar as Christians are citizens of both orders, yet the calling of each is distinct. The sojourning exiles seek the welfare of their cities (Jer. 29:4–7) even as they long for the city which is to come (Heb. 11:10). In this paradigm, church and state have distinct roles with limited overlap in the present age. For example, Christians are free to serve as political leaders or civil servants. And Christians are to live and vote in accordance with Christian righteousness. But leaders should not rule and decree in the name of Christ as if they know Christ's mind on every policy matter that government must address. The exception to this is areas explicitly addressed by Scripture that dually partake in government's God-given jurisdiction. These are common-grace matters that require moment-to-moment wisdom. The political leader who is a Christian understands that their task is to rule justly in accordance with reason, wisdom, and moral righteousness, not to advance a "Christian government." It is perfectly acceptable for Christianity to influence a nation; it is not acceptable for a nation to have a Christian preamble in its constitution declaring that the entire nation is covenantally joined under the shared recognition of Jesus Christ. Central to religious liberty is the conviction that the state does not have the authority to declare what is or is not Christian.[9] We should not blur church and state for the sake of seeking moral consensus. But neither should we allow for an oppressive secularism that cordons off religion's influence in shaping society. In the case of the former, the state sees itself as a functionary of God's mission, and in the latter, the state sees itself as inviolably insulated from the claims of divine authority that shape the worldview of some of its citizens. The mission of the church, according to Carl F. H. Henry, is "to declare the criteria by which nations will ultimately be judged, and the divine standards to which man and society must conform if civilization is to endure."[10]

Eschatology is central to an understanding of religious liberty, because it provides a promise of future judgment without confusing the role of the church with the role of the state. Because the kingdom of God is given witness through the church, the church can never be coterminous with the operations of the state or nation. Nor can the church insist on a totalized Christian social order short of Christ himself enacting his fully realized reign. This is not at odds with the Great Commission's commandment to disciple all nations. It merely serves to remind us that while we strive to preach Jesus's lordship in all times and places, we cannot attain a uniformly Christian society apart from the consummated eschaton, desirable as that is. This is a concession not to Christian failure to influence society or to the catacombs as the rightful place of the Christian in society but to the present order of how things are expected to be in a fallen age.

All of these realities—present reality, coming judgment, institutionalized church witness—bear enormous consequence on forming a doctrine of religious liberty and the separation of church and state rooted in the kingdom of God.

The Authority of Christ

"And he has given him authority to execute judgment, because he is the Son of Man." Jesus's words in John 5:27 provide a critical foundation for the intersection of the kingdom of God and religious liberty. As king, Jesus has sole, absolute authority to execute judgment over the conscience of every human. "Authority" refers to the legitimate office given by God to a person or entity to command obedience for the sake of overseeing and fulfilling a task consistent with its calling. All earthly authority is derived and ordered by God; it is not absolute or sovereign. Only Jesus has ultimate authority, and that authority is to oversee the rule of his kingdom—that it expands and its righteousness is incarnated (Matt. 28:18; John 19:11).

This truth is reflected in a striking Revolutionary War–era sermon by Elisha Williams. According to Williams, "If Christ be the

27

Lord of the conscience, the sole King in his own kingdom; then it will follow, that all such as in any manner or degree assume the power of directing and governing the consciences of men, are justly chargeable with invading his rightful dominion; He alone having the right they claim. Should the king of France take it into his head to prescribe laws to the subjects of the king of Great Britain; who would not say, it was an invasion of and insult offer'd to the British legislature."[11]

According to Williams, Jesus's status as king gives him authority over jurisdictions intended only for God's purview. A king or government that binds people's consciences over religious matters is interfering with Jesus's domain. This is true not only when a state attempts to formalize a relationship with a religion but also when a state attempts to prohibit citizens within its jurisdiction from acting in accord with their consciences. We are to leave room for conscience freedom because Jesus has the only infallible competency to judge the conscience. The state understands its jurisdiction by what it does not have jurisdiction over: the soul and the conscience. The government may possess the authority to kill the body, but it cannot damn the soul. Nowhere in Scripture is the state authorized to judge the conscience.

Because Jesus Christ is Lord over the conscience, no human institution or individual can legitimately usurp Jesus's authority. The state is designed to pursue and execute justice regarding temporal and interpersonal affairs, not referee whether an individual's grasp of divine claims is true or false. For Christians, who believe that Jesus Christ is king, it is right and proper to speak of the reign of Jesus as enacting this imperium—the power to command and to judge (Ps. 2). He has the authority and the power to execute judgment over spheres that governments or rulers do not have sanction over.

One goal of this chapter is to set forth a vision for the kingdom of God that informs an understanding of the relationship between church and state and that posits a doctrine of religious liberty. Religious liberty assumes a theory of church-state relationship, but the category of church-state relationship is broader than just religious liberty. The kingdom of God sets the horizon for larger debates on the proper relationship between church and state. It is not the church versus the state that is preeminent in the development of a thoroughly Christian conception of religious liberty but the nature of the kingdom being eternal and authorized by a sovereign Christ as distinct from a secular and penultimate age, an age that is passing away and evil (1 Cor. 2:6; Gal. 1:4).

The kingdom of God establishes the intelligibility, relevance, and urgency of religious liberty to Christian social ethics. Christianity teaches that history is advancing toward an ultimate conclusion, evidenced by an inaugurated though not-yet-consummated kingdom. As a result, what happens between resurrection and consummation gives rise to the necessity of consciences responding freely to the gospel. The reality of a future kingdom advances the legitimacy of an era, an "eschatological gap," in which individuals are permitted to engage in false worship without fear of government intervention.[12] Yet Christ's coming kingdom will judge false belief at the end of history. Religious liberty is not an eternal principle but a temporal doctrine that helps us manage social and religious differences. These truths find ultimate expression in the kingship of Christ. Apart from Jesus's kingship and the uniting of all things in him (Eph. 1:10), which authorize his claim to execute ultimate judgment over the conscience (2 Cor. 5:10), religious liberty lacks a Christocentric foundation.

The kingdom of God denotes the authority of Jesus Christ as king. The theme of kingship is also the primary foundation for establishing a doctrine of religious liberty. The New Testament is replete with examples of Jesus and his apostles attesting to his kingship (Matt. 25:34; John 12:12–15; Acts 17:7; Phil. 2:9–11; Heb. 1:8–9). But what is kingship apart from the king's ability to render just, final judgment? Presbyterian theologian Edmund Clowney observes that "the God-man is Lord of all: his salvation brings judgment as well as redemption (Ps. 96:13; John 5:21); his rule in heaven now governs all creation, and he will put down all evil forever (1 Cor. 15:24–28; Heb. 1:4; Col. 2:15; Phil. 2:9–11)."[13] It is precisely because Jesus is the ultimate judge that humans and human institutions cannot judge erring consciences over religious matters (Heb. 9:27). Nowhere in the New Testament is the conscience held to ultimate account except before God. Indeed, where religious obligation meets the objections of the state or nongovernmental entities, the New Testament teaches that defiance is the right response (Acts 4:18–20).

Yet *how* does Jesus's kingship promote religious liberty, pluralism, or religious diversity? Using "tolerance" as the semantic equivalent for religious liberty, John Piper has advanced a provocative thesis that Jesus is both the source of tolerance and the end of tolerance. Piper's religious-liberty framing is particularly useful in developing a theocentric and Christocentric rendering of religious liberty. Citing 2 Thessalonians 1:7–10, Piper teaches that Jesus's eternal judgment produces a time-limited tolerance within a penultimate age: "Jesus Christ, the source and ground of all truth, will himself one day bring an end to all tolerance, and he alone will be exalted as the one and only Lord and Savior and Judge of the universe. . . . Since Christ alone, crucified-for-sinners, has the final right to kill his religious enemies, therefore Christianity will spread not by killing for Christ, but by dying with Christ—that others might live. The final triumph of the crucified Christ is a call to patient suffering, not political success."[14]

We leave to Christ what belongs only to him. But notice the consequences of Piper's argument. A commitment to religious liberty leads to a patient trust in Christ's exclusivity and authority and a posture of humility toward religious diversity, knowing that domination or coercion is ineffective to bring about belief. This is, in some respect, freeing. Christians will understandably reject the false tenets of their neighbors' beliefs, but a Christian understanding of judgment will also allow them to love their neighbors as people made in the image of God for whom dialogue and persuasion are possible. We are not called to avenge God for not being worshiped but to leave room for his wrath (Rom. 12:19). There may be no greater foundation for promoting cultural peace than the convictions that our neighbors are made in God's image and that Jesus is Lord.

Christ's ability to execute judgment over false belief is bound up with the authority granted to him as King and Lord. Piper correctly notes that if Jesus will bring false belief to an end, no other source—including ourselves—has that adjudicating authority. The role of Christ as King thus sets up a hierarchy, wherein the kingdoms of the world are subjugated to the eternal judgment of Christ's kingship (Rev. 1:5). Because judgment is final and ultimate, tolerance and, by extension, religious liberty are not eternal goods that last into the eschaton. Religious liberty must not be taken beyond the bounds of its temporal purpose. Thus, the eternal reality of judgment makes room for false belief in the present era.

Piper's christological foundation for religious liberty forms the basis for a doctrine of pluralism.[15] Piper argues that the spiritual nature of the kingdom of God prevents any form of religious coercion: "God himself is the foundation for our commitment to a pluralistic democratic order—not because pluralism is his ultimate ideal, but because in a fallen world, legal coercion will not produce the kingdom of God."[16] Theologian S. M. Hutchens similarly grounds his doctrine of religious liberty in "divine forbearance."[17] Hutchens, like Piper, works backward from judgment to a foundation for religious liberty: "Toleration" results from awaiting "condemnation and judgment."[18] He therefore rejects any "rights"-based language associated with religious liberty for fear of promoting the idea that those in sin and error possess positive rights to defy God's lordship. He writes, "The time given in which no action is taken in judgment must be regarded as a limited period of grace, and is never a 'right.'"[19]

Baptist historian Jason G. Duesing likewise argues that Jesus's kingship has implications for religious liberty. The fact that a "future day is coming when the name of Jesus will go forth and all creatures will bow and confess him as Lord"[20] means, writes Duesing, that religious liberty exists within a defined era and that knowledge of Christ's return and judgment "should serve as a warning to all outside of Christ that freedom to worship other gods without the judgment of the one true God will come to an end."[21]

Moore similarly champions a kingdom-of-God-centered approach to religious liberty. In *Onward*, Moore notes that the "question of religious liberty is, first and foremost, a question of the kingdom of God."[22] He draws on the themes of eschatology and kingship to approximate the shape of religious liberty in the current era of history.

> Those who would pretend to enforce the kingdom with tanks or guns or laws or edicts do not understand the nature of the kingdom Jesus preached. The risen Christ promised that the "one who conquers" will be given "authority over the nations and he will rule them as with a rod of iron" just as, Jesus said, "I have received authority from my Father" (Rev. 2:27). The "conquering" here though is not about subduing enemies on the outside, but about holding fast to the gospel and following the discipleship of Jesus to the end (Rev. 2:25–26). We are not yet kings over the world (1 Cor. 4:8), but are instead ambassadors bearing persuasive witness to the kingdom we have entered (2 Cor. 5:11, 20). This is not the time of rule, but the time of preparation to rule, as we, within the church, are formed and shaped into the kind of Christlike people who, at the resurrection, can sit with him upon the thrones of the cosmos (Luke 22:24–28; Rev. 3:21).[23]

For Moore, the nature of the kingdom of God assumes a doctrine of religious liberty defined as persons' ability to respond to the gospel apart from influence or coercion. The eternal nature of the kingdom of God restricts the power of the state (it has term-limited and penultimate authority), helps locate where the rule of Christ is presently manifest (the church), determines the method of evangelistic witness (persuasion), and marks out to whom the conscience is ultimately accountable (Christ). It is the already and not yet of God's kingdom that gives space for others' claims of lordship to have temporary freedom.

Religious liberty therefore gives shape to the reality that not all has been brought under Christ's reign (1 Cor. 15:28). Religious liberty exists because God's retribution awaits. Elsewhere, Moore argues that this passing age represents a "temporary suspension of doom. After this, the grace of God is not extended—only his justice, and that with severity."[24] Christ has not given authority to his church to judge the consciences of unbelievers, nor is that the role of the state. Christians are to use persuasion rather than coercion to engage others. The right understanding of the rule of God thus acts as a buttress against religious and political utopias.[25] It also means that the state should be nonpreferential toward religion, because its role is not to enforce or referee religious belief.[26]

By putting absolute judgment within the realm of the ultimate (the kingdom of God)—not the penultimate—Christians can make temporary room for dissenting, false belief. This is due to neither convenience nor concession but is a theological principle following from the reality of inaugurated eschatology. This does not mean that dissenting beliefs share equal merit with biblical orthodoxy. Rather, it means that no human or government authority can judge, end, or mete out punishment for false belief. Only Jesus has that power in his coming kingdom. Consider the words of the apostle Paul: "The times of ignorance God overlooked, but now he commands all people everywhere to repent, because he has fixed a day on which he will judge the world in righteousness by a man whom he has appointed; and of this he has given assurance to all by raising him from the dead" (Acts 17:30–31). As Paul's words reveal, humanity's current ignorance will not go unchecked. God has given Jesus the ability to judge the world "in righteousness." This implies that all judgment will be meted out with perfection. God will receive the honor due his name that was robbed from him by false religion.

Christians know where the arc of history bends and how erring ideologies will be addressed. We combat "philosophy and empty deceit" (Col. 2:8), but not through carnal warfare of the flesh—using suppression or coercion. Instead, we work to "destroy arguments and every lofty opinion raised against the knowledge of God, and take every thought captive to obey Christ" (2 Cor. 10:5). Christians can be patient with false religions and ideologies, because Christ promises perfect justice. Our duty is to combat them, not to insist upon their necessary banishment. As Christians, we have no part to play in punishing false belief. We argue and plead with it, but we do not smite it. We reconcile ourselves to a world in which unbeliever and believer coexist.

Baptist ethicist Evan Lenow finds the parable of the wheat and the tares (Matt. 13:24–30) illustrative in demonstrating that future judgment prevents coercive action: "True judgment is left up to God. It is not the job of the government to judge and remove these people for their unbelief. God will judge them, and his judgment is final."[27] Because sorting out the wheat from the tares belongs to God exclusively, "Jesus was apparently taking a position against coercion in matters of religious conscience. Discernment is the responsibility of the church, but judgment belongs only to God."[28] The promise of sorting the wheat from the tares is the assurance of impending judgment.[29]

John Locke presented a similar argument for religious liberty on the grounds of judgment. Locke deferred to Jesus Christ for the ultimate decision distinguishing heresy from orthodoxy. Since that decision rests outside the hands of government or individuals, individuals, in humility, must refrain from judging one another concerning religious affairs within the civil domain: "The Decision of that Question belongs only to the Supreme Judge of all men, to whom also alone belongs the Punishment of the Erroneous."[30]

By refusing to bring history's future judgment into the present, Christians can extend an account of religious liberty to their unbelieving neighbors with whom they disagree. Religious liberty, therefore, is not a political idea searching for religious justification. Rather, religious liberty is rooted in the very nature of Christ's kingship and sovereignty.

Religious Liberty and the Subordination of Earthly Rule

The kingdom of God as the center for religious liberty subordinates the authority of earthly rulers to the reign of Christ. This has immense implications for the power that Christians ascribe to the state. If the state lacks ultimate power and cannot mediate God's saving rule, then the state's claim over and reach into religious matters by definition are limited. "Limited government" ought not be a buzzword for conservative politics but rather a guidepost for how Christians understand the state. Oliver O'Donovan notes that Christians have a duty to stand in the gap and remind the state of its limited power: "The most truly Christian state understands itself most thoroughly as 'secular.' It makes the confession of Christ's victory and accepts the relegation of its own authority. It echoes the words of John the Baptist: 'He must increase; I must decrease' (John 3:30). Like the Baptist, it has a place on the threshold of the Kingdom, not within it."[31] O'Donovan's claim rescues "limited government" from the banks of partisanship.

While I reject the idea that the state can make a formal "confession of Christ's victory," those who occupy the levers of power would do well to understand their authority in relationship to that of Christ. A state that does not see itself as a god is a state not only subscribing to the First Amendment but also obeying the First Commandment. By focusing on the kingdom of God, Christians recognize that the state's authority derives from a higher power. To again quote O'Donovan, even where Christians find themselves at odds with the state, "the only corresponding service that the church can render to this authority of the passing world is to help it make that act of self-denying recognition."[32] The state that actively refuses to see itself as an arbiter of the divine or over all affairs is a state acting in accord with the New Testament.[33] (One of the tasks of a Christian ethic of religious liberty, then, is to remind policy makers that they are accountable to a divinely established moral order, such as natural law—the moral theory that a God-given and self-evident universal moral order exists that acts of reason and practical deliberation, in theory and in practice, can grasp as intellectually knowable and function as behaviorally directive.) This comprehension of the moral order and its basic goods defines and identifies which actions are imminently reasonable and worth pursuing—even apart from an *immediate* appeal to divine revelation—by achieving the purposes or goals consistent with goods constitutive of human nature's design. Natural law provides an account of public and personal morality that all persons, in principle, could agree on. Natural law is action guiding and action explaining by providing an account of the directiveness we intuitively act on to achieve the ends consistent with our design.[34]

Due to natural law, legislators can rule justly without committing the state to a formal religious or metaphysical commitment. As Henry writes, "It is not the role of government to judge between rival systems of metaphysics and to legislate one among others. Government's role is to protect and preserve a free course for its constitutional guarantees."[35] This does not lead to an empty-headed "moral neutrality" but speaks to the reality that government must make moral decisions without saying that one metaphysic and one alone must ground a moral norm.

Elsewhere, Henry argues that "the Church's most important concern concerning law and order is that government should recognize its ultimate answerability to the supernatural source, sanction, and specification of human rights and duties, and hence of government's limited nature and role as a 'minister' of justice. This recognition implied a congruity between the social commandments of the Decalogue and the principles expressed in the laws of the State."[36] Henry's call is not to a formal church-state union but to a government whose rulers understand their allegiance to a supernatural foundation. Thus, language like "In God We Trust" may be hopelessly vague, but it is and ought to be the maximal claim a state may make concerning religion, and this is for moral grounds only. Thus, Christians are to pronounce that the power of the state and its policy makers is limited and circumscribed, whether the state is cognizant of this or not.

The edict that Christ's name be carried to kings (Acts 9:15) is not a call for church-state establishment. It is a call to kings to repent, to rule justly, to understand that their power is term limited and passing away (Col. 1:16; Rev. 11:15). A political ruler can have a biblically shaped conscience and even rule by that conscience, but they cannot formally ensconce their religion in law. It is neither legitimate nor necessary. This is because the justice and wisdom obtained through the natural law are not in tension with biblical justice but are more firmly and expressly established by it. The greatest hope for social reform and the just society in this penultimate age is not found ultimately in public policy alone, but in rulers who confess Christ as true King and turn to sanctified reason to rule in accord with true justice for the sake of the common good. Likewise, religious liberty means that a political leader or political body is not limited by a religious test but only by a test as to whether the leader or body can obtain to the ideals of justice.

There is no evidence in Scripture that a church-state establishment is a prerequisite for the state to be just or for society to be moral. Rather, natural law exists to accomplish both. We can arrive at just government and a moral society without a church-state establishment or civil religion by relying on the natural law pattern of creation order established in Genesis 1–2 and reestablished in the Noahic covenant of Genesis 8–9 (which I will explore further on). At the same time, we should acknowledge that natural law is not a neutral idea. When I speak of natural law, I am speaking of a natural law *tradition* that ultimately originates in the eternal mind. While the tradition assumes a realist metaphysic and ontology, the tradition posits the intelligibility of the natural law apart from the immediate appeal to religious presuppositions.

To formalize a state's relationship with a church or religion is to exceed the jurisdiction of the state's authority, an authority it does not possess (Matt. 16:18–19). Neither is a state's reliance on religion a necessary proof that it will be just. The United States' history with slavery is a testament to how civil religion can be both a source of continued oppression and a source of liberation. The test of fitness to rule is justice. So a thoroughgoing political theology of the type being argued for in this chapter is going to irritate progressivism because it insists on the good—and even the necessity—of religion for civil society. But it will also irritate various conservatisms by refusing to reduce religion to a socially useful totem subordinate to some other purpose than salvation.

All that has been said thus far has been pointing toward the question of the state's authority over religious affairs. The answer thus far is this: it has remarkably little, if none at all. The proper end of any earthly government is to uphold justice and secure the basic rights of all human beings, to promote the common good, and to restrain and punish evil deeds citizens commit against each other. From a Christian vantage point, we hope the state aims to achieve temporal peace so that the gospel might spread, rightly protecting the freedom of the church to fulfill the Great Commission. In response, the church respects the civil powers granted to the state by pursuing righteousness in humble citizenship (1 Tim. 1:2). The state plays an indirect role in citizens obtaining the spiritual good. Promoting access to the common good only, the state gives space to citizens to discern and pursue the spiritual good. The state removes impediments to the spiritual good by upholding the common good. Christians are to be faithful citizens who view the state as a legitimate expression of God's authority on earth established for their and society's welfare. They must ensure that it keeps to its temporal jurisdiction and not ascribe to it authority over sacred affairs.

In the view advocated here, the only "authority" a state may have over a religion is to restrain a religion where it incontrovertibly threatens the common good in such a way that no one of goodwill would disagree. Here, the authority concerns civil affairs, not doctrinal ones. As Lenow notes, drawing from Romans 13:1–7, government is established to ensure "civil peace, not doctrinal purity."[37] This speaks not only to a scriptural argument but also to a natural law argument. The very nature of religion as a conscience-dependent experience would seem to entail that because the state cannot effect religious belief, it has no authority over religion qua religion. The state's commission is to treat all religions equally and to adjudicate only those offenses that are criminal in nature. Leaving aside legal debates about the free exercise clause of the First Amendment, the greater theological implication is both profound and simple: aside from instances in which religion is causing an indisputable harm and danger to society, the state lacks the mandate to adjudicate theological affairs. The fact that a nonconfessional state is the ideal is separate from the requirement that a robust public square exist where different religious traditions can debate matters of deep moral importance. I am arguing not that legislators or voters should be less religious but that the state should be nonconfessional.

Even when the state needs to investigate harmful actions stemming from religious motivation, the state cannot adjudicate whether the harm stems from correct or incorrect theology. Rather, a state can observe the effects of a religion's teaching in society and then reasonably discern that a teaching is causing harm and act to restrict that religion on the basis of its outcomes. What it must do in this situation, however, is withhold adjudicating whether the religion is true or false. This distinction accords with the words of John Leland, one of the architects of America's religious liberty regime, who thought that the government should punish bad outcomes that result from religion, not religion itself: "The duty of the magistrates is, not to judge of the divinity or tendency of doctrines; but when those principles break out into overt acts of violence, then to use the civil sword and punish the vagrant for what he has done, and not for the religious phrenzy that he acted from."[38]

Before questions of harm, though, we must understand the state's proper place within the unveiling of God's kingdom. Hendrikus Berkhof has argued that with the resurrection and ascension of Christ, the powers have been defanged, so to speak. Their power is term limited, and their authority is prescribed. Absolute authority is not theirs. But politics and statecraft remain a creational ordinance stemming from God's design for the world. And when political orders thwart God's design by exceeding their just authority, expect politics to take on a very religious-like fervor.

Christians can be politically homeless only by way of ultimate commitments, but to deny the penultimate importance of political order—as though indifference is virtuous—is to invite a latent Gnosticism. Political detachment, in extreme form, casts off the creational ordinance of Romans 13. We must understand earthly political orders are "still the framework of creation, preserving it from disintegration."[39] As Robert A. Markus writes, "The powers of this world are posed between the eschatological kingdom and the realm of Satan or the Antichrist, and they have a choice between serving the one or the other. By claiming absolute powers not subject to God's authority, by usurping quasi-divine prerogative over human beings, in short, by seeking to escape the conditions imposed by the triumph of Christ's cross over them, they betray the purpose for which they are sanctioned."[40] Thus, we might reasonably conclude that if a state deems itself an arbiter over religious affairs, it is not only transgressing its circumscribed role but also assuming a demonic undertaking of a false mantle of authority.

One of the most significant passages that gives witness to the limited role of the state is Matthew 22:17–22.[41]

> "Tell us, then, what you think. Is it lawful to pay taxes to Caesar, or not?" But Jesus, aware of their malice, said, "Why put me to the test, you hypocrites? Show me the coin for the tax." And they brought him a denarius. And Jesus said to them, "Whose likeness and inscription is this?" They said, "Caesar's." Then he said to them, "Therefore render to Caesar the things that are Caesar's, and to God the things that are God's." When they heard it, they marveled. And they left him and went away.

As Catholic philosopher Francis J. Beckwith notes, the traditional interpretation of this passage is that Jesus says the church and government have different spheres of authority.[42] Beckwith also notes that Jesus's question to the Pharisees about whose image is on the coin begs an additional "unsaid" question: Who or what has the image of God on it? Beckwith writes, "If the coin represents the authority of Caesar because it has his image on it, then we, human beings, are under the authority of God because we have his image on us."[43] This authority distinction has far-reaching implications, according to Beckwith, because it confirms the theory of limited government: "Thus, both government and the church, though having separate jurisdictions, share a common obligation to advance the good of those who are made in God's image."[44]

Theologian Wayne A. Grudem has argued similarly that Matthew 22 helps demarcate the limits of the state. "'The things that are God's' are *not* to be under the control of the civil government (or 'Caesar')."[45] At the same time, what belongs to the government is not exempt from God's rule. Rather, God decrees that the government has certain legitimate powers. On this account, all power, rule, and jurisdictional authority are grounded in God's decree. James K. A. Smith argues that this passage should not be read as Jesus "carving up distinct jurisdictions of authority."[46] The legitimate sphere of government authority is not an "uncontested sphere of secular right."[47] Smith goes on to say that Jesus offers the state legitimate sanction in the same sense of "granting someone the right to occupy a building that has been condemned to demolition" because Jesus understands the state to have a limited and derived authority given by God.[48] Jesus is offering a politics determined ultimately by future judgment, not independent sphere sovereignty.

Civil affairs such as taxes belong to Caesar's sphere, while religious affairs belong to God. Jesus's words restrict the civil realm but also the church as well, by insisting that his hearers must allow those duties divinely mandated to the state by God and not encroach on them. Thus, anarchy and totalitarianism are outside the purview of the New Testament's witness on church-state relationships and religious liberty. Oscar Cullman argues that Jesus's interactions with the state reveal that "he does not regard the State as in any sense a final, divine institution: on the other hand, we see that he accepts the State and radically renounces attempts to overthrow it."[49] Cullman posits that Jesus saw the state as "circumscribed" with a particular "duality": "On the one hand, the State is nothing final. On the other, it has the right to demand what is necessary to its existence—but no more. Every totalitarian claim of the State is thereby disallowed."[50]

In what context is Jesus's announcement made? Jesus's announcement that Caesar's claim is limited supports the idea that the kingdom of God is the overarching entity that assigns the state its proper jurisdiction of administering justice only (Rom. 13:1–7). H. Richard Niebuhr captures the spirit of the jurisdictional issues at stake by reminding us that discussions about religious liberty are ultimately about issues of authority and allegiance to ultimate ends: "Religion, so understood, lies beyond the provenance of the state not because it is a private, inconsequential, or other-worldly matter, but because it concerns men's allegiance to a sovereignty and a community more immediate, more inclusive, and more fateful than those of the political commonwealth."[51]

O'Donovan argues that, from the vantage of Christian theology, the "state exists in order to give judgment, but under the authority of Christ's rule it gives judgment under law, never as its own law."[52] I take this to mean something a bit different than O'Donovan may mean. Rather than under the guise of "Christendom," states make judgments *under* law—subordinate to Christ whether acknowledged or not. This is entirely consistent with the framework of this chapter if the governing authority is operating from a conscience shaped by either the gospel or natural law rather than seeking to advance Christianity in law as a way of legitimizing it *for the sake of* social order.

From the perspective of the state, then, it is possible to see how religion helps to buttress the claims of an overweening state. According to Peter J. Leithart, "So long as the church preaches the gospel and functions as a properly 'political' reality, a polity of her own, the kings of the earth have a problem on their hands. . . . As soon as the Church appears, it becomes clear to any alert politician that worldly politics is no longer the only game in town. The introduction of the Church into any city means that the city has a challenger within the walls."[53]

While any state will be tempted to exercise its powers too broadly and aggressively, a Christian understanding of religious liberty provides the state with its own divine calling. Rather than understanding the state as being all-encompassing or tasked with an oversight outside its competence, Christian thought understands the state as ordered to protecting the common good by restraining evildoers and giving freedom for that which is necessary and essential to a flourishing society. In this way, the church serves the state by calling the state to its proper domain. This is a positive rather than a pessimistic vision of the state. A church that takes seriously its call to proclaim the kingdom of God will thus challenge the state to be true to its limited calling, allowing the church to do what Paul calls for: "I urge that supplications, prayers, intercessions, and thanksgivings be made for all people, for kings and all who are in high positions, that we may lead a peaceful and quiet life, godly and dignified in every way. This is good, and it is pleasing in the sight of God our Savior, who desires all people to be saved and to come to the knowledge of the truth" (1 Tim. 2:1–4). It would appear, then, that there is an inextricable link between the state functioning as it ought with its limited purview and the church going about its mission of evangelization. In this way, the church's mission includes the announcement of the self-limits of the state's authority.

As Sherif Girgis and Ryan T. Anderson argue, the state's respect for religious liberty acts to "impose universal limits on the state's authority."[54] As those authors note, the limited jurisdiction of the state's coercive power allows civil society (and I would argue primarily the church) to make moral claims on the state.[55] Indeed, it is by understanding its limits that the "most truly Christian state understands itself most thoroughly as secular" (a concept given fuller explanation in chap. 3).[56]

The Kingdom of God and the Soteriological Aspect of Religious Liberty

Issues of salvation can never be separated from questions central to the kingdom of God, because God's rule simultaneously manifests his saving rule. As Baptist theologian Barrett Duke notes, "The doctrine of salvation itself contributes to our understanding of God's design for religious liberty."[57] If entry into the kingdom is contingent on regeneration, the nature of regeneration raises questions about the medium or vehicle through which individuals are saved. It is a question of process and agency. The kingdom of God intersects with themes relevant to religious liberty: the conscience, justification by faith alone, and the voluntary nature of saving faith. The interior logic of the gospel demands features consistent with religious liberty.

The conscience, in tandem with the will, is the vehicle that makes individuals realize guilt and their need for salvation (more will be said about the function of the conscience later). The conscience indicts in the sense that it convicts individuals of wrongdoing (Rom. 1:21; 2:14–16) while also directing the inner person to their need for absolution (2 Cor. 1:12; 1 Tim. 1:19). The conscience is one aspect of humanity's nature, making a person rational and "free to think for himself as responsible to God for the use of his intellect. As a moral being, he is free to choose good or evil and is responsible to God for his choice."[58] Entry into God's kingdom depends on the conscience being convicted of sin and persuaded by the gospel (Acts 17:2–4; 2 Cor. 5:11), which means rationally self-chosen without external coercion. Before we examine how one's faith is to be exercised, we must recognize the relevance of religious liberty for how salvation is obtained: in a person recognizing guilt and the need for redemption. Thus, the kingdom of God is received by faith and not by external factors or consideration. One cannot be blackmailed, coerced, or lured into the kingdom of God.

In the New Testament, a person receives salvation and is transferred from the domain of darkness to the kingdom of light through faith (John 3:3; Rom. 1:16–18; Col. 1:13). The different understandings of "faith" sparked the Protestant Reformation and are partly responsible for the division of Christendom. One might reject the idea that justification by faith is connected to religious liberty, but that requires examining the nature of faith. Faith is settled trust in the finished work of Jesus Christ to secure salvation. Faith must operate personally, freely, and voluntarily in order for there to be saving faith.

Justification by faith denotes the personalist nature of salvation: humans (the lawbreakers) standing before God (the lawgiver) asking on what grounds they are to be saved. No action of another individual, church, or state can substitute for God's grace and a person's faith. A proper account of religious liberty thus rejects all forms of proxy baptisms in which an individual is converted apart from *both* divine agency and individual responsiveness. From this vantage point, a Protestant confessional gloss on religious liberty emerges.

Baptist theologian Jonathan Leeman argues that the "grand mistake of Christendom" is nothing less than infant baptism. According to Leeman, this practice, which coincided with medieval church-state relationships, was wholly problematic because it "treated the membership in the church and state as two overlapping circles, thereby usurping the authority of the church."[59] By making church and state membership one and the same, an unregenerate church polity was a logical outcome. A dominantly unregenerate polity worked out like leaven, over time, will lead to a form of Christian nominalism and civil religion. Hence, religious liberty requires a conversionist account of salvation for it to be most coherent. A Christian account of religious liberty relies on a doctrine of justification by faith by insisting that individuals enter God's kingdom individually and conscientiously, thus negating a porous relationship between church and state membership.

If the kingdom of God manifests itself through the conscience brought to faith through justification, then asking institutions or persons to mediate salvation on behalf of individuals, apart from God working through sinful persons, is ruled out. Hughey notes that the absence of government's ability to effect spiritual regeneration assumes that "no earthly power has the right to enforce obedience to God, since his authority over the spirit of man has not been delegated."[60] Or as Paul writes in 1 Timothy 2:5, there is only "one mediator between God and men, the man Jesus Christ." This is significant because it relativizes the role that any outside force could play in accomplishing an individual's salvation. Because individuals are fallen, "people are incapable of fully interpreting the will of God in all matters for other people, and they are certainly incapable of properly enforcing spiritual standards."[61]

This notion of fallibility, however, also speaks to the question of agency. In the salvation framework inherent within Christianity, individual salvation results in belonging to a community, but individual salvation rests in an individual assenting to God's call to salvation. Thus, salvation cannot be accomplished or mediated on behalf of individuals. "The kingship of Jesus," writes O'Donovan, "is such as can be recognized only by those who recognize it on their own account; it lacks accessibility to public opinion."[62] In the New Testament, salvation is a self-disclosed reality; it is not conferred wholesale on nations or others for the sake of others.

This personalist nature of faith at the root of religious liberty is reflected in the voluntary nature of the kingdom of God. Coerced faith is a contradiction in terms. "Any law of church or state," J. Philip Wogaman writes, "designed to make people be Christian would, if obeyed, more precisely succeed in making them *not* be Christian."[63] This is why forced conversion is futile. Individuals cannot be made to believe one matter or another. They might be deceived or deluded, yet the nature of faith is that assent to faith is voluntary. Individuals can be coerced into religious performance and religious observance, but faith can never be effectuated externally. The nature of true faith requires that faith be grasped and acted on freely and sincerely. A faith arrived at apart from deep conviction is not faith.

A. F. Carrillo de Albornoz notes how religious liberty is a precursor to authentic faith: "Humanity, as it is presented in the biblical revelation, is intelligible only in the hypothesis that the purpose of God is better served by leaving man free to make choices for which he alone bears the consequences, than by restraining him or coercing him in order to keep him from making mistakes."[64] At the same time, the way Christ advanced the kingdom during his earthly ministry militates against the claim that Christians can act either triumphantly or coercively in religious dealings: "The basis of religious liberty is the very fact that Christ did not come in heavenly splendor and worldly majesty to subjugate any possible resistance and force all and everybody into subjection. Christ made himself a servant and humbled himself even unto the death of the cross. . . . Or to use a theological term which at any rate is familiar to people of Lutheran tradition: 'The foundation of religious liberty is the fact of the *theologia crucis* (theology of the cross) over against the *theologia gloriae* (theology of glory).'"[65] This is a profound insight. When understood properly, religious liberty affirms the pattern of incarnational ministry that marked the Lord's ministry. The Lord of the universe chose the meekness of human flesh and the scorn of rejection, rather than military conquest or political power, to advance his kingdom. Religious liberty is thus a surrender to the way of the cross, not power or domination.

Conclusion

The kingdom of God is the plausibility structure of the Christian imagination around religious liberty. Before religious liberty is an intrahuman doctrine meant to settle disputes within political communities, it is fundamentally a response to the relationship humanity has to God. In this framework, religious liberty is tectonically situated to address fundamental ideas related to Christ's authority, the state's authority, and the nature of saving faith. In this, it is *primarily* a theological doctrine with an anthropological application. That is not meant to diminish the significance of anthropology to the theological task of religious liberty, but only to determine that before religious liberty is a political ethic, it is a *theological* ethic.

3

Religious Liberty and Christian Secularism

TO RESCUE RELIGIOUS LIBERTY from the sole domain of political philosophy, Christians must place religious liberty in the story of creation, fall, redemption, and restoration. Unless an idea can be understood from within the story line of Scripture, it will fail to be understood as Christian.

Why root religious liberty in creation, fall, redemption, and restoration? For one, we need the story line provided by the horizon of the kingdom of God to shape our understanding of religious liberty, and the kingdom of God only makes sense against the backdrop of creation, fall, redemption, and restoration.

Second, religious liberty needs to be a publicly accessible ethic grounded in creation itself and bound to the current age while also looking toward its fulfillment in the age to come, where, as I have argued, there will no longer be religious liberty. Religious liberty must be understood as a *social* practice irrespective of whether the recipients of such liberty are Christians. In other words, non-Christians should stand to benefit from a Christian account of religious liberty even if they do not recognize it as Christian in origin. This is so, as I will argue, because the desire to worship God and to make meaning in one's life—to constitute one's self—are creational realities existing within each person regardless of whether the person worships or makes meaning accurately. Religious liberty, understood as the ability of a creature to orient themselves properly to God, is a creation ordinance.

God created humans to relate to him as vice-regents in their quest to exercise dominion over the world (Gen. 1:26–28). In Eden, "liberty" did not exist so much as the choice to obey or to rebel. We all know how the story went. As sin entered the world, the casting off of God's authority brought about a schism between God and humans. Humanity's right understanding of God, once answered by God's loving-kindness, was exchanged for imitators. Rather than looking to God, rebellious humans looked elsewhere to justify their existence and find answers to life's deepest questions. Fundamentally, they worshiped other gods. This is why the First Commandment declares, "You shall have no other gods before me." God was not acknowledging the existence of other gods but only humanity's desire to make gods of *something*. Religious liberty by no means excuses idolatry but explains how to relate to the idolatry of humanity apart from God's final judgment.

As the story unfolds, the drama of redemption is enacted. The people who become members of the covenant of redemption are marked out for a priestly role on God's earth. From Abraham to Moses to David to Christ, a nation, Israel, becomes a people drawn from among the nations to take part in God's divine reclamation project. This mission of God, while temporarily a governmental project in the nation of Israel, is never understood chiefly as a governmental project, though Christianity would take on great political significance. The mission of God's people has an eternal scope while taking place on a temporal stage. As the drama unfolds, unbelief and rebellion persist. What is to be done with unbelief? We know that unbelief will not be a reality in the new heaven and new earth, but what of the present age? God does not honor religious differences. He demands that all humanity give him the glory he is due. All false religion will be judged. But this judgment belongs to Christ alone and will come later.

A crucial reality confronts us in the biblical narrative. Among the governments and nations of the world, aside from Israel with its unique place in time and history, religious idolatry is not something that civil authorities are authorized to combat. Humanity's idolatry is condemned broadly (Rom. 1:18–32) in relation to humanity's Creator, but governments do not have the authority to hold liable their inhabitants' idolatry, only their injustice. In between the descent into sin and the second coming of Christ, an intervening period of time—*now*—exists when religious rebellion has free rein. If there is no evidence in Scripture that governments (apart from Israel's example, now expired) are given the sword to execute justice against the greatest injustice of all—disobeying God—what does this mean for how we understand religious liberty?

In the last chapter, we saw how God's kingdom provides the backdrop for a Christian understanding of religious liberty. Because Christians are promised the kingdom's coming judgment, we can be patient with religious plurality in the present. But more must be said about the time between Jesus's resurrection and the consummation of history. If the kingdom of God establishes the inevitability of final judgment, what does that mean for the intervening or interim period of history? This leads to a Christian idea of secularism. Secularism describes the era of what I am calling "contestability"—the idea that it is normal and expected for irreconcilable disagreement and competition to exist among religions and ideologies vying for acceptance in the public domain. To establish this idea of Christian secularism, I will rely on recent scholarship on the Noahic covenant and its implications for religious liberty as a temporal creational ordinance that allows for the peaceable existence of false religious belief.

The Covenant of Re-creation and Religious Liberty

Baptist theologian Jonathan Leeman and Presbyterian theologian David VanDrunen have offered the most sophisticated accounts of a distinctly Christian rendering of religious liberty by grounding it in the Noahic covenant. The Noahic covenant is God's promise to sustain and preserve a minimal social order for the world's continued existence. Hence, it has also been called the "covenant of preservation."[1] O. Palmer Robertson writes that "the covenant with Noah binds together God's purposes in creation with his purposes in redemption. Noah, his seed, and all creation benefit from this gracious relationship."[2] It "provides the foundation for the world-wide proclamation of the gospel."[3] The Noahic covenant does not teach that all are saved through the Noahic covenant by virtue of their existence; rather, the Noahic covenant is a form of saving grace only in that the world is not destroyed by sin. The Noahic covenant provides the stage, as it were, on which the story of redemption unfolds. The world is a platform for the covenantal drama to unfold and for society to continue. Without the Noahic covenant, Christ would have no world to come into, which means that an incarnational anticipation is built into the preservative function of the Noahic covenant. The Noahic covenant, therefore, has only an indirect redemptive purpose.

Applying equally and universally to all persons of the world irrespective of their religious commitments, Genesis 8:20–9:17 establishes God's decree for procreation, proper eating, and retributive justice in a postflood world.[4] Why God focused only on these three aspects may seem odd, but understood properly, they are the building blocks for society's continued sustainability—families must populate the earth, families must fruitfully provide for their well-being, and there must be a system of justice to ensure a stable social order for families to live within. In short, the Noahic covenant is God's promise to maintain the conditions for humanity's survival and to not destroy the world through another worldwide flood. VanDrunen refers to the three creational aspects of the Noahic covenant as familial, enterprise, and judicial institutions.[5] He grounds the modern political order in the minimalist contours of the Noahic covenant, a project I find common cause with.

The Noahic covenant mirrors the cultural mandate of Genesis 1, except it modifies the mandate by accounting for a world in which sin is the norm. The Noahic covenant preserves a common social order in which humans interact with one another. This covenant assumes the reality of sin and braces for it by constraining it through the establishment of justice and right order (Gen. 9:5–6). More important, the Noahic covenant still operates and will continue on until future judgment—or "while the earth remains" (8:22). This means that all of earth's inhabitants share in the blessings of common grace established by the Noahic covenant. And the realities of procreation, eating, and justice are realities not exclusive to Christians alone.

By virtue of the Noahic covenant's reconstitution of the social order in Genesis 8:20–9:17, Leeman argues that "God has not authorized human beings to prosecute crimes against himself."[6] When we look at the requirement for justice within the Noahic covenant, Leeman asserts, we see that the penal code of Genesis 9 adjudicates wrongs between fellow human beings only, not between human beings and God. This does not mean that God grants a right to rebel; rather, it prohibits humans from vindicating God through retributive or punitive actions. Humans are not given the task of criminalizing wrong belief, and it is difficult to imagine what enforcements would be used to ensure correct belief. All of this suggests that personal religion is outside the realm of civil enforcement. While ultimate justice awaits those who refuse to acknowledge God, the act of false belief is not a form of social injustice in light of the Noahic covenant. Instead, the Noahic covenant concerns the bare minimum operations for society's continued existence in view of sin. The Noahic covenant reveals that adequate social cooperation can occur apart from absolute agreement on religious matters for society to remain legitimate and ordered toward the common good.

God does not require accurate religious belief for participation in the reconstituted social order, so religion is not a biblical criteria for membership in a political community. This is further demonstrated in that social life and social tranquility are predicated on the routine domesticity set down in the Noahic covenant—family life, moral uprightness, justice, and industriousness. Thus, the Noahic covenant sets boundaries on what are legitimate and illegitimate grounds for exclusion within a political society; such things as race and religion have no bearing on a person's ability to cooperate civilly and meaningfully within society.[7] We are called to a common life together as participants of a common human nature, not a common religion. The Noahic covenant implies that while society cannot exist without a common morality, it can exist without a common religion. Of course, this can be the case only if not stretched too far. The Noahic covenant is not a call to eliminate God from the public square, and surely, where common grace, natural law, and justice are upended or unrecognizable, no society can long maintain itself. Where the natural family, justice, and human industry are jettisoned, society's continued viability would necessarily be called into question. VanDrunen posits that a robust common good may not even be fully attainable by the Noahic covenant's standards but rather calls for a "modest" common good, a degree of "*some* shared moral vision, but this vision need not be substantively rich in order to sustain a peaceful coexistence."[8]

What this means, practically, is that only forms of worship that physically harm other persons should be restrained or punished in light of the minimalist social order of Genesis 9:5–7. What God establishes in Genesis 9 is a justice system meant only to punish wrongs and mediate disputes between humans. Leeman writes, "The God of the Bible gives governments authority to prosecute crimes against human beings, not the authority to prosecute crimes against himself. As long as people remain unharmed, false religion should be tolerated publicly and privately. This is the call to free exercise."[9] VanDrunen echoes this: "Insofar as God delegates judicial authority to human judges, he commissions them to administer penalties proportionate to wrongs done to fellow humans, not penalties proportionate to wrongs done to him."[10]

Leeman's and VanDrunen's paradigms offer the possibility of rooting religious liberty within a doctrine of God and in creation while grounding it in a biblical eschatology that is advancing through the development of covenantal theology. This means that religious liberty inheres *within* God's design for the present social order—that is, it is not merely a contingency of history but divinely orchestrated. On this account, religious liberty is objectively grounded in the fabric of creation and the social order. It is no mere construct but speaks to the reality that not all forms of sin—namely, unbelief—are criminal. On this account, religious liberty is a postflood creation ordinance.

The Noahic covenant also grounds the idea of the free exercise of religion. Because God has not established civil order to seek out and eliminate false worship, false worship is to be "tolerated." Thus false belief is not punishable, leaving room for false belief to be exercised. Leeman's overture to "authority" complements the limited jurisdiction that the state oversees: to administer law and adjudicate claims between persons, not between persons and God, since the relationship between God and humans is an interior one. There are areas of thought and belief to which the state cannot lay claim—determining true or false belief is one of them.

The canopy of Genesis 9 and the Noahic covenant serves as a precursor and backdrop to the jurisdiction of the kingdom of God in the drama of redemption. As the kingdom of God establishes the demarcations of what is eligible for judgment, it also establishes the demarcations of what is not—namely, lesser authorities have neither the authority nor the competence to adjudicate theological matters. Only God can execute judgment against false religion or erring belief. (Only the local church exercising its rightful authority over those it considers members has the ability to execute judgment against Christians who indulge in unrepentant heresy and immorality.) The argument grounded in the Noahic covenant complements the promise of Christ's future kingdom judgment. While the Noahic covenant is a covenant of creation, it is operative only "while the earth remains" (Gen. 8:22). The Noahic covenant concludes when the kingdom of God is consummated in full. In grounding this doctrine of "religious tolerance" in the Bible, Leeman appeals to Christ's kingdom, which is given present institutional authority in the local church. Hence, Leeman's emphasis on the "keys of the kingdom" as the cipher that unlocks the authority of the local church also provides a crucial insight into limiting the authority of the state over religious affairs.[11] Grounding religious liberty in the Noahic covenant allows erring religious consciences to be free from government penalty.

Appealing to the Noahic covenant and a biblically based system of natural law where God orders the world through universal moral norms dictated by reason and conscience,[12] VanDrunen observes that "God established the Noahic covenant with the entire human race and gave no religious qualification for participation in its blessings and activities."[13] Here VanDrunen states that natural law theology "implies the propriety of recognizing a right to religious freedom."[14] It is a function of natural law insofar as acting on religious reasons deemed as obligatory by the person helps fulfill their goal of honest living. It is worth noting that VanDrunen's characterization of religious freedom makes it less a good to be celebrated or a positive "right" and more an implication and accommodation of the Noahic covenant. Therefore, VanDrunen expresses a "modest appreciation" for liberal notions of religious freedom and secularism while acknowledging that what the two agitate for in their more extreme forms is opposed.[15]

It is important to note the universal scope of the Noahic covenant, but it is also important to recognize that it does not carry jurisdiction over false worship. God expects humans to operate in the common realm through a commitment to conscience and natural law, not proper worship. This should be intuitive, for in rejecting this idea, one must reject the proposition that a non-Christian can live a moral and fulfilled life. A human does not need to be a Christian in order to meaningfully participate within a culture.

The Noahic covenant is designed to providentially sustain the social order through institutions that make life and society manageable. VanDrunen therefore argues that the neglect of a penalty for false worship when God reorders the world postfall offers a "crucial" biblical-theological foundation for religious freedom.

> If God called all human beings generally to the pursuit of procreation, eating, and justice (and whatever other obligations this covenant entails), without excluding people for reason of religious profession, then excluding people for this reason is inherently problematic. Also significant is how Genesis 9:6 commands the pursuit of justice and authorizes the use of coercion through the *lex talionis*, which concerns *intrahuman* disputes and the injuries one person inflicts upon another. It does not speak of human beings prosecuting each other for wrongs inflicted upon God. Therefore, to prohibit a person from engaging in a particular kind of religious practice, which does not injure another person but allegedly injured God, seems to transgress the boundaries of rightful human authority under the Noahic covenant.[16]

There are thus two prongs for religious liberty. First, God did not intend to endow earthly governments with the authority to prosecute crimes against him. Second, according to VanDrunen, religious liberty is primarily aimed at preserving society. It functions downstream from God's command for intrahuman justice: "God delegates to human beings the authority to impose punishments for wrongs insofar as they are injuries inflicted upon each other."[17] Religious liberty thus "keeps the peace" as a function of common grace. And indeed, religious liberty is a keystone to civil tranquility and is a vital ingredient to stable social order.

Critically, VanDrunen believes that there is no "ultimate" right to religious freedom but only a penultimate right instituted by God because, ultimately, the arc of history will culminate in Christ judging all false gods and ideologies.[18] Said differently, persons made in God's image do not have a right to deny God what is owed to him (Exod. 20:3). But VanDrunen concedes that there is a "penultimate natural law right to religious freedom before fellow human beings, and this right is granted by God."[19] I agree with this assessment. A natural law right is the protection of a moral faculty one determines to act on based on reason and conscience. The moral faculty, as such, is essential to a person grasping and actualizing their duty to act in accordance with the truth. Civil authorities have a duty to protect the natural rights of their citizens such that citizens can lead meaningful, free lives. A right protects the faculty, but it does not protect all uses of the faculty that are miscarriages of a faculty's true end. Hence, when we talk about protecting religious liberty, we are not agreeing with every viewpoint of one's religious beliefs, but protecting the faculty that informs their grasp of what is true. This right underlies the importance of codifying a penultimate or civil right to religious liberty among humans and, by extension, the political institutions they form. Offering a summary of his argument, VanDrunen states:

If God has called the entire human race (regardless of religious identification) to participate in the cultural life of society while he preserves this present world, then no human being has the authority to exclude other human beings from full participation because of their religious profession or practice. The covenant with Noah is a common grace *blessing of God* (Gen. 9:1). Therefore the minimalist natural law ethic concerning procreation, eating, and justice (9:1–7) does not merely involve obligations but also a privilege that God grants to all people to be active members of civil society—and this despite the ongoing blight of human sin (8:21) and the specter of a final judgment in the distant future.[20]

Judgment over matters concerning religion belongs to God. It is not only wrong but also unjust for society and government to impose burdens on or create obstacles for people of different religious persuasions to make them cooperate within the social order. This is possible to say not only out of overtures to "tolerance" or "inclusion" but also by way of theological deduction. Seen in this light, a refusal of society or government to allow people to live out their religious convictions—when there is no threat of harm—is not only an affront to God's jurisdiction but also a failure of the government or society to understand its own obligations.

VanDrunen and Leeman offer some of the most unique, trenchant, and substantive biblical-theological formulations for grounding religious liberty in contemporary social ethics. Perhaps most rewarding, both authors establish religious liberty as a biblically sanctioned function of the social order rooted in a reconstituted creational order. Creatively, they do so by making religious liberty a function of postflood creation ordinances while also keeping in mind the unfolding of biblical history.

Both Leeman's and VanDrunen's arguments bear witness to the already/not-yet nature of the kingdom. Because the kingdom of God awaits fulfillment, the Noahic covenant allows religious diversity without exclusion or penalty to exist in the present. Leeman's and VanDrunen's arguments remind us that it is not the job of humans or governments to punish individuals for false, erring belief.

Christian Secularism

What results from VanDrunen's and Leeman's frameworks is akin to what I call a Christian doctrine of secularism. Christians are confronted with two realities: (1) religious diversity exists, and (2) religious diversity is not something to celebrate since the hoped-for goal of Christian mission is conversion. Christian secularism seeks to address these propositions head-on by seeking neither to suppress diversity through coercive means nor to celebrate it. A doctrine of the secular sees the reality of erring beliefs as an expected but lamentable component of the present age and a forewarning of coming judgment. This concept of the secular supplies the needed building block to help us understand the different realms to which the conscience is accountable. It also gives eschatological shape to the expectation or normalcy of wrong belief in a penultimate age.[21] Secularism, according to Luke Bretherton, is "a way to talk about the need to coordinate with non-Christian others the pursuit of the kingdom of God with pursuit of penultimate goods." This results in an age in which the common life is not "dominated by the church, yet . . . is open to transcendent claims."[22] And indeed, religious liberty ought to be cherished for allowing Christians to proclaim transcendental arguments without fear of penalty or harm.

With the establishment of a reconstituted created order in the Noahic covenant and the dawning of Christ's ministry, which awaits ultimate consummation, a Christian idea of the secular emerges. This concept is essential to an eschatological foundation and orientation for religious liberty. Augustinian scholar Robert A. Markus posits that Christianity, and specifically Augustine, is largely responsible for developing the concept of the secular.[23]

Before Augustine, history was understood as immanentized—that is, as capable of bringing the divine within the present age, merging the two. While Christian eschatology shares a similar concept within an already/not-yet understanding of inaugurated eschatology, Christian theology allows for the two ages to overlap without making them coterminous. The overlapping era is the saeculum. It is the current age, not the eternal age. Yet the two have merged into the present with the promise that the current age will pass away. And as I will argue, a doctrine of the secular (a penultimate age) is only discernable by appeal to an eternal, ultimate age (the kingdom of God).

By "secular," I am not referring to broader trends in the contemporary West to harass and marginalize religious belief from the public square, such that the public square becomes "naked."[24] Rather, in keeping with the historical definition, secularism is rooted in the saeculum, which is "that intermediate and temporary realm in which human affairs unfold before the end."[25] VanDrunen defines it as an "age preceding the second coming of Christ" or "the life of this present age that is distinct from the life of the age to come in the new creation" that authorizes a "common social space."[26] A secular age is not nonreligious. Rather, the secular is a deeply religious and shared space of contested belief. Christians believe that the holy and the sacred exist within the order of redemption and are manifested in the mission of the church. But they exist alongside a social order that is open to people of different faiths. A secular age does not reject religion or metaphysical arguments; it is open to both and understands that the common era is not bound by one exclusive religious order. The kingdom of God has broken into the secular age but will ultimately terminate it at judgment. James K. A. Smith defines the "secular" as the "not-yet" of the kingdom awaiting universal fulfillment and recognition. The secular age is situated between the ascension and the final manifestation of the kingdom, "between ascension and Parousia."[27]

Michael Horton argues that secularism is defined by "God's different covenantal relationships in different epochs of redemptive history."[28] The language of "different epochs" captures the eschatological orientation necessary for our understanding of religious liberty. The secular epoch establishes the legitimacy of religious diversity but understands that it will not last; God will not relate to unbelief at the end of history like he does now. Horton further defines the secular age as one that is not "nontheological" but rather a "time in which cult and culture have not yet been reunited"; "creation, providence, and common grace" sustain it.[29] A secular age is governed by natural law, while the church is governed by the Spirit. A secular age is merely an attempt to keep the two ages distinct from each other without one overwhelming the other. One age is passing away (1 Cor. 2:6), and the other is eternal. In Christ, the two overlap.

Markus posits that the ancient use of the term "secular" was "roughly equivalent to what can be shared with non-Christians."[30] This claim that the secular represents the shared space of culture is similar to the claim made by VanDrunen—namely, that after the flood, God designed the social order to be inhabited by diverse peoples whose religious moorings are not the basis for inclusion in or exclusion from the social order, since only God can adjudicate the rightness and wrongness of religion. The secular allows for a multitude of religious expressions to inhabit a shared cultural space together. From this perspective, the secular age grants the theological legitimacy of pluralism as a feature of the social order, not a deviation. Again, this is not to argue that religious liberty or pluralism is an absolute, eternal good. It is not. As Markus notes, "The secular is that which belongs to this age and will have no part in the age to come, when Christ's kingship will hold universal sway. Political authority and institutions, with all the agencies of compulsion and enforcement, are destined for abrogation when the rule of God in Christ is finally revealed."[31] It would be even more accurate to "lament the reality of directional pluralism" in the saeculum, "even as it concedes that this is to be expected."[32]

Religious liberty, like pluralism, is provisional and exists only in a secular era.[33] Secularism does, however, provide a foundation for a social ethic of religious liberty. Markus observes that the "authorities" (Rom. 13:6) retain their legitimacy, but not absolute legitimacy over all affairs. This is because the powers exist to settle intrahuman disputes, not religious ones. From a Christian vantage point, the powers are not destroyed "but dethroned, kept on a short leash."[34] Even still, the division between eternal and secular realms advocated here, like religious liberty, is not eternal. At an appointed time, the secular age will conclude, and shared, contested social space will not be permitted as Christ vanquishes his enemies (Ps. 2; 1 Cor. 15:24–25; Heb. 10:13). As Oscar Cullmann observes, "Only in the kingdom of God will there no longer be two realms, for there God will be 'all in all.'"[35]

A Christian doctrine of the secular helps us see how the gospel must go forth in a secular age: patiently and persuasively. As Oliver O'Donovan argues, "Secularity is a stance of patience in the face of plurality."[36] The legitimacy of secularism is the rejection of coercion. Living in a time when unbelief has equal say in the public square requires the church to "improvise forms of witness in response to the prior work of Christ and the Spirit, who are drawing creation into its eschatological fulfillment."[37] The legitimacy of unbelief in the present is not to relativize its consequences or insist that unbelief is morally benign. Christians, rather, are to be the people exposing the bitter fruits and incoherence of unbelief by insisting upon the divine, perfect standards of God set forth in his Word. What secularism betokens is how we respond to the existence of unbelief: Do we respond through patient persuasive pleading or coercion? Belief in a secular era results in a confidence that the church's mission goes forward without coercing or enticing others. But a Christian doctrine of the secular also desacralizes the temptation to fuse the religious and the political, thus compromising the church's mission and infringing on non-Christian religious liberty.[38] Secularism is a bulwark against the pursuit of utopia. In this sense, the secular reconfigures this age as one in which neither triumph nor despair is the right posture. It is an age of moral realism, a paradoxical age when revival and decline occur in perennial jousts.

The secular also points to the victory of Christ. It is a patient trust in final victory. Smith argues that the triumph of Christ has political ramifications, signaling to the state its limited jurisdiction in a secular age: "The political is now inherently eschatological. Christ has disarmed the powers, made a public show of them, and delegitimized their claims to be mediators of ultimacy."[39] One of the great political testaments to the church, then, is the church holding the United States accountable, for example, to its own maxim that it is "one nation under God." While the state might understand this stance from the position of civil religion, the church sees such a pronouncement as an eschatological reality that Christ has triumphed over it.

By witnessing to the state that its powers are limited, a Christian doctrine of the secular lets the state administer law and execute justice while also providing ample freedom for religious diversity and persuasion. Citing 1 Timothy 2:1, O'Donovan argues that the purpose of secular authorities is to ensure a space for "men and women to be drawn into the governed community of God's kingdom."[40] Secularism, then, is an instrumental good whose highest purpose is to ensure common space while also issuing a call to humility. This is what Markus calls Augustine's "radical agnosticism"—an appropriate posture given that Christians do not know how long the secular period will last or where it will lead. Secularism also counteracts the temptation to declare Christian triumph over the world prematurely, since, according to Augustine, "the Two Cities are inextricably intertwined and mingled with each other, until they shall be separated in the last judgment."[41] A shift of this nature in our understanding of the secular age has the ability to fundamentally reconfigure how we understand not only religious liberty but also the Christian posture toward the world. It is by no means one of withdrawal, but it is the jettisoning of expectation that faithful Christian witness necessarily entails worldwide adoption of Christian norms, desirable as that is.

Penultimate Secularity and Contestability

VanDrunen argues for a "penultimate secularity" or "finite secularity."[42] This is not an ideological secularity that tries to cordon off shared cultural spaces from religion; it is, rather, a theological secularity that grounds human difference in the covenants of creation and redemption. The coming kingdom of Christ, through which Christ will execute judgment on false belief, creates a "penultimate secularity" that grounds a doctrine of religious freedom for the present age. This penultimacy gives rise to the concept of contestability—the idea that what is expected in our age is a contest between competing religious claims and wherever consensus can be reached, it is evidence of common grace. This has enormous practical implication: if I can offer an explanation for why someone believes differently than me that is grounded in an eschatological reality, it frees me from trying to use coercive or illiberal means to silence or marginalize erring religious viewpoints. The larger eschatological horizon of coming judgment ties these themes together.

When surveying the available options for how religious liberty and church-state relations should be structured, we see that two popular paradigms on the opposite ends of the spectrum emerge: a paradigm of theocracy in both soft and hard forms, and what I call "seculocracy." Theocracy has different forms but is most often associated with political rule directly by God or under God's authority, which rulers mediate. Softer forms include Christian nationalism, the idea that Christianity accords the nation-state with a covenantal identity, morality, and destiny. Hard theocracy is associated with theonomy, a school known as Christian Reconstructionism, which seeks to implement biblical law into statutory law. Seculocracy, by contrast, is the effort to eliminate or reduce religion's influence in culture. This drives such organizations as the Freedom from Religion Foundation and the rise of New Atheism.

Seculocracy and theocracy share a mutual commitment to an absolutized orthodoxy given centralized authority in the present age. Both are opposed to the organic differences of society and work to overcome them through domination or harassment. For theocracy, that orthodoxy is derived from religious norms. For seculocracy, that orthodoxy is derived from naturalistic means but often held with similar religious fervency and yielding quasi-religious commitments. When seculocracy and theocracy interact, the result is a "clash of orthodoxies" that sends societies into never-ending cycles of conflict and tumult.[43] Modern-day America is a picture of this contest, where a growing class of nonreligious citizens clash with their religious counterparts, evincing that political disputes are intractably metaphysical in nature.

Both theocracy and seculocracy are unhelpful in forming societies capable of reasoning through deep conflict and providing reciprocating avenues of liberty to one another. How a polity responds to this conflict speaks to deeper assumptions about the role of the church in influencing society. Is the collision over worldviews to be expected, or should Christians expect to attain a level of cultural dominance in laws and social norms? My argument, and one that risks a certain mischaracterization, is that total Christian dominance within a society is not to be expected in the present age. Existence short of the new creation will be bombarded by a reality of religious and ideological difference.

This is not to say that Christianity cannot, will not, or should not influence or even transform a given context. Of course, it can and should. To say otherwise would call into question the work of such individuals as William Wilberforce and Martin Luther King Jr., who expressly relied on religion to make society more just. Instead, we must adjust our expectations for cultural and religious triumph. Christianity is not a political program. The gospel does not create a new political agenda actionable within government qua government. Christianity, with its belief in common grace and natural law, is meant to shape consciences and help the world be the best version of itself as justice is recognized. Christian secularism does not mean that Christians should throw up their hands or give up declaring "the criteria by which nations will ultimately be judged, and the divine standards to which man and society must conform if civilization is to endure."[44] It means, instead, that Christianity acknowledges the reality of the secular age and works within it, regardless of what level of dominance it achieves. The fractured, sinful state of the contested era does not delegitimize the era in the eyes of God or seal the era off from Christian influence. Christian secularism simply focuses on the conflict of desires, wills, and moralities that are misdirected. Christians, as Jeremiah told the exiles, are to "seek the welfare of the city" (Jer. 29:7). There is no promise that such seeking will ever be finished—apart from the dawning of the new creation.

As a Baptist, I believe that Christianity must always resist the temptation to instrumentalize itself, or to subordinate itself to the needs of culture and state. Moreover, the Christian faith does not require social and political legitimacy, but social and political legitimacy requires a degree of transcendental rootedness in order to be sustained, which Christianity posits. A Baptist account of religious liberty would strongly advance a nonconfessional government alongside a vibrantly confessional civil society. In contrast to theocracy and progressive secularism is a third way—the Baptist way—one that understands that for society to long endure, society must be radically nonsecularist in its accounting for truth, rights, and justice.

At the same time, the church ought to expect bombardment and assault on its teaching. This means that the hand-wringing and complaints about the decline of the Christian faith in the West have a ring of theological shallowness, hollowness, and historical myopia. To the fearful Christian, I would simply say, "Do you remember how the church came into being?" By divine mandate. And if the church is an institution of divine origins, perhaps our hand-wringing and despair over the ruins of Western civilization can lead us to remember that the martyrs of the early church went to their deaths knowing that from death came life.

I can make this argument because I do not believe there is, in a secular age short of the coming of Christ, a "golden era" of the church. Every act of Christian mission requires trade-offs. And who is to say that Christianity's waning cultural "influence," now being whittled into unbelief, is not also a testament to the Lord purifying his church apart from the expectation of cultural dominance? There will be ups and downs, successes and failures. The Western church in the twenty-first century should remember that history belongs to the Lord and not to our triumphs. Or as Horton argues, a Christian doctrine of the secular means that "we can preserve the secular or common from both secularist ideology and from Christian triumphalism."[45]

As Isaiah Berlin quipped, one of the greatest challenges and opportunities for liberal democracy is that its foundation assumes "that human goals are many, not all of them commensurable, and in perpetual conflict with one another."[46] We should expect these incommensurable goals of society to remain in conflict until the consummation of history. Such conflict, then, awakens Christianity to the need for its own social space to persuade, preach, and proclaim. The liberty we want for ourselves is the same liberty we must impart to others.

This paradigm prioritizes the coming judgment of the kingdom of God. Further, its formulation of penultimate secularity and contestability—the interrogation of religious and moral truth claims aimed at achieving consensus about the goods of human nature and human society—becomes the modus operandi. In an essay that criticizes neo-Kuyperianism for incorrectly expecting fallen societies to attain to the standards of the kingdom of God in a penultimate era, VanDrunen argues that Christians should make peace with social difference:

> Religious and metaphysical pluralism is at the very least a fact, a basic reality of Western society at the present moment and for many centuries past. More than that, religious and metaphysical pluralism is what Scripture suggests we should *expect* in society during this interim, inchoate period between the comings of Christ. . . . Religious and metaphysical pluralism will not be eliminated this side of Christ's second coming, however much we may try to wish, to preach, or to persecute it away.[47]

VanDrunen makes contestability a feature of the current era of the church's mission. Rather than something to be overcome, contestability offers a vision for the church to be a voice for pluralism. It also corrects attempts to enact totalized orthodoxies by calling for restraint and sober-mindedness. To be sure, Christians are to unswervingly proclaim the gospel, but they are to do so expecting to meet challenges within a secular age.

Thus, in place of seculocracy and theocracy, which work to overcome ideological difference and pluralism through often illiberal, coercive means, we might adopt what I call "contestulocracy." It places interrogation, debate, and liberty at the forefront for settling disputes over religious, moral, and ideological difference. It is an ethic of humble truth seeking, and expecting deep disagreement is one of its features. Contestulocracy urges patience, persuasion, and a limited view of the state's power to play referee regarding religious truth claims. Such a position militates against totalizing extremes but also prohibits the government from either ideological secularism or "neutrality." Contestulocracy understands that the public square is ground zero for intense ideological, religious, and political battle.

Steven D. Smith observes that, historically, religious freedom in America "was not one of secularism or neutrality but rather open contestation."[48] An emphasis on contestability will require the church to develop a more chastened understanding of Christianity's dominance in any given society and to see the challenge of social difference as a welcome feature constitutive of Christian mission. This contestability model is Augustinian; it recognizes that humans and human societies are fragmented, paradoxical, corrupted, and imperfectible apart from God establishing his kingdom, yet they are simultaneously enmeshed within a shared social space. In short, contestability reconfigures the expectations of common life by revealing that ideal social arrangements are often designed to minimize avarice and violence. In Markus's words, the ideal social arrangement is one that holds "the wicked in check, to enable the virtuous to live untroubled among them."[49]

Penultimate secularity and contestability align closely with the currents of liberal democracy, the root political order of Western civilization that prioritizes individual rights, the rule of law, and limited government.[50] Jeffrey Stout deploys an Augustinian vision for liberal democracy that is highly commensurable with the vision for religious liberty advanced in this chapter. Stout argues for a social order

> that can secure private space in which we can form friendships and families and voluntary associations. In these spheres, not in the sphere of political doings, we find the closest thing to true happiness available in this life—analogues to the form of association the blessed enjoy in God's Kingdom. Politics at its best makes

room for such happiness and such associations. It also opens up the space in which individuals can pursue the spiritual life as they understand it.[51]

In conclusion, the kingdom of God not only subjugates the state but also grants the church the ability to remind the state that the church's power and declarations are eternal. As Leeman observes, "The local church possesses the power of eschatological declaration. The state possesses the power of temporal coercion."[52]

Once again, O'Donovan reminds the state that its claims and power are temporal: "Secular institutions have a role confined to this passing age (*saeculum*). They do not represent the arrival of the new age and the rule of God. They have to do with the perennial cycle of birth and death which makes tradition, not with the resurrection of the dead which supersedes all tradition. The corresponding term to 'secular' is not 'sacred,' nor 'spiritual,' but 'eternal.' Applied to political authorities, the term 'secular' should tell us that they are not agents of Christ, but are marked for displacement when the rule of God in Christ is finally disclosed."[53]

An eschatology of the kingdom determines the shape and confines of a Christian doctrine of the saeculum. This, in turn, authorizes a doctrine of religious liberty based on the normativity of religious diversity.

Secular Ideology and the Impossibility of Religious Liberty

A principled commitment to religious liberty would be unintelligible apart from its foundation in God's transcendent plan for history, humanity, and redemption. But transcendence on its own terms is not enough, for a religion that believes utopia is possible in the present age will be a religion (or ideology) incompatible with freedom. This is why Christianity is uniquely situated to make the argument that dissent from a reigning orthodoxy is permissible when the age is understood as contestable. Christianity teaches that God has come to earth but that earth has not yet reached its climax. The eschatological orientation of the Christian faith ensures that transcendence is kept front and center while keeping puritanical and exacting forms of Christianity from being realized in the present. This can be accomplished only within a framework of inaugurated eschatology.

Humanity is fallible in its ultimate judgments on religion because humans lack the knowledge and judgment to know which religion is ultimately true (eschatology). A concept of transcendence means that human dignity and freedom dwell inviolably in human nature because humanity is a creation of God—not the state. This is true regardless of whether humanity's right to liberty is acknowledged by the governing authorities or civil society (anthropology). Lastly, a concept of transcendence means that humanity cannot save itself, that human longing for redemption is central to human experience, and that redemption is achieved only through free responses to the gospel (missiology).

Whenever religious belief is placed within the domain of human authority (whether governmental or social), religious liberty is threatened. This is because fallible agents are not equipped to make discriminating judgments on another's understanding of religion. To the extent that a truly secular ideology attempts to furnish a type of eschatological judgment without an account of transcendence underwriting it, it erodes religious liberty. Without an account of transcendence and ultimate judgment, a lasting ecosystem of religious liberty is impossible.

Once again, the categories of penultimate and ultimate come into play. Where ideologies confuse the penultimate for the ultimate, these ideologies will work to rectify or remove whatever impediments prohibit the ultimate from enactment. Whenever an ideology or movement functions as an agent of absolute judgment over religious, moral, or ideological dissent in order to further its own vision of political utopia or social justice, it engages in what is known as "immanentizing the eschaton."[54] According to Eric Voegelin, attempts to enact a state of perfect justice will lead to disastrous, oppressive, even tyrannical outcomes. In this account, utopias are parasitical to liberty because utopias bring about a sweeping eschatological and secular form of judgment. John Murray Cuddihy writes that these notions of the "perfect community" that are driven by an eschatological interpretation of history's fulfillment (e.g., "progress") will not allow for tolerance, patience, or civility.[55] Whether they would countenance liberty is questionable as well. Such is the result of what Richard John Neuhaus calls the "naked public square," one devoid of an adjudicating authority higher than the community itself.[56] Religious liberty is therefore premised on the notion that correct judgments about God are not judgments that people can make for others *or* be enacted uniformly throughout society without disastrous consequences.

Henry Van Til taught that "culture is simply the service of God in our lives; it is religion externalized."[57] Religion is that which becomes comprehensive and totalizing to a person's existence. Whether there is a notion of "God" in this paradigm is irrelevant. Something godlike inevitably fills the vacuum left unoccupied by transcendence. As G. K. Chesterton aptly put it, "The special mark of the modern world is not that it is skeptical, but that it is dogmatic without knowing it."[58] Again, according to Van Til, "Even Communism, like Nazism, has its gods and devils, its sin and salvation, its priests and its liturgies, its paradise of the stateless society of the future."[59]

Bound up in this "politics of redemption" is an attempt by philosophers and activists to "direct their political prescription toward some future event of ultimate significance, trying to hasten its arrival by human action."[60] This account of history supplies ideologies with a comprehensive account of justice yet is supplied with its own humanistic eschatology, anthropology, and missiology. The offer of ideological utopia being brought to completion in the present explains why there is no principled commitment to give space to dissenting viewpoints.

Consider this thought experiment: If the present age is sufficient for approximating perfect justice and redressing all social ills, then whatever fills the vacuum left by God's absence functions in the role of divine judge and divine mediator. Divine judgment is then placed in the hands of nondivine beings who attempt to execute judgment for the sake of justice.

In a perspective void of transcendence, if an account of the world disagrees with this worldview, why countenance it? If steps can be taken to eradicate the perceived social pathology in the present, why not take steps—perhaps even through violence or suppression—to quash what the majority considers inappropriate dissent? If the present age is all there is in one's secular horizon, and if the closest approximation to justice that can be known is mediated through an eschatology of the present, why countenance an idea such as religious liberty or freedom of conscience if the liberty to hold and act on those ideas impedes progress or aggrieves an offended party? This conflict is why, ultimately, clashes over religious liberty are not battles between religious persons and nonreligious persons. The debates around religious liberty are clashes over how perfected a society can become in the present age and whose version of the perfect society will prevail. A movement will foster liberty for those who disagree only to the extent that it understands its own limitations.

Leeman notes that the absence of divine judgment simply results in human judgment functioning in the same capacity: "When you remove the God of glory and the God of judgment who created all humanity in his image, this is where the story of freedom, rights, and equality culminates. I dare say, the American Experiment, divorced from God, makes same-sex marriage, transgender-bathroom debates, and the end of religious tolerance inevitable. Every person becomes his or her own god."[61]

This judgment happens by rejecting transcendence as a mediating source of authority altogether. Secular ideology that attempts to enact its vision of social justice or political utopia is trying to bring heaven to earth or bring perfect justice into the present. It is displacing transcendence altogether. So much of the secular fervency to pronounce judgment stems from Christian theological concepts related to judgment and salvation now translated for the purpose of illiberal causes. Joseph Bottum, in a 2014 essay, aptly describes the underlying religious faith of secular progressivism: "Our social and political life is awash in unconsciously held Christian ideas broken from the theology that gave them meaning, and it's hungry for the identification of sinners—the better to prove the virtue of the accusers and, perhaps, especially, to demonstrate the sociopolitical power of the accusers."[62]

This echoes the maxim of Carl Schmitt, who observed how "all significant concepts of the modern theory of the state are secularized theological concepts."[63] This owes to the secularization of society in which God is displaced by humanistic idealism. This concern over enacting a secularized form of quasi-religious judgment finds purchase in non-Christian viewpoints as well. Commenting on the thought of Jewish intellectual Irving Kristol, Tom Wilson observes that secular liberalism's gutting of transcendence leads, ultimately, to authoritarianism hostile to human and religious liberty.

> Stripped of any belief in the kind of higher consolation that makes sense of life's inevitable injustices and humdrum frustrations, the demands that people place on the political system "become as infinite as the infinity they have lost." Eventually the democratic regime is no longer able to justify or defend itself against the expectations of a citizenry that experiences no spiritual nourishment. Indeed, those expectations become unappeasable in the limitless material improvement that they insist government must provide

and that capitalism promises. Without a religious culture, the slide into statism, if not authoritarianism, seems to become irresistible.[64]

Concerns about an immanentized political utopia are prescient and explain why a society built merely on reason will not persist with maximal liberty in the long run with these types of philosophical social movements at the helm. James K. A. Smith observes that with humanity at the center and the question of God's authority rejected from common understanding, "modernity inherited Christian introspection but lost/rejected the God encountered in this interiority. Therefore new (transcendent) expectations are thrown on society/government, the result which is despair, since modernity inherits the Christian burden to 'judge for yourself' without the good news of God's judgment in Christ. Hence we spiral into self-conscious despair and cling ever more tenaciously to 'secular' institutions—that is, institutions that are passing away and cannot save us."[65]

Reasoning beings require debate and inquiry, which progressive social canons cannot countenance if ultimate redress of social wrongs can be achieved in the present. In essence, ideologies fall prey to the tendency to exchange the penultimate for the ultimate. The Christian American founder John Witherspoon made a similar observation, noting that opposition to civil liberty will lead, inevitably, to the decline of religious liberty.

> The knowledge of God and his truths have from the beginning of the world been chiefly, if not entirely, confined to those parts of the earth, where some degree of liberty and political justice were to be seen, and great were the difficulties with which they had to struggle from the imperfection of human society, and the unjust decisions of usurped authority. There is not a single instance in history in which civil liberty was lost, and religious liberty preserved entire. If therefore we yield up our temporal property, we at the same time deliver the conscience into bondage.[66]

According to Witherspoon, something inheres within the transcendent that makes other forms of liberty possible. This is not coincidental. Even political philosopher Alexis de Tocqueville (though not an orthodox Christian) understood the relationship between transcendence and the limitations of human judgment when he wrote that "despotism can do without faith, but freedom cannot."[67] The antidote to illiberalism and coercion is the reemergence of the divine foundation of political freedom. "The way of deliverance from human authoritarianism," writes Thomas Smail, "is the rediscovery of divine authority."[68]

Conclusion

A transcendental foundation to religious liberty prevents nondivine agents from presuming divine agency. By giving judgment to Christ alone at the end of history, Christians can allow for wrong belief. This is not out of indifference but because Christianity believes that judging, ending, and redressing all wrong belief cannot be achieved fully either in the present era or by human hands. The future of religious liberty, then, is a battle of competing eschatologies: Whose vision for the fulfillment of human destiny will win?

Inherent to Christianity is the rejection of totalized or absolutized visions for social order itself. This does not mean, however, that a social order is cordoned off from religious influence. Whenever secular liberalism, Nazism, communism, or any other ideology attempts a comprehensive vision for society, it commits what is, at root, an eschatological heresy. Drawing on themes from Augustine, Markus argues that Christianity resists seeing politics or social movements as agents of perfection in the current era: "Christian hope deflates all ideologies and utopias: in their place it sets provisional goals, to be realized piecemeal, and to be kept flexible and perpetually subject to revision and renewal in the light of political experiences seen in an eschatological perspective. It resists political programmes, which seem to make an ultimate claim on men."[69] He continues, "Christian hope, just because it is eschatological, resists the investing of immediate projects, policies and even social ideals, with any absolute character."[70] Divesting any movement, ideology, or political structure of its tendency toward infallibility may be one of the most urgent and prophetic tasks for the church in society. As Dietrich Bonhoeffer suggested, "Does one not in some cases, by remaining deliberately in the penultimate, perhaps point all the more genuinely to the ultimate, which God will speak in his own time?"[71]

One of the more important postures for Christians to develop in a culture that rejects divine judgment, but nonetheless settles on judgment according to its own standards, is to reassert the primacy of eschatological judgment in its religious pronouncements. Indeed, John the Baptist's forewarning of Jesus's reign must become the posture of the church toward a society that would erringly believe in its own infallibility: "Repent, for the kingdom of heaven is at hand" (Matt. 3:2). Only for a culture made aware of its fickleness and error will the reality of future judgment pose an adequate rival, for as Richard J. Mouw and Sander Griffioen argue, a "theocentric position treats all our human points of view as ultimately accountable to divine authority," and erroneous ideologies and religions "will not be treated kindly in the coming Judgment."[72]

PART 2

ANTHROPOLOGY

4

The *Imago Dei* and Religious Liberty

I have often wished myself a beast. I preferred the condition of the meanest reptile to my own. Anything, no matter what to get rid of thinking! It was this everlasting thinking of my condition that tormented me. There was no getting rid of it. It pressed upon me by every object within sight or hearing, animate or inanimate. The silver trump of freedom had aroused my soul to eternal wakefulness. Freedom now appeared, to disappear no more forever. It was heard in every sound, and seen in every thing. It was ever present to torment me with a sense of my wretched condition. I saw nothing without seeing it, I heard nothing without hearing it, and felt nothing without feeling it. It looked from every star, it smiled in every calm, breathed in every wind, and moved in every storm.[1]

Frederick Douglass's words capture a profound truth: we are agents of meaning, discovery, and truth. If only he had been kept ignorant, Douglass avers, he would not have known the promise of liberty. But reading empowered him. Reading of liberty, and knowing what one could become, meant reorienting his life toward one goal: the attainment of his freedom. Douglass recognized that his personhood was inadequately acknowledged apart from his freedom. Here was a person who came to better understand that the injustice of his condition demanded his freedom. From that point forward, a mind came alive.

Douglass's narrative reveals a deep truth endowed in every human: we have a desire for freedom and true, authentic living. Douglass's quest reveals another fundamental truth of what it means to be made in God's image: we are not automatons or animals but deeply moral creatures seeking the freedom to live our lives before God as we understand the duties of honest conviction.

Christian anthropology begins with the belief that humanity is made in God's image, the *imago Dei* (Gen. 1:26–27). It is the most axiomatic truth of human identity. Yet "image of God" language has become so common among Christians that the term has been emptied of its power. Absent from most Christian reflections on religious liberty is its connection to the image of God. What does the image of God mean, and what does it imply about religious liberty? That is the task at hand.

Because humans are made in God's image, humans are, at an irreducible level, religious beings. Before describing what it means to be religious and truth seeking, we must explain the aspects of how bearing God's image in its *substance* participates in the economy of religious liberty. It necessarily leads to other important questions: What is our purpose? How do we come to understand truth? What role do reason and conscience play in a person's search for and grasp of ultimate truth? What does the use of reason signify about humanity's unique status in creation? Toward what is humanity's freedom ultimately directed?

In answering these questions, we can begin to understand second-order questions such as the following: Do humans have a right to err in their religious beliefs? What role, if any, does the government have in adjudicating matters of religious truth and conscience? These are but a few of the questions relevant to the discussion of how humanity's image-bearing status relates to a Christian formulation of religious liberty.

To discuss the image of God and its relationship to religious liberty is to engage in a number of complex topics: (1) what it means to be made in God's image; (2) how our moral agency as self-constituting creatures helps us understand the purpose of what personal agency, or liberty, actually is. The purpose of this chapter is to put forward an anthropological account of religious liberty grounded in the doctrine of the image of God that finds ultimate telos in Jesus Christ, the true image of God (2 Cor. 4:4; Col. 1:15; Heb. 1:3). The fact that humanity is created in God's image provides the foundation for positing a practical doctrine of religious liberty that is both intelligible and inviolable in a penultimate age.

God's Image Explained

God created us to relate to him, to know him. As Augustine wrote, "Thou hast made us for thyself, O Lord, and our heart is restless until it finds its rest in thee"—declaring that humanity's nature is in search of God.[2] Restlessness implies process and struggle, which implies agency and comprehension. How is that rest obtained? Relating to God and knowing God assumes the ability to allow that relationship to flower. Being created by God means we owe our existence to him, and that dependence is a prerequisite to the liberty of the Creator-creature relationship.

The question of religious liberty immediately directs us to the foundation of personhood (of how we conceive of the idea of the person) and agency. Scholar Larry Siedentop argues that Christianity birthed the very idea of the individual.[3] Prior to the advent of Christianity's influence on the world's stage, human identity was tribal—not individual but group assigned. Whatever problems that extreme forms of individualism can be accused of, the idea that the human person bears a unique significance in their own person is a gift of the Judeo-Christian tradition to the world and poses enormous consequence for human rights.

In the eyes of the Creator, each and every person is stamped with glory. That God gave a sense of dignity, self-consciousness, and individuality to the person implies that the image of God is the ground on which humans "apprehend and participate in an intelligible order. Such a conception puts front and center the rational and moral capacities of the human being and their role in personal, social and political life."[4] The question of religious liberty thus acknowledges full personhood—our existence, our grasp of truth, our obligations to God, our ability to respond to God. Given the relevance of the image of God for human nature, it should not be surprising that it offers an attractive framework to make religious liberty a Christian anthropological enterprise.

The Image of God in Biblical Theology

Our highest distinction as humans is that we are created in the image of God, as Genesis 1:26–27; 5:1; and 9:6 depict. This doctrine distinguishes humanity from animal life and the rest of creation. Only humanity is said to be made in God's image and tasked with dominion.

Plumbing the depths of the image of God in the Bible is no simple matter.[5] The concept denotes both mystery and ambiguity, because the Bible "nowhere fully defines what it means for people to be created in the image of God."[6] John F. Kilner argues that the concept centers on humans being connected to and reflecting God. He believes this doctrine reveals humanity to be God's "crowning glory" of creation that reflects "who God is and what God does."[7] John M. Frame argues that bearing God's image constitutes humanity's essential "resemblance" and "representation" of God.[8] Wayne Grudem defines "image bearing" as meaning that "man is like God and represents God," since the Hebrew for "image" (*tselem*) and "likeness" (*demut*) refer to something that resembles God but is not identical with God.[9] Crucially, humanity is not synonymous with the image of God itself. This distinction is important because it forges a difference between humanity, which is made in God's image, and Jesus Christ, the true image of God.

Kilner argues that descriptions or attributes of being made in God's image have more to do with purposes and consequences of the teaching than what "actually defines" the image itself.[10] Thus, bearing God's image has more to do with the totality of one's existence and status as a creation of God than outright functional attributes. Frame states that "everything we are" somehow reflects God, even the totality of our nature itself. This includes our soul, body, reason, volition, and propensity for goodness.[11] Humans are not identical to God, but we are made to be like God in features such as our moral aspects, spiritual aspects, mental aspects, and relational aspects. We can know God in ways that the rest of creation cannot.[12] Yet humanity is also unlike God because of sin's distortion of every part of our being.

Representation is also central to bearing God's image. Bearing God's image intensifies the idea of royal representation found in the ancient Near East. In that context, to "image" bespeaks loyalty to the image the object bears. Adam was to represent God as his vice-regent in the world, commissioned to exercise dominion and authority on God's behalf (Gen. 1:28; 2:19).[13] According to David C. Innes, "Human beings were made to mediate God to the creation as vice-regents, as markers of his government and ambassadorial agents of his rule."[14] Our agency as image bearers is to reflect God's redemptive rule to the creation around us.

Theologians have attempted to organize different categories to explain the image of God. Anthony A. Hoekema, in his classic volume *Created in God's Image*, combines image and likeness to render the expression as "an image which is like us." According to Hoekema, this indicates that humanity represents God in certain aspects but is not the image itself.[15] Hoekema also argues for "structural" and "functional" categories related to bearing God's image. According to Hoekema, structural categories include "his [humanity's] gifts, capacities, and endowments," while functional categories include "his actions, his relationship to God and to others, and the way he uses his gifts."[16] Millard J. Erickson has set forth the substantive, relational, and functional views.[17] According to the substantive view, God's image in humanity results in a "definite characteristic or quality within the make-up of the human";[18] the image of God constitutes humanity's overall nature. The relational view teaches that the image of God is about humans' ability to relate to God.[19] The functional view assigns the image of God to a person's actions, particularly in exercising dominion.[20]

For our purposes, being made in the image of God means that humans have a special ontological status that is similar to God's but not synonymous with God. Having the image of God is not so much about what humans *do* as the capacities that define who we *are*. Because of our status, we have been assigned the task to rule on God's behalf and to exercise loving dominion over creation, "a divine commission to exercise rule in this world in the likeness and under the authority of God the supreme king."[21] Yet we possess essential attributes and capacities, such as reason, that allow us to go about the task of our calling to exercise responsible stewardship over creation.

Jesus Christ as the Image of God

The New Testament's treatment of the image of God fleshes out the Old Testament's. In the New Testament, Jesus Christ is revealed as the true image of God, not just made in the same likeness of God as humanity is. While humanity bears the image of God, Christ is himself the image of God (2 Cor. 4:4; Col. 1:15; Heb. 1:3). According to Kilner, "Ultimately, the image of God is

Jesus Christ. People are first created and later renewed according to that image. Image involves connection and reflection. Creation in God's image entails a special connection with God and an intended reflection of God. Renewal in God's image entails a more intimate connection with God through Christ and an increasingly actual reflection of God in Christ, to God's glory."[22]

Image bearing demonstrates the nature and fulfillment of human createdness and salvation. Each individual bears God's image in hopes that they might mature into God's image, Jesus Christ. According to the apostle Paul, one's salvation begins the process of becoming conformed to the image of Christ. Thus, discipleship is about believers becoming like Jesus Christ. Christ and his moral perfections are therefore the backdrop that helps us discern and identify what it means to be made in the image of God (Rom. 8:29; Col. 3:10). Christ is the true image, and the path of discipleship is being conformed into Christ's image (Rom. 8:29; 1 Cor. 15:49; 2 Cor. 3:18).[23] This means that the agency we have as image bearers is constituted for the purpose of knowing Christ more fully.

Moral Agency and the *Imago Dei*

We have agency as humans because God has agency.[24] The link between these two realities is a doctrine of humanity and moral agency rooted in God's being and humans being made in God's image.

Individual moral agency is central to the question of religious liberty. Jim Spivey grounds religious liberty in a question of creation, noting how "religious liberty begins with the will of God as the creator of humanity."[25] Matthew J. Franck similarly argues that "the truth about religious freedom begins with men and women as *imago Dei*, the image of God."[26] This question of moral agency is rooted fundamentally in "God's nature and in his dealing with persons."[27] Moral agency refers to the status of a person as a free, rational creature whose ability to grasp truth and live in accord with it furnishes foundational aspects of their personhood. This may be an overly complex way of saying that God designed humans to order their lives according to the truths they come to grasp. Moral agency includes the many "dimensions of one's personhood—reason, conscience, will, emotions, body, and soul."[28] Since we are not cogs but enfleshed persons with personalities, we desire to make meaning and seek after truth by which to order our lives through intellective acts of reason. And it is these categories of createdness that help posit a doctrine of religious liberty.[29]

Spivey uses creation and humanity's status as image bearers in configuring religious liberty's significance.

> Being created in God's image, each person possesses infinite dignity and is a rational, moral agent with a conscience capable of responding to him by faith. Faith is a gift from God, not of human origin or institutional fabrication. This faith elicits voluntary obedience from the rational soul: the equal and independent right of every person to choose without coercion. The individual conscience is sovereign before people, but it is neither independent from God nor controlled entirely by the person. Conscience bears a divine imprimatur which, beyond human will, brings awareness of God and conviction of divine law.[30]

If human beings are anything less than free to reach their own conclusions by way of reason and conscience, they lack the moral agency central to authentic living. Living with integrity means living with one's principles integrated through the whole of one's life. Moreover, unless persons are freely disposed to respond to religious truth arrived at on their own terms, they lack the culpability that renders them eligible for judgment.

The image of God is fundamentally a creational reality. In examining the religious nature of humanity's design, we need to examine the constitutive aspects of bearing God's image that make religious liberty an essential component to being human. Because God's image bearers are rational and volitional creatures endowed with both inviolable dignity and the powers of discerning reason, humanity possesses qualities or aspects of personhood that make a concept like religious liberty constitutive of their truth-seeking nature. The ability for an image bearer to engage in conscious and rational reflection about transcendent realities resulting in moral action relies on an assumption of freedom and how that freedom is acted on.

From a biblical perspective, people bear God's image for the purpose of glorifying him with their total person (1 Cor. 10:31). We are to surrender every part of ourselves to Christ. Thus, an anthropological account of religious liberty based on Christian grounds understands that agency, in its totality, ought to be used for the sake of individuals conforming themselves into the image of Jesus Christ (Rom. 8:29). This entails a connection between authentic personhood and the goal of freedom. A person is most free and authentic when living in conformity with Jesus Christ. As free agents, however, humans have used their freedom to disobey and rebel against God. Such is the whole reason for God's plan of redemption as described in Scripture. But the choice to honor God or to disobey him is central to the biblical narrative. In Genesis, the command to eat from any available tree except one contained a sub-text that there was an option or choice to obey or to disobey (Gen. 2:16–17). Humanity has not used its choice—or its liberty—in accordance with God's design for obedience. But true liberty is realized in proportion to obedience to God's law (Ps. 119:45).

Hoekema argues that personhood and moral agency are aspects of what it means to be created in the image of God: "To be a person means to be able to make decisions, to set goals, and to move in the direction of those goals. It means to possess freedom—at least in the sense of being able to make one's own choices. The human being is not a robot whose course is totally determined by forces outside him; he has the power of self-determination and self-direction. To be a person means, to use Leonard Verduin's picturesque expression, to be a 'creature of option.'"[31]

A "creature of option" is both poetic and nuclear in its consequence. An approach to religious liberty that emphasizes the image of God and the image-bearing worth of every created person means that error and idolatry are the result of the misuse of the freedom that exists in a penultimate, contested era. Because Jesus is Lord of the conscience, Christians must resist penalizing or restricting any person's beliefs or convictions that don't pose direct threats to the common good. Religious liberty is thus scandalizing, because it presumes the very existence of human error and the corrupting consequences that stem from it.

Frame situates the image of God as related to moral excellence and moral agency, thus constitutive to bearing God's image is our capacity for moral awareness: "Our reasoning power, creativity, ability to use language, ability to sense moral distinctions and to make moral choices, and above all our religious capacity distinguish us from animals and make us like God. But beyond these, remember the fundamental principle: everything we are images God."[32] For Frame, moral agency is an essential feature of bearing God's image. Monkeys and elephants do not reason about God's existence; humans do. We do not judge an animal's actions the same way we judge a person's actions. Why? Because human actions have a degree of sophistication and intention. While we are never less than our instincts, Christian anthropology suggests that reason assigns a higher degree of judgment to our actions than is excusable solely on instinct. We are humans, a reality stemming from our divine design. In examining the religious nature of humanity's design, we must ask, What is it, exactly, about bearing God's image that makes religious liberty an essential component to being human?

The following sections discuss how moral agency—that is, our responsibility to honor God with our lives—requires reason, freedom, and the conscience. Each of these are components of what it means to be made in God's image as a moral agent and are implicit in a doctrine of religious liberty.

Reason

Reason refers to the cognitive process through which a person discerns truth. When we observe that 2 + 2 = 4, we use our mental faculty to understand this truth. Reason is a tacit faculty we use every waking moment. Reason helps us evaluate and follow the rules of conscience. It acts to distinguish truth from error. Reason aids us in our search for understanding by searching after moral purpose and clarity. This is not to say that reason is infallible. From our own experience and judgment, the opposite is true. But reason is knit into human existence. Reason directs us toward what we individually believe is true and ultimate.

Humanity's moral agency—its ability to choose between right and wrong, to discern truth, to reflect about realms and ideals outside of us—is central to a doctrine of religious liberty. Whether one agrees that reason constitutes an essential attribute of bearing God's image or that reason is but one consequence of bearing God's image, reason is a central feature of human design that results from bearing God's image and is important to a Christian account of religious liberty that takes seriously humanity's nature as truth-seeking creatures.

Early Christian theology placed an inordinate focus on reason as the most important element of bearing God's image. Jeremy Waldron says, "For almost the whole of the Christian era, *imago Dei* has been associated with man's capacity for practical reason."[33] Reason was a dominant attribute of the image of God in the work of Irenaeus, Clement, Origen, Athanasius, Augustine, Cyril of Alexandria, Thomas Aquinas, and John Calvin, owing to how Greek philosophy and scholasticism influenced early Christian theology.[34] The focus on reason is not unmerited, for rational capacities "reflect God's reason, and enable man now, in a sense, to think God's thoughts after him. Man's moral sensitivity reflects something of the moral nature of God, who is the supreme determiner of right and wrong."[35]

91

Others object to the notion that reason constitutes an essential, exact attribute of bearing God's image. Kilner dethrones reason as the apex of humanity's image attributes. According to Kilner, the Bible does not provide sufficient textual evidence to make reason an essential component of the image of God. "The key question," Kilner writes, is not "does it appear biblically sound to see people as 'uniquely rational, spiritual,' but instead, 'why should we think that this is what constitutes being in God's image?'"[36] No direct reference in the Old or New Testament makes reason the "primary concern."[37]

A potential negative consequence of inordinately focusing on reason is persons being denied full dignity because of impaired reasoning skills, in the case of mentally handicapped persons, or because their reasoning capacities are not fully developed or have atrophied, in the case of young and old persons. In addition, an overemphasis on reason can lead us to miss the effects of sin on human reason. Distinguishing whether one attribute in particular is what constitutes image bearing is less important than preserving the overall economy of being an image bearer.

Whether reason is a constitutive element or a consequence of bearing God's image, reason has immense significance, because it is antecedent to other aspects of the God-human relationship. Kilner stipulates how reason bears significance to the image of God:

> By creating humanity in God's image, God has created an unbreakable connection with humanity, with the intention that humanity would live with rational and spiritual attributes that in some small but wonderful measure reflect God's own. Reason, then, is one of the human attributes that ought to flow from being in the image of God—it is not, in itself, what constitutes being in God's image. It is a particularly strategic capacity since it is a prerequisite for other human attributes that flow from being in God's image, such as rulership and relationship.[38]

Carl F. H. Henry goes so far as to see humanity's ability to reason as a central feature of a human response to revelation.

Knowledge of God is indeed wholly dependent upon divine revelation, but man was divinely made with rational and moral aptitudes for intelligible communication with his Maker and for the joyous service of God. The possibility of man's knowledge of divine revelation rests in the created capacity of the human mind to know the truth of God, and the capacity of thought and speech that anticipates intelligible knowledge and fellowship. Man's rationality is therefore one span of the epistemological bridge whereby he knows theological truth. That man's reason is a divine gift for recognizing God's truth is a main tenet of the Christian faith. Human reason was a divine endowment enabling man to have knowledge of God and his purposes in the universe. The functions of reason—whether concepts, forms of implication, deduction and induction, judgment and conclusions, and whatever else—are not simply a pragmatic evolutionary development but fulfill a divine intention and purpose for man in relation to the whole realm of knowledge.[39]

Henry captures how reason is a principal component of the relationship between God and humanity. According to John David Hughey, reason demonstrates that human beings are "free to think for [themselves] and [are] responsible to God for the use of [their] intellect."[40] It is also considered a cognitive ability wherein persons can "apprehend something of God himself and his order and purpose in the world."[41] Reason allows humans to reflect on purpose and divine meaning; it makes humanity responsible before God. Persons may discern truths of general and special revelation because they possess reason. By making humans creatures of reason, God decreed that humans would respond to external stimuli hoping to find truth. The aptitude for apprehension is what makes reason essential to religious liberty.

While not speaking in explicitly Christian terms, James Madison provides helpful insight into the integrity of reason that complements a Christian understanding of humanity's cognitive nature as image bearers.

> As long as the reason of man continues fallible, and he is at liberty to exercise it, different opinions will be formed. As long as the connection subsists between his reason and his self-love, his opinions and his passions will have a reciprocal influence on each other; and the former will be objects to which the latter will attach themselves. The diversity in the faculties of men, from which the rights of property originate, is not less an insuperable obstacle to a uniformity of interests. The protection of these faculties is the first object of government. From the protection of different and unequal faculties of acquiring property, the possession of different degrees and kinds of property immediately results; and from the influence of these on the sentiments and views of the respective proprietors, ensues a division of the society into different interests and parties.[42]

Madison's comments illustrate a scriptural truth: reason is essential to humans' grasp of truth and must, by definition, be free. Government has a duty to preserve the rights of conscience, since reason helps govern action. Reason allows a person to understand who they are and what they are responsible for before God.

Madison avers that the job of government is not to promote diversity qua diversity, as though all opinions that consciences reach are equally true. Rather, government ought to recognize and protect the free exercise of one's cognitive faculties.[43] Madison states that the duty of government is to respect the individual as a rational creature whose reason directs them toward intelligible ends. Thus, government must recognize and protect aspects of personhood that uphold the integrity of personhood.

The use of reason, though, is not abstract. Rather, reason is also "practical" in that the ability to apprehend truth "involves also the ability to shape our lives and actions in accordance with that apprehension."[44] Reason is "passionate [and] ordered to our ultimate end in the presence of God."[45]

Reason is not divorced from christological categories. All reason is done in the shadow of divine reason. One of the paramount truths of Christology is that the logos of God is Jesus Christ (John 1:1–3). Jesus is the divine ordering principle of the universe and also the image of God. He is the reason that reason exists and is an intelligible operation of the mind (Col. 1:15–20). If the image of God is Jesus Christ, and the logos of God is Jesus Christ, the use of reason is directed toward and fulfilled in reason's grasp of Jesus Christ. Siedentop makes the compelling argument that it is Christ himself who makes reason and rationality intelligible: "Individual rationality, rationality in all equally, is purchased at the price of submitting to God's will as revealed in the Christ. . . . In the Christ, both the power of God and the wisdom of God are revealed. Jesus is the Christ because his death and resurrection give humans, as individuals, access to the mind and will of God."[46] Human use of reason is meant to reflect the divine mind of the Trinity, that the person exercising their reason might come to understand the mystery of saving faith.

Freedom

Only in obedience to a power above humanity can humanity truly attain liberty. Properly understood, liberty is not the freedom merely to do what one wants but the ability to do what one ought. This is why Scripture speaks of people being free only in proportion to their obedience to Christ (Gal. 5:1–7; cf. Ps. 119:45). "Where the Spirit of the Lord is, there is freedom" (2 Cor. 3:17) is not a reference to ground the American experiment but a profound scriptural truth. The true irony of liberty is that it flourishes only under law. Through the "law of liberty" individuals are freed to experience the blessings of a life ordered toward divine blessing

(James 2:12). Human freedom is grounded in bearing God's image, but "true freedom is spiritually based and originates in the person of Jesus Christ."[47] Freedom is not an intrinsic good in Christian thought; it is an instrumental good that directs us in the path of obtaining righteousness. Image bearers were not made for liberty qua liberty but for a state of excellence, which is found ultimately in Jesus Christ. To reduce humans to liberty-maximizing agents is to rob them of the good for which their nature is designed. Humans crave limits, and the absence of limits does not make society better but worse. Moreover, without tethering liberty to God's purpose for its use, liberty is gutted of its deepest connection to obtaining the good. Liberty assumes a particular telos. If God is removed, all that is left of liberty is choice. A miscarriage of "liberty" can be found in the often and justly ridiculed formulation of former Supreme Court Justice Anthony Kennedy, who famously declared in a 1992 Supreme Court opinion on abortion rights, "At the heart of liberty is the right to define one's own concept of existence, of meaning, of the universe, and of the mystery of human life."[48] This is a debased and vulgar conception of liberty. It vitiates any stable conception of ordered liberty, leaving all meaning to subjective interpretation. On the one hand, this is a risk posed with the exercise of liberty. On the other hand, to valorize a conception of liberty such as this as the sine qua non of political liberty is to invite moral anarchy and social chaos. Edmund Burke spoke of the "dust and powder of individuality."[49] This is striking imagery for our conversation around liberty. Burke understood that a social compact for society to unite around is hopelessly fleeting when persons in society define individuality untethered from institutions that anchor their accounts of truth, goodness, and beauty according to loyalty, custom, and tradition.

True liberty, rather, is ordered to reason's grasp of the truth. Imperfect as a person's reason may be, political discourse should always associate liberty with its directiveness toward proper ends.

But what of freedom not yet brought under the rule of Christ? What does freedom mean as a creational reality available to sinful agents? We ought to understand an agent's penultimate use of liberty as a vehicle for possibly turning away from sin and toward Christ. Under this penultimate rubric of liberty, the misuse of liberty is what grounds our ultimate culpability as responsible creatures before God.[50] The wrongful use of liberty is given space, since that same space also enables the right use of liberty to flower. Furthermore, the common good is undermined when government acts to eliminate all error. In that sense, the remedy is worse than the disease. Erring uses of freedom are protected only insofar as there is no legitimate threat to the common good.

For humans, who image God, the ultimate pursuit of human freedom is greater conformity to Jesus Christ. Human conformity into Christ's image requires the freedom to exercise the faculties that make sanctification and maturity in Christ possible. Thus, freedom is part of God's plan for humanity to enjoy relationship with him (Rom. 8:21; 2 Cor. 3:7; Gal. 5:1).[51] Amos Niven Wilder observes that biblical language of "repent," "follow me," "choose this day," "believe in thy heart," and "return" all signify the eschatological nature of humanity's freedom before God.[52] And Siedentop states, "If faith in the Christ can free humans from the bondage of sin, then each must have a potential for freedom, a free will."[53] Freedom is thus "transcendent" and "existential" because it calls for an "eschatological summons" in response to God's revelation.[54] If the gospel calls for greater conformity to Christ, then freedom before God—seen primarily through theological lenses—is the foundation that allows image bearers to reach their highest purpose. Indeed, as J. Philip Wogaman argues, "Unless man is externally free to bear witness to God, the inner intention of the covenant between God and man remains frustrated."[55]

In Colossians 3:10, Paul refers to the redeemed self as the agent "being renewed in knowledge after the image of its creator."

Human destiny is defined by its initial purpose, which is fulfilled by knowing God in Christ. The freedom to respond to the gospel is the same freedom that brings one into greater conformity to Christ. All of this, it is worth stressing, is grounded in the reality of humanity bearing a distinct mark given to it at its creation. A reaffirmed creation established by Jesus's bodily resurrection means that each individual image bearer requires the freedom to engage their moral agency with the highest possible telos: redemption in Christ. Religious liberty is thus animated toward the truth of redemption, and redemption includes the capacity of those who bear God's image to recognize the fulfillment of their image in Jesus Christ. As Oliver O'Donovan writes, "We must complete our account of Christian freedom by saying that the Spirit forms and brings to expression the appropriate pattern of free response to objective reality."[56] Such is the essence of liberty. Human freedom is fundamental to salvation. Humans have supernatural ends to their existence, and freedom is a prerequisite to their fulfillment.[57]

Here, I do not mean to conflate ultimate freedom before God (a creational reality based in our relation to God) with penultimate religious liberty (a social reality based in law). Rather, we must differentiate between a theological freedom (ultimate freedom) and legal freedom (penultimate freedom).

At the ultimate level, the logic of the gospel—such as free/uncoerced response, voluntary/personal assent, acknowledgment of guilt, and faithfulness in obedience in how one lives out the obligations of the gospel—ought to necessarily lead to the reality of there being a penultimate, social, or legal doctrine of religious liberty.

But at the penultimate level, the absence of religious liberty does not, at one's interior, prohibit actual belief. This reflects a fundamentally theological reality: no government can effect or impede actual true belief. Opposition to religion, however, hampers the outward expression of inward reality which can, in turn, be harmful for the good of religion in society and deleterious to the ways people organize their lives in response to their religion. In time, this hostility to religion could atrophy religion's presence in society and create an environment (or moral ecology) that is hardened to the goods and claims of religion; namely, that religion helps individuals align themselves with ultimate reality, resulting in true, authentic living.

Religion, as such, is a matter of internal volition and affection before it is imminently practical. Downplaying the conversionary aspects of religion is inimical to religious liberty, in my view, as it makes religion a matter of cultural identity and social practice rather than the heartfelt grasp of ultimate reality. Religion is never less than practical in its outworking in our life, but it is more—it is a personal encounter with the divine.

All that to say, conversion qua conversion does not hinge on a social or legal doctrine of religious liberty inasmuch as those who live in hostile regimes can still have consciences and affections that have been transformed. Conversion, internally, does depend on principles of religious liberty for individual persons, as noted above. There is thus a freedom before God and a freedom before the state. The former (inner freedom before God) explains the intrinsic and metaphysical properties of religious liberty while the latter freedom (external freedom before the state) births extrinsic and legal properties that testify, accurately, to what religion is, its role in persons' lives, and how it should be accommodated in society.

A 1960 statement by the World Council of Churches echoes the teleological nature of freedom in relationship to Christ: "In Jesus Christ, God has both restored and redeemed his human creation, made in his own image. A particular man was and is the bearer of God's majesty and purpose. In Jesus Christ, he has called humanity to a destiny for the pursuit of which every man must be free."[58]

Freedom is of course central to the ordering of political communities, but more foundationally, it is oriented toward a greater purpose and higher plane. Freedom is to be used not so much for "choice" but for union with Christ. Exercising freedom comes with a responsibility to steward that freedom for its ultimate purpose. Christians can defend a robust account of religious freedom on the grounds that image-bearing persons are meant to hear and respond to the gospel with the totality of their personhood. Liberty is granted to those who reject Christ in hopes that their ultimate responsibility to him will be realized through a voluntary response.

At the same time, as there is an ultimate use of freedom, there is a penultimate use of freedom. The penultimate use of freedom is using one's reason to respond to the conscience's apprehension of either moral or religious obligation. A defense of religious freedom for non-Christians issues, then, from the hope that non-Christians will use the availability of freedom to "come to the knowledge of the truth" (1 Tim. 2:4). But again, the ultimate use of one's freedom is bound up with God's calling on humanity, which is to reflect his perfect image, Jesus Christ (Heb. 1:3). A. F. Carrillo de Albornoz writes that the "revelation of God in Jesus Christ requires a free response and, therefore, any other kind of response is incompatible with its intrinsic nature."[59]

James E. Wood observes that "freedom is primarily, or in essence, an inner state, in which no external authority may exercise control over a person."[60] In no sense can a person be understood as religiously free if they are compelled to accept or reject moral or religious convictions. Neither can faith be effectuated by coercion. The inner freedom of human beings as rational image-bearing creations serves as the foundation for a social doctrine of religious liberty. Because people are in their essence made to be free, society and its institutions cannot coerce belief.[61] God desires "voluntary spiritual allegiance" since, according to Henry, "coerced decision is of little spiritual value."[62] Moreover, coerced belief is false belief, which undermines personal moral agency. According to John Finnis, when religious liberty is extinguished, "we are unable to be authentic, and fail to make our actions genuine realizations of our own freely ordered evaluations, preferences, hopes and self-determination."[63]

Freedom also concerns how God reveals himself to individuals and their response to him. "An essential characteristic of the gospel," writes Wood, "is that God has chosen to make himself known in love and that, therefore, he does not use force to win our allegiance."[64] The very coming of the Lord Jesus in humility, rather than in triumph, captures God's posture toward us. God brought his mission to earth through an infant rather than through conquest.[65] Niels Søe writes that "the basis of religious liberty is the very fact that Christ did not come in heavenly splendor and worldly majesty to subjugate any possible resistance and force all and everybody to subjection."[66] Wood states, "For faith to be faith, it must be voluntary, personal, and [a] free act, an act born of freedom. Faith is not faith if its voluntary character is abridged by coercion. Freedom is integrally bound up with God's revelation of himself and in his relations with persons. In God's very disclosure of himself, freedom is a part of that revelation."[67]

Freedom, then, is not simply the exercise of one's choice. Freedom, rather, is a comprehensive estate understood as constitutive to image bearing and personhood. Søren Kierkegaard writes that freedom is at the core of personhood. Freedom is a benchmark that expresses the underlying essence of human nature: "Man is himself primarily and genuinely in his free choice. If then our Lord will draw people to himself, he cannot force them to surrender. For then he would not get their real selves, but something different. Then he would have drawn the object of his 'drawing' in away from their own selves in such a way that finally he would not have them drawn, but changed into a kind of impersonal machinery."[68]

A biblical account of religious liberty must also consider how sin's effect on humanity impacts freedom. As Barrett Duke notes, because individuals are fallen, "people are incapable of fully interpreting the will of God in all matters for other people, and they are certainly incapable of properly enforcing spiritual standards."[69]

A doctrine of sin, therefore, reminds us that "the sinful nature of man negates the possibility of the absolutizing of human authority, religious or political, and by limiting all human authority provides an important foundation for religious liberty."[70] While sin results from distorting one's freedom, sin also buffers against earthly claims of infallibility. A doctrine of religious liberty, then, accounts for humanity's sinful proclivities to coerce or punish the unbelieving or to weaponize religious faith.

In the end, deducing the significance and priority of freedom is essential to distilling the consequences that follow from bearing God's image: "True freedom is whole and, indivisible—it embraces political freedom, moral freedom, spiritual freedom, freedom of thought, freedom of belief, freedom of expression, free enterprise, a free press, free elections, but supremely freedom to perform the will of God. Religious freedom is basic to all else; it offers humankind not only freedom not to worship Caesar, but freedom to worship Caesar's God, who is the ground of all human duties and rights."[71] True liberty is found in obeying God's law. Liberty without telos is license; liberty under law is blessing.

Image bearing is of foremost importance to the question of religious liberty because true freedom and true humanity are bound up in the culminating reality that Christ is the true image of God. Freedom is freedom toward a particular telos or purpose. Biblical passages that deal with liberty teach that liberty is fulfilled in direct relationship to Christ (John 8:36; Acts 13:38–39; Rom. 6:22; 8:1–4; 1 Cor. 6:12; 2 Cor. 3:17; Gal. 5:1, 13–14; Eph. 3:12; 1 Pet. 2:16). Therefore, image bearing, as it relates to religious liberty, is oriented toward the ability to know Christ as the perfect image. The image of God is about the freedom to discern who the God-man, Jesus Christ, really is. Christians require a christological component to religious liberty because, anthropologically, true freedom orients persons toward liberation in Christ, who is God's perfect image.

The Conscience

One of the early roots of religious freedom was the conscience.[72] The conscience is the primary rudder of a person's moral intuitions. There are two layers of the conscience, so to speak, developed from Aquinas: *synderesis* and *conscientia*. Synderesis refers to the natural moral inclinations that individuals have as image bearers and moral agents possessing the "law . . . written on their hearts" (Rom. 2:15). Think of synderesis as the content of the moral law. Conscientia is the inner judgment of a person acting either congruently or incongruently with the moral law. Synderesis cannot be altered, as it simply reflects the moral deposit God gives to humans. Individuals can decide and act (conscientia) inconsistent with what their inner judgment knows to be true (synderesis).[73] When a person lies, for example, their conscience (judgment) is disobeying truth. The conscience acts as judge and jury to the imprint of the moral law.

Humans are morally constituted, and the conscience helps direct humans toward their proper end, an end that satisfies both the moral law written on the heart and the obligations to act on the basis of moral and religious truths that originate from God himself.

As Carrillo de Albornoz helpfully defines it, the conscience is "our imminent and native faculty for reaching moral judgments, conclusions, and decisions." It is the "last norm and rule of action and decision."[74] The conscience acts as a buffer between the individual and whatever authority structures would seek to tamper with or impede one's grasp of religious truth. Indeed, "the recognition of conscience, in turn, created the possibility of moral appeal against imposed authority—whether by church or state."[75] The conscience can be considered the "inner voice" of a person that brings about "natural moral sense," which "incites or binds" individuals in their moral agency.[76] The conscience is the internal God-given guide for discerning moral judgment. As such, the conscience is an instrument of reason. The conscience makes one's convictions intelligible. The conscience is the wellspring of directiveness that animates a person's life.

Gary T. Meadors defines the conscience as "an aspect of self-awareness that produces the pain and/or pleasure we 'feel' as we reflect on the norms and values we recognize and apply. Conscience is not an outside voice. It is an inward capacity humans possess to critique themselves because the Creator provided this process as a means of moral restraint for his creation."[77] The conscience is the moral aspect of humanity bearing God's image. As individuals ascertain truths, they order their lives around them. This is why individuals are willing to die for the sake of their conscience. People will not sacrifice themselves for falsehood. Whether apocryphal or not, Luther's declaration that to go against the conscience is "neither right nor safe" bears witness to this.

Reason and the conscience are essential characteristics that distinguish humans from the rest of creation.[78] Evangelical theologian Carl F. H. Henry asserts,

> Man differs at one essential point from all other creatures. He alone bears the *imago Dei*—the image of God. Only he has, as part of his essential nature, the forms of reason and morality. Only he is given a distinctive content of knowledge. Because he is so made, he cannot escape ethical responsibility. . . . This intriguing phrase—the *imago Dei*—is not an archaic Latinism; it embraces the essential nature of man as he is on the basis of creation. Hebrew-Christian thought views the *imago Dei* with primary emphasis on the conscience. It holds to an unchanging moral standard on the basis of Divine creation and preservation. And it says that man possesses an ineradicable ethical content. But it does not limit man's knowledge to this aspect of experience. The moral *imago* does not stand alone. It is part of a comprehensive Divine-human relationship that distinguishes man as unique in the creature world. The *imago* embraces at once the forms of rational as well as of moral experience and a knowledge of God as the Truth and as the Good.[79]

The conscience is essential to a Christian understanding of personhood because the conscience, as reason's capacity for moral judgment, is what distinguishes humanity from the rest of creation. The operation of the conscience helps individuals solve the greatest mystery of their existence: To whom do I belong? To God? To the state? To an ideological end? A Christian view of the conscience is not hyperautonomous. Rather, the conscience is what individuals obey to pursue transcendent meaning and self-ordering. The self-constituting nature of the conscience helps humans understand themselves as "persons, not things, creatures with dignity, and subjects of rights, beings made in the image of God."[80]

The conscience is the central place for decision making and judgment. According to Wood, "Man's one and only means of learning God's will for him is the voice of his own conscience."[81] The conscience is the spark of moral intuition that conforms individuals to God's will or leads them to rebel against it. Thus, the conscience is ordered toward truth, regardless of whether truth is fully grasped. A harbinger of the conscience, then, is its essential freedom. But defending the conscience defends the freedom of the faculty of the conscience, not the conclusions that the conscience reaches, for the conscience is not a morally neutral center of operation. According to Scripture, the conscience can be seared and driven by subrational instincts that override the conscience, thus implying guilt (1 Tim. 4:2; Heb. 10:22). Scripture says that the conscience needs to be redeemed.[82] Consciences go awry. To defend the conscience is not to sanction it, nor is it to grant a "right" to blaspheme God. Rather, we defend the freedom of the conscience because "no one should be compelled to act contrary to conscience" and "no divine or good power motivates one to act against conscience."[83] In this sense, from a Christian view, a person has a negative right to religious freedom. A person has a right to be left alone and unmolested in their conception that God is correct or incorrect. This is not a "positive" right that affirms all religious inclinations but a negative right not to be coerced, because those with erring consciences, though in error, are under the belief that they are acting truthfully.

A person should not assent to something their inner self does not believe. A person is to believe only that which accords with what their conscience believes is true on the basis of reason. In the words of the *Catechism of the Catholic Church*, the conscience "formulates its judgments according to reason, in conformity with the true good willed by the wisdom of the Creator."[84] Persons are to obey and follow judgments they believe to be true. The weightiness of the conscience over religious matters shows that coercion does not work: conforming to a religion or ideology accomplishes only insincerity and falsehood. Disturbing the conscience by compelling an individual to violate it, then, represents a personal fragmentation that jeopardizes integrity and sanctity.

Christopher Tollefsen notes how important it is for humans to be free to exercise convictions based on belief: "The exercise of conscience—the making of the moral judgments that is necessary to these enterprises—and the pursuit of religion, thus have a claim to be the most central aspects of an agent's attempts at upright self-constitution, aspects which, if intruded upon in unreasonable ways, would cut to the heart of an agent's ability to act, and constitute herself as a person."[85] Standing for the dignity of the conscience means upholding the faculty of the conscience to arrive at truths that may oppose Christian orthodoxy. As shocking as that may sound, to deny anything less is to deny religious freedom. The awakened conscience, as a vehicle of honest belief, is that which can either redeem or damn, quite literally. The conscience is to be persuaded, never coerced, as an individual comes to recognize truth and falsehood by their own volition.[86]

The integrity of the conscience is grounded in the reality of duties that the conscience apprehends. Consider John Henry Newman's words:

Conscience has rights because it has duties; but in this age, with a large portion of the public, it is the very right and freedom of conscience to dispense with conscience, to ignore a Lawgiver and Judge, to be independent of unseen obligations. It becomes a license to take up any or no religion, to take up this or that and let it go again, to go to church, to go to chapel, to boast of being above all religions and to be an impartial critic of each of them. Conscience is a stern monitor, but in this century it has been superseded by a counterfeit, which the eighteen centuries prior to it never heard of, and could not have mistaken for it, if they had. It is the right of self-will.[87]

According to Newman, the role of the conscience is to discern moral duty and to exercise one's duty based on that discernment. Notice that Newman is also critiquing general appeals of "conscience" that are made in order to license immorality or self-autonomy. In Newman's thinking, the conscience acts to discern truth, not simply to respond to whatever impulse or idea comes to mind. Ethicist Daniel R. Heimbach refers to this as the "ordered liberty" component of religious liberty. This is a view of freedom that sees religious liberty as guided by moral restraint to oblige a law higher than human law. This is "freedom *for* as opposed to freedom *from*."[88] The conscience ought to lead someone to align with the truth that is written on the heart. The conscience subservient to mere human autonomy is under an exploitative form of freedom. Freedom subservient to the upright conscience is where the true function of the conscience is found. This paradigm rescues religious liberty from concerns of ethical or religious relativism. In this view, ordered liberty "presumes that real moral authority is objective, enduring, and universal, and is certainly not anything controlled or made up by those living by it."[89] From this perspective, the freedom of the conscience implies limited political authority stemming from the freedom that God grants to the individual as an element of their nature, not as a subsidy from the state.

God created us with a conscience. The conscience will be accountable to God (Rom. 2:12; 3:20). As Andrew David Naselli and J. D. Crowley note, "The guilt that your conscience makes you feel should lead you to turn from your sin to Jesus."[90] When we violate our conscience, we are indictable before a holy God, as our response to our conscience reflects our obedience or disobedience to God. The conscience is therefore a vehicle of indictment. On the theological level, all consciences are indicted as having fallen under the judgment of God (Rom. 1). According to Henry, "The Bible teaches that all human beings, irrespective of nationality or race or religion, have some intellectual and moral light and that conscience hails them anticipatively before God's judgment throne. It condemns nonperformance of what humans know to be right as insistently as it deplores inexcusable ignorance of the right."[91] Here Henry avers that the light of reason—even in a fallen world—is what condemns us in our sins of omission and commission. Romans 1, the infamous passage of humanity's fretful condition before God, teaches that fallen humans actively rebel against God's law. To rebel, we must first know what is right. By knowing that we do wrong, we know there must be a right; and if there is indeed a "right," we are obligated to follow it, even though we cannot. This suggests that humanity's greatest problem is not primarily epistemological but ethical. We know the content of the moral law, but we continually violate it, to which our conscience bears witness.[92]

In the interest of holding consciences truly accountable, consciences must be free. Thus, a doctrine of the image of God, one that takes seriously human beings' status as morally free creatures, must hold the conscience to be free because the conscience makes individuals indictable. Indeed, the "continuing answerability" of believer and unbeliever alike weds our freedom to our responsibility before God.[93] As Sherif Girgis and Ryan T. Anderson argue, religious liberty implies that people are free to be "deluded about matters of cosmic importance around which they have ordered their lives—even *damnably wrong*."[94] A person deserves to be condemned only if that person has truly violated a law born witness by the conscience. God gives humans freedom, then holds them responsible for how they use it.[95] Henry elsewhere argues that it is the answerability of the conscience to God that makes a person "ultimately responsible not to his fellow men but to God for the decisions he makes and the options he pursues."[96]

The image of God in every person means that genuine conversion requires a free conscience. Coercion in defense of religious allegiance is a "contradiction" of "God's ways with men as well as a lack of trust in the power of the Holy Spirit."[97] Individuals must be brought to conviction and repentance through the operations of heart and mind. Freedom, therefore, is not just an abstract political doctrine but the essence of true faith. Individuals must be free to be wrong because by recognizing their errors, they repent and turn to Christ.

Should "religious liberty" or "religious freedom" simply become "freedom of conscience"? If the conscience governs actions issuing from deep-seated convictions, collapsing religious freedom into conscience freedom would allow broad acceptance by those who do not claim to be religious. In this framework, the common root between the religious and the nonreligious is the function of the conscience. Everyone has strong opinions, but not everyone has strong opinions based in religion, so why not argue on terms that everyone is familiar with?

An appeal to the conscience alone severed from the foundation of eternal law (the traditional source of moral law) can too easily collapse into claims of moral anarchy or relativism, since it claims no authority beyond or outside itself. This is simply untenable within a political community. The conscience must be accommodated to the greatest degree in a free political community, but it cannot be understood as absolute. A person may not commit murder under the guise of their conscience's desire, even if done sincerely. One cannot receive a conscience exemption to abuse a child. This is self-will run amok, a perverted self-rule that exploits the idea of self-constitution and threatens the common good. While the state may not want to arbitrate every moral dispute in a political community, it cannot leave everything to the conscience alone. It must establish some foundation for morality. This has traditionally been religion, which recognizes the divine source of morality. Rex Ahdar argues that "freedom of conscience" is best understood as a "supplement" to religious freedom.[98] We must understand the conscience as a means of violating or upholding the law written on the heart. This is necessarily a religious reality.

Religion acknowledges a source of morality outside one's self. This does not mean that one's religion is correct but that when one seeks to order one's life around a transcendent authority, religion can at least offer a more enduring source for morality than just the individual himself or herself.

Conclusion

The human person as made in the image of God best grounds an anthropological account for religious liberty that is distinctly Christian in origin. Religious liberty, then, is not simply a political question; it arises from a theology of creation—that humanity bears a unique origin, design, and purpose in its constitution. Apart from recognizing the special ontological uniqueness of humanity and the uniqueness of their capacities to constitute themselves, the idea of protecting the religious freedom of individuals with whom you disagree moves away from a principled account of religious liberty and into the category of consensus and convention, both of which are subject to changing human attitudes about the acceptability and popularity of certain groups in society.

5

That They Should Seek God

IN HIS CLASSIC *THE GREAT DIVORCE,* C. S. Lewis depicts an exchange between a spirit and a ghost shuttling between heaven and hell. The ghost, who was a theologically liberal bishop when alive, and "Dick" (the spirit) converse about intellectual curiosity, myth, and the truthfulness of the Christian faith. In the course of the conversation, the bishop is incredulous that Dick would take the simple myths of Christianity *literally.* The bishop, like all modernists, has dispensed with such fables. He believes in the intellectual fashions—that inquiry, questioning, and doubt are goods unto themselves—which led him to reject most of Christian doctrine.

Dick disagrees that intellectual curiosity is good for its own sake. He says that knowledge and truth seeking are designed to lead to a conclusion. Dick has bad news for the bishop: despite his honest seeking and honest rejection of the Christian faith, "errors which are sincere in that sense are not innocent." Truth seeking and inquiry are not endless pursuits. Dick says, "Once you were a child. Once you knew what inquiry was for. There was a time when you asked questions because you wanted answers, and were glad when you had found them. Become that child again: even now. . . . Thirst was made for water; inquiry for truth."[1] In this exchange, Lewis testifies to something axiomatic in our discussion of religious liberty—it protects the search for religious truth that comes to define the most important parts of a person's life.

Meaning Making and Personhood

Because humans are made in God's image, we are at root moral and religious beings.[2] If divinely created, we are also divinely animated, oriented to the divine, and fulfilled by the divine. To say that humanity is religious in its fundamental nature is to convey that God ordered persons to seek the divine. In this account, atheism is not only a rejection of God but also a rejection of human nature, for to negate the divine is to suppress an orientation residing deep within the interior of humanity. Note that Scripture never defends God's existence. God is the grand assumption of Scripture.

As *Homo adorans*[3]—the "worshiping human"—humans are God-seeking creatures. Our seeking often leads to idolatry, but we seek nonetheless. Paul declares in Acts 17:26–27, "And he made from one man every nation of mankind to live on all the face of the earth, having determined allotted periods and the boundaries of their dwelling place, that they should seek God, and perhaps feel their way toward him and find him." This passage reveals that humans are oriented to seek God and that our quest is in fact God given. To seek God is not to seek after the quixotic; it is to seek to know God, to come into knowledge of ultimate reality and the deepest truths one can ascertain to order their lives around. To orient one's self to God is to know joy (Pss. 16:11; 73:25–26).

Baptist scholar Barrett Duke has argued based on Acts 17 that it "seems reasonable to deduce from this passage that God intends for humans to have the freedom to search after him."[4] Luke Timothy Johnson likewise argues that Paul is "remarkably positive toward the legitimacy of Gentile religious longing."[5] Even as there are echoes in the Old Testament for YHWH to redeem the nations, the New Testament confirms and makes explicit God's mission to bring salvation to the ends of the earth (Matt. 28:18–20). Behind humankind's religious nature is a divine imprint that puts a longing for transcendence and alignment with transcendence inside every human heart. Augustine's maxim "Thou hast made us for thyself, O Lord, and our heart is restless until it finds its rest in thee" declares that humanity's nature is in search of God.[6] This quotation is a coda that is both descriptive of human nature and prescriptive for why religious liberty is intrinsically tied to the very nature of humanity.

Humans are inherently religious, such that humankind tries to "achieve a harmony with whatever transcendent order of reality there may be."[7] Sociologist Christian Smith goes so far as to call humans "believing animals."[8] Cognitive science affirms that religion and the answer for meaning it provides are embedded in human nature.[9] Steven D. Smith writes that "religion engages this meaning-seeking dimension of our nature by offering a sort of Grand Story or metanarrative that confers meaning by explaining what the cosmic and human drama is all about."[10] Christopher Tollefsen asserts that humanity's inherent religious and ethical nature means that religion takes on a "radically architectonic status in an agent's life."[11] By this, religion becomes the animating center of our lives. "The good of religion," writes Tollefsen, "will now potentially be implicated in every possible circumstance calling for choice."[12]

If religious impulse is central to humanity's design, then tampering with religious nature fundamentally violates personhood. As the authors of *Religious Freedom: Why Now?* state, "To repress religion then is not to frustrate some odd quirk of human nature, somehow separable from the 'true' interests of human beings. Instead, it is to repress the variable yet inevitable religious choices and experiences of actual human beings. . . . Religious repression is the denial of the very essence of what it means to be human."[13] They soberly note that "religion is so profoundly intertwined with human existence that it cannot be repressed except at the price of undermining individuality and disrupting society."[14] If religious impulse is intrinsically tied to human experience, then the moral and religious conclusions that free persons arrive at must be self-chosen and voluntary—that is, a community cannot believe on behalf of an individual, nor can conclusions be transposed on an individual that they themselves did not grasp on their own. Only an understanding of human freedom and human nature that respects as fundamental the image of God as the foundation for religious inquiry can furnish a doctrine of religious liberty that sees religious instinct as an inseparable, integral aspect of human fulfillment. In fact, the image of God is the starting point for establishing why it is that human beings search after ultimate meaning to begin with—it is intrinsic to who God made them, even those who believe wrongly yet still attempt to make religion central in their lives.

Religion functions, therefore, as a vehicle through which humanity not only derives ultimate meaning but also sets out to live in accordance with this meaning. How "religion" functions in this paradigm does not necessarily require belief in the divine. Like Ronald Dworkin, I do not equate religion with theism but define religion as a meaning-making enterprise inside a world.[15] In other words, agnostics and atheists have sincere "ultimate beliefs" about the world, and these are also taken on faith.[16] As David Foster Wallace has similarly argued, every person is "religious" insofar as every individual is seeking to live their life by an ultimate authority, deriving meaning and purpose from it. Every person attempting to discern what is true—even if grasped erringly—is participating in a truth-seeking endeavor.

Religious belief orients people's lives. As Pope Benedict XVI declared, "Religious freedom should be understood, then, . . . as an ability to order one's choices in accordance with truth."[17] This is a profound framing for why religious liberty is integral to human dignity. It parallels Paul's understanding that religious belief leads us to act in ways that are faithful to that belief (Rom. 12:1–2; 1 Cor. 10:31). All that we do is bound up in what we believe. How we grasp God dictates the form of life we will live. Since God is the Creator and Sustainer of life, it only makes sense that persons would give their full selves to God. This means that nothing of a person's life falls outside the canopy of God's glory. A person who has given themselves and their life to God cannot compartmentalize their psyche. To live all of life for God's glory, then, means to live a life to its highest possible good. It is to live *coram Deo*, "in the presence of God" (see Rom. 14:7–8). Only a being so powerful, glorious, good, and beautiful as God can explain why people are willing to sacrifice their existence for such conviction. Sidney Greidanus observes that "freedom of religion will require freedom of choice in every area of life, freedom to respond in a way that is consistent with one's religious beliefs. The Bible clearly teaches that a choice for the covenant of God must direct subsequent choices in every area of life."[18]

People do not live and die for mere choice alone. They live and die according to the conviction that unless lived authentically, life is not lived in earnest. Therefore, when someone cannot live out the deepest convictions of their belief system, their self-transcendence and self-possession are violated. A lack of freedom to engage in religious devotion works to thwart human nature and human fulfillment.

Religious Liberty and the Commonality of Human Experience

Religious liberty can be difficult to translate to a nonreligious person in a secular era (especially if they profess to be free of all religious devotion, which I dispute). Nonreligious individuals view religious liberty as a religious idea; religious individuals view it as a basic human right necessary for an authentic life. The result is a contest between those who see religious liberty as essential to fulfilling basic human goods and those who see it, at best, as a political construct to achieve political tranquility or, at worst, a holdover from a bygone era that nefarious actors use for their own insidious purposes. A chasm emerges between those who see religious liberty as essential to what it means to be human and those who see it as an impediment to progress. Given this polarization, can we make the case for religious liberty as a social good?

There is a way to distill religious liberty to a form that everyone can understand. Everyone, whether overtly secular or even quasi-religious, understands three categories explained by virtue of their creational status as image bearers: adoration, authenticity, and authority. Knowingly or unknowingly, every person at their fundamental level operates according to these categories. This is because, according to ethicist J. Daryl Charles, humanity is "rational, perceiving, intuiting, and conceiving."[19] Everyone worships something (adoration); everyone wants to live truthfully (authenticity); and everyone has an ultimate standard for what they value (authority). These concepts are the building blocks of religious liberty that presumes an anthropology consistent with both Christian theology and the lived experience of those who would not subscribe to a particular religion. It bears repeating: everyone relies on these concepts to bring meaning to their lives. It is impossible to deny their reach and exercise in every living person. Each category is crucial to understanding why religious liberty is vital to the human experience of being rational, truth-seeking persons made in God's image.

Adoration: Who or What Is Worshiped?

Christians confess that the triune God is the Lord of the universe and is to be worshiped (Pss. 29:2; 33:8; 95:6). For Christians, worship is not just a rote practice. Worship is why we exist and gives us a joyful orientation to the world. We do not worship out of compulsion or fear. We worship because we believe that worship is the telos of purpose: to exult in the Lord and refract his glory in our lives. God demands our worship as God, but he does not coerce it.

Worship has a corresponding impulse in the non-Christian life. Adoration means to adore, to worship or venerate, to give highest devotion, praise, and love to someone or something. Everyone adores. Everyone has something at their core that drives them and contends for their attention and affections, whether it is a favorite sports team, a hobby like traveling, or an understanding of the divine. Whatever the object of adoration, its purpose is to help anchor a person's life and give it meaning.

It is possible to rephrase the question "What is worshiped?" to "Where is ultimate meaning found?" "Religion" is a catchall category that answers these questions. Is ultimate meaning found in the state? In organized religion? In entertainment? In science? A person may not recognize this as true for themselves, but what they build their life around is, functionally, their god. This is a descriptive statement about human nature: persons will inevitably give their lives to *something*. The question is whether the object of one's adoration is morally praiseworthy. Money, sex, and power are the functional gods of this age. To doubt that people are ordering their lives around these pursuits is to deny the obvious.

As soon as the object of worship is identified, an important question follows: What right, if any, does someone or something (such as the state) have to prevent someone from worshiping? The presumption of liberty and the significance of human agency mean that the burden to prove why someone should be restricted from exercising their agency and respective faculties is high. As a result, religious liberty is a capacious concept that includes those activities that also aptly fit under the category of personal freedom. If religious liberty is about alignment with truth, religious liberty gives space to pursuits of truth that Christians hope, in time, will lead one to come to know ultimate truth (John 14:6). The argument here is both substantive and rhetorical in hopes that it will allow those who do not practice an organized "religion" to better understand why formal religious worship is equally deserving of broad liberty protections.

If someone's liberty to find meaning in life is not restricted because it does not lead to criminal wrongdoing or is not a threat to social harmony, then the liberty that allows someone to find that same meaning in God should also not be restricted. This conclusion will necessarily make some uncomfortable, since it has the possible consequence of being interpreted as treating all pursuits equally. Is a person's desire to escape the world's pain through drunkenness or serial monogamy on the same level as a person's pursuit of God? Of course not. Moral and religious relativism should be rejected in the strongest terms possible. Freedom is only as virtuous as its ends; it is an instrumental good to help attain a noninstrumental good.

But even with that qualification, unless the state desires to eliminate all forms of personal vice, the state should leave room for citizens to experience the negative consequences of freedom. Civil society, not the state, should be the seedbed of fostering humane moral ecologies in which people are taught to shun behaviors that impede human flourishing. But not all such behavior should be criminalized. Political bodies should be able to make judgments concerning what is criminal that reflect the convictions of the communities they represent. In doing so, they should differentiate among what is disfavored, what is repugnant, and what is criminal. The responsible exercise of liberty will require freedom while at the same time the establishment of limits to protect against the negatives of excess liberty. Deliberative bodies serve the common good and religious liberty by distinguishing immoral actions from those that are merely sins to those that verge into criminal wrongdoing. As the adage goes, all crimes are sins, but not all sins are crimes. The common good requires a consistent and fairly applied moral system, one whose moral theory can construct a case for determining what types of vices to penalize versus merely to discourage. But a government of exacting moral rectitude will channel the very worst of Inquisition-like powers. According to Ryan T. Anderson and Robert P. George, this form of government can become intrusive and does more harm to the common good:

> Thomas Aquinas famously taught that the law should not command every virtue or prohibit every vice. Attempts—in the name of the human good—to penalize every form or instance of immorality would actually *undermine* the human good (by, for example, giving power to governments that is too easily abused, or intruding improperly into the lives of families and other institutions of civil society, or imposing a legal burden that is too heavy for most to bear). And so, he taught, the state should limit itself to punishing the graver forms of immorality, those that do the most harm, and those against which the force of law can be effective. Thus, we see in Aquinas one "pre-liberal" limit on government power: Government should not attempt to promote the common good in ways that are likely to undermine or harm it. Indeed, sometimes restricting the liberty to do wrong—a liberty to which no one has a moral right— rather than promoting the common good can actually harm it.[20]

Not all uses of liberty are equal. As stated in the previous chapter, liberty, at root, is an instrumental good to be used to maximize the attainment of human goods. Maximizing human goods through the proper use of liberty also entails, in a fallen world, the misuse of liberty. In this framework, the diversity of views that come to exist around religion are not valued for their own sake as though all views are equal. Rather, liberty is a concession to the reality of religious diversity that yields the fulfillment of a basic good, such as grasping religious truth, that people come to realize in different ways. Catholic natural law philosopher Robert George argues similarly:

> Neither diversity nor uniformity can ever be an end rationally sought for its own sake; and any instrumental value that either may possess is dependent on the specific nature of any given instance of diversity or uniformity. Only one thing need be remembered to dispel the unease that results from a combination of the feeling that a maximum of diversity is always good and the suspicion that a perfectionist conception of anything is bound to decrease diversity: a sound perfectionism recognizes both that human flourishing is advanced by having a broad array of morally valuable choices and that a diversity of evil choices contributes nothing of practical value to human beings. In the pluralistic perfectionist theory which I shall advance, diversity is respected not for its own sake, but precisely for the sake of the diverse goods, to be realized in diverse reasonable ways, by diverse human beings, with diverse talents, interests, and backgrounds, facing diverse challenges and opportunities, in and through their diverse reasonable choices and commitments.[21]

Such is the reality with which we must reckon. Individuals have a penultimate right to guide their lives by their conscience. This is not relativism inasmuch as the recognition that people in a fallen society will direct their adoration toward conflicting ends, some of which are unprofitable and may be rightfully prohibited. Moreover, a state that sets out to police all immoral behavior (and false worship) is a state that will end up posing a greater threat to the common good than one that allows some misdeeds to occur for the sake of liberty. With the exception of legally prohibited actions, a person cannot be directed away from an unprofitable end by external force. Instead, through persuasion, a person will need to conclude for themselves by use of their own reason and settled judgment that something is unprofitable.

Authenticity: What Is True Living?

Imagine that a state passes a law that requires someone to believe in something or to act in a way that goes against their conscience. This would not be authoritarian but totalitarian. Active drafting of one's person into something one knows to be false is tyranny. Not only would the state be overreaching, but the person would also experience deep inner conflict. Being coerced into believing in or acting on what one believes is false or immoral creates internal fragmentation and disturbance. The state is also creating false adherents to its system, which is a hallmark of puppet regimes who propagandize with either deluding or eye-rolling effect. Imagine an oppressed person being made to believe that their oppressor is virtuous. This would be unspeakably inhumane. As Robert George writes on the relationship between authenticity, religion, and religious liberty:

> We human beings have always wondered whether there is anything greater than ourselves, that is to say, an ultimate, or at least more nearly ultimate, source of meaning and value which we must take into account and (if personal) with whom we can enter into friendship and communion. The question is both sensible and important. If there is a God (or gods, or non-deific ultimate realities), and if harmony and communion with the ultimate is possible for human beings, then it is obviously good to establish such harmony and enter into such communion. People, of course, come to different conclusions about religious matters: hence, the truly radical religious pluralism one encounters in the world. Yet, no one can reasonably ignore the religious question. One's answer to it, even if atheistic or agnostic, profoundly affects one's life. One is bound, in reason, to explore the religious question and act on the basis of one's best judgments. Moreover, no one can search for religious truth, hold religious beliefs, or act on them authentically, for someone else. Searching, believing, and striving for authenticity are interior acts of individual human beings. As interior acts, they cannot be compelled.[22]

121

All of this reflects the human impulse to live authentically. To live authentically is to live in such a way that a person's actions align with their convictions. Now, there are better and worse understandings of authenticity. In contemporary society, an obsession with "identity" has fostered a culture in which the highest good a person can attain for themselves is to "live their true self" or to "live their truth." On the one hand, there is an admirable aspect to this insofar as a person desires to be honest with themselves in a nonexploitative way. On the other hand, this concept has become solipsistic and self-serving, resulting in scenarios in which people abscond from responsibility, reason, and the moral law in service to the "cult of the imperial self."[23] A concept of authenticity that begins and ends with the human horizon will be not only profoundly robbed of the fullness of living in accord with God but also profoundly unsettling, as the script for fulfilled living disintegrates into a cacophony of competing voices. Living authentically, in its fullest sense, means allowing oneself to live in accordance with the dictates and demands of the conscience.

Living authentically requires the free exercise of God-given faculties for that purpose. The artist who creates masterpieces is not simply drawing or painting but creating an image that reflects the creativity and beauty they observe. A presumption toward liberty ensures that honest living, whether through moral expression, aesthetic expression, or religious expression, should be unhindered. The person who lives authentically is a person who is seeking to order their life around truth. The person who says, "I cannot go on living like this" is a person who has learned that a certain mode of existence is untenable with their sense of fulfillment. Again, I do not mean to be interpreted as relativistic. The person who grounds their existence in what is ultimate is a person who will seek to live honestly and authentically in conformity with it. To do anything less would be to live out of sync with their grasp of the universe and their place in it.

A fundamental question emerges: Will a person be able to engage in the activity that gives them authentic fulfillment? Perhaps someone thinks that the thrill seeking of mountain climbing makes them happiest. A person who finds delight and joy in mountain climbing will want as few obstacles as possible between them and a mountain. Or if an individual's religion teaches them that orphaned children are to be cared for, they will not want society to take action that impedes their ability to care for children. Liberty and religious liberty are constituent participants in this idea of authenticity because having the opportunity to act on what drives someone ensures that their deepest convictions are not restricted and that they are following their conscience.

Everyone has a code of ethics and morality, regardless of whether they consider themselves religious or not. Each person has deeply held convictions and moral codes that they prioritize and use to dictate all their actions, words, and decisions. This is true of the atheist as much as the overtly religious. Religious liberty thus protects all persons.

The skeptical reader might respond, "So are you saying that someone has the right to be wrong in what they value as authentic conviction?" Yes, and no. Religious liberty, ultimately, is not a license to do anything that seems right; it is ultimately about exercising a God-given conscience toward God-honoring ends. John Henry Newman wrote, "Conscience has rights because it has duties."[24] When the conscience apprehends a duty and responds to it, authentic living is the result. Authentic living is not coterminous with unbounded autonomy. Tollefsen provides helpful pushback to this notion that religious liberty, the conscience, and freedom of conscience result in radical relativism: "Conscience is a judgment of reason, and an upright will acts in accordance with reason. But reason is oriented towards the truth. So, while any attempt at self-constitution is successful just insofar as it constitutes a person in this or that way, the perfection of self-constitution is self-actualization in accordance with the truth about human well-being."[25] To act "in accordance with reason" means that a person acts in accordance with how their mind perceives truth. The mind's grasp may be wrong, but it grasps nonetheless. The presumption of liberty entails that we protect the pursuit of self-constitution as a penultimate vehicle in hopes that a person comes to know the ultimate. It certainly entails that there is a chance that people will abuse that liberty. We do not defend the end of their authenticity but the faculty that drives them to order their lives around the pursuit of the authentic.

The right to authentic living is not an absolute right at all costs. When governing bodies reach legitimate conclusions that someone's expression of authentic living is causing harm to themselves or to society, they have the right to intervene.

Authority: Who Has Ultimate Judgment?

To speak of authority is to speak of the source or object that commands ultimate obedience in life. It is the substance that gives shape to all other aspects of life. Whereas it may be possible to consider adoration and authenticity instrumental goods meant to direct a person toward their fulfillment, authority is the end to which a person directs their worship and experience of true living. Authority, then, is the backdrop against which a person configures the basic existence of their life. It is the plausibility structure and moral imagination that coordinate to give shape to one's social imaginary. To quote Charles Taylor, the social imaginary is "that common understanding which makes possible common practices, and a widely shared sense of legitimacy."[26] This type of authority mediated by the social imaginary is one where "people think about the world, how they imagine it to be, how they act intuitively in relation to it."[27] It is, at root, their authority.

Even nonreligious people believe that someone, something, or some ideology has ultimate say over life's meaning. An authority need not be divine to be the guiding force in life. In fact, the sources from which most people derive their sense of moral purpose in this world seem more and more nondivine.[28] The nihilist responds that the highest authority is the eventual dawning of nonexistence. The existentialist builds existence and authority on surrealism. The atheist responds that rationality is the highest authority. The hedonist pleads for pleasure's highest authority. The Darwinist says that nature's systems and processes are the highest authority. A North Korean citizen is supposed to believe that its country's leader is the highest authority. More trivial and ephemeral sources can just as easily work their way to the top of a person's affections. Consider social media. The preponderance of likes, retweets, and otherwise socially affirming actions can be the primary horizon through which a person mediates their existence. Authority forms a person's moral dictates and behavior. To that end, authority takes the driver's seat of life—it tells them where to go and how to get there. Authority, like adoration and authenticity, is a void that will be filled by something.

Not all claims of authority are equal. The fact that Western civilization is in the throes of a crisis of authority indicates that people have very different ideas about what is authoritative. But still, everyone has an authority. Determining the proper balancing of liberty with authority, a truly just authority will be one that allows its devotees to obtain the end for which they strive. And because society is imperfect, an era in which competing claims of authority challenge one another is normal and expected. As political philosopher Leo Strauss wrote, the political question of just order "par excellence" will be "how to reconcile order which is not oppression with freedom which is not license."[29]

A just government will understand that its authority is not absolute. Rather, a government is there to allow for the existence of nonstate authorities that compete to guide the lives of its citizens. But the question remains: Whose view of authority is truly ultimate? This is difficult to answer, because the authority to make ultimate decisions about right and wrong is debatable as people seek to discern for themselves what is true. Government will have to determine the degree of freedom it will give to evil even as it defaults to human liberty. A feature of liberal democracy is a commitment not to answer that question, ultimately, at the level of government but to allow citizens to work through reliable procedures to balance immorality with the common good.

To be clear, a culture that is unable to agree on even the basic standards of morality and that defaults to a protracted and procedural liberalism on all matters will be an impoverished culture. But a government without procedural ways to resolve tensions nonviolently will be authoritarian. This tension does not mean that questions of morality derived from competing authorities are off-limits. Indeed, the moral gravity and the moral obviousness of some given actions correlate with their universal recognition (all societies criminalize theft and murder). It means only that government does not make explicit metaphysical commitments to any one authority (outside its own authority, of course). Everyone believes that their source of authority is ultimate, and it may in fact drive their way of life, but that does not mean that others will be persuaded by a person's authority. As previously argued, government is simply to recognize the contestable nature of plurality and seek consensus and compromise among its citizens.

When government props up any one ideology or religion as the official position, freedom is squelched, happiness deteriorates, and societies live in deep, irresolvable conflict. This is why religious liberty is about a market of ideas that allows different authorities to freely compete for acceptance. Problematic as it may be to reduce something like religious liberty to the idea of market competition, it doubtlessly has elements of truth to it: people should be free to pursue the religion and authority that accord with their judgment and acceptance. We may not like this, but we must accept that an authority cannot become an authority for a person apart from that person's grasp of it. The state can impose its authority, even on the unwilling, at least at some level. The same is true of God: just because someone does not believe in God does not mean that they will not be under God's judgment. Still, an authority, at least of the type described here, needs to be recognized in order for authority to be ascribed to it. Authority by proxy is thus ineffective not only as a religious matter but also as a matter of how people live in a free society. Religious liberty allows the various authorities to test their credibility and legitimacy against one another.

The founders of America understood that God's authority is higher than government's and that government should not try to play God or obstruct humanity's response to God. James Madison states:

> It is the duty of every man to render to the Creator such homage and such only as he believes to be acceptable to him. This duty is precedent, both in order of time and in degree of obligation, to the claims of Civil Society. Before any man can be considered as a member of Civil Society, he must be considered as a subject of the Governour of the Universe: And if a member of Civil Society, who enters into any subordinate Association, must always do it with a reservation of his duty to the General Authority; much more must every man who becomes a member of any particular Civil Society, do it with a saving of his allegiance to the Universal Sovereign.[30]

If this seems old hat by now, that is because Americans have grown accustomed to this arrangement. When Madison wrote this, however, it was revolutionary. To conceive of government as limiting its authority by ceding primary authority to an individual's relationship to God, as a matter of philosophical principle, was a breakthrough in political philosophy. Madison was not an orthodox

Christian, yet his comments align with Matthew 22—namely, that ultimate authorities precede and trump penultimate authorities. Madison reminds us that the first claim on a person does not come from the state but from God and that person's understanding of who God is.

From a Christian perspective, ultimate authority resides in God. The state is not ultimate. No ideology is ultimate. Jesus Christ is ultimate. From a Christian perspective, any secondary authority (like the state) that tries to be the primary authority (God) is mistaken.

The explanation offered here does not settle all ongoing disputes about religious liberty. It helps expose why society, in fact, is so fraught with conflict. Why? Because everyone has their own version of orthodoxy that can easily conflict with or undermine another's. In a pluralistic society, striving after common denominators that allow everyone to experience as much freedom as possible is the desired end (a theme I will pick up in a later chapter).

The spirit of adoration, authenticity, and authority can be summarized using Deuteronomy 10:12–13: "And now, Israel, what does the LORD your God require of you, but to fear the LORD your God, to walk in all his ways, to love him, to serve the LORD your God with all your heart and with all your soul, and to keep the commandments and statutes of the LORD, which I am commanding you today for your good?" God has authority over creation, requiring something of it because of his ultimate power to command obedience; God requires adoration and desires this in authentic form issuing from an authentic self.

The image of God subsists in all persons despite the conclusions they reach about the existence of God and how and whether this God wants worship. The model advocated above signals that we cannot erase the image of God in its religious and ethical dimensions. All persons generate convictions. They live by them (authority), in service to them (authenticity), and to delight in them (adoration). Whatever the taxonomical debates about "religious freedom" versus "conscience freedom," everything can be tucked under the penumbra of religion. As H. Richard Niebuhr argues, to deny God is not to deny the gap that God ought to function in: "To deny the reality of a supernatural being called God is one thing; to live without confidence in some center of value and without loyalty to a cause is another."[31]

Humans desire to worship. Humans desire to bring their worship into every corner of their lives in whatever form that takes. And humans give to God or whatever functions as their god the highest place of authority. These basic truths form the backbone of why a Christian understanding of humans as persons who share a common constitution, a likeness made in God's own image, is integral to religious liberty.

The Image of God as the Foundation for a Human Right to Religious Liberty

The foundation and security of human rights remain two of the most elusive challenges to modern thinking. Despite secularism's quest to ground rights in something enduring and bedrock, its inconsistency in its application, in areas such as abortion, demonstrates the unsoundness of its secular foundations.

Religious liberty is among those issues typically assigned to "rights" protections.[32] To speak of religious liberty as a "right" is to speak of it as something more substantive than a social construct. Attaching "right" to it establishes it as a fundamental precept necessary for human flourishing.[33] While religious liberty's connection to rights will be established further on, here we note that it is important to establish a foundation for rights from a Christian perspective. Shorn of ultimately theistic foundations, an inviolable doctrine of human rights is at best tentative, arrived at by the consensus and conventions of political communities. A clear and principled account, then, will be difficult to obtain, since it collapses inevitably to speculation on the part of society and majorities. Echoing this, Carl F. H. Henry argues that "objectively grounded human rights are logically defensible on this foundation of the supernatural creation of man with universal dignity."[34] Human rights originate in humanity being made in God's image. Because humanity bears a unique relationship to God in ways distinct from other parts of creation, this special status confers protections and freedoms consistent with God's design for human nature. This is also where religious liberty's inviolability is anchored as an entailment of human rights.

The Image of God and Human Rights

No doctrine has better aided a foundation for human rights than the image of God.[35] When looking at the implications of the image of God for endeavors such as human rights, politics, and social ethics, ethicist T. B. Maston writes, "It is doubtful if there is any one concept more basic for democracy and Western civilization in general."[36] Humanity has profound dignity and worth because of its elevated creational status. Human rights are thus predicated on humanity possessing a certain ontological status. This status has been the subject of endless interpretation, but theologians and ethicists from across the spectrum agree that the fact that humanity is created in the image of God has profound implications for a doctrine of human rights. If humanity is a special creation of God, then we are compelled to protect and valorize the status of humanity both in society and in law.

If humans are a creation of God and not simply autonomous beings born of evolutionary processes, then the relationship of humans to their Creator and the rights or duties they bear are key to unlocking the fullest understanding of humanity's identity, nature, and purpose. Apart from a theistic foundation, there is little hope for framing human rights as inalienable and inviolable.[37] A failure to anchor rights to a metaphysical foundation will mean that "secular notions of jurisprudence collapse routinely into revered human convention."[38] This is the predicament of modernity: How does it uphold human rights while denying that humanity is objectively deserving of rights?

A divine foundation for human rights provides a better, fixed, and objective account and referent for protecting those rights than the shifting sands of opinion, custom, convention, political philosophy, or social science. As theologian R. Albert Mohler Jr. writes, "Human rights and human dignity are temporary abstractions if they are severed from their reality as gifts of the creator. The eclipse of Christian truth will lead inevitably to a tragic loss of human dignity. If we lose religious liberty, all other liberties will be lost, one by one."[39] Without a metaphysical foundation, discerning the purpose of rights is a vain pursuit. According to Kevin P. Lee, "Endless seeking of rights becomes banal without some understanding of what rights are for."[40] The purpose of rights is found in returning to the doctrine of the image of God at creation.

Humans have duties, and by fulfilling those duties, they flourish and find their destiny. A human right protects someone's ability— both positively and negatively—to perform what they ought. Rights are directed toward goods commensurate with reasoned reflection about human nature and human nature's fulfillment. Robert P. George states, "Human rights exist (or obtain) if it is the case that there are principles of practical reason directing us to act or abstain from acting in certain ways out of respect for the well-being and the dignity of persons whose legitimate interests may be affected by what we do."[41] In chapter 3, I defined a "right" as the protection of a moral faculty. The moral faculty, as such, is essential to a person grasping and actualizing their duty to act in accordance with the truth. In this scheme, government protects speech, religion, and association in order to allow people to live, assemble, and worship according to the duties of conscience and reason. Rights are ordered toward authentic, truthful lives. The risk to society that comes with granting such rights—that they might be abused—is more worthwhile than squelching human freedom. In other words, we grant a capacious understanding of liberty grounded in rights-based language since the opposite situation is worse than the risk of abusing one's rights.

From the vantage point of Genesis, humans have a duty—or right—to obey God, and this obedience involves exercising dominion over creation. Thus, any reason we speak of rights thrusts rights back on their corresponding responsibility. We protect what we believe a human is designed to fulfill. A right is not merely a negative protection from government interference; it is a positive right to a particular good that helps us achieve our purpose consistent with our design. From this viewpoint, then, a right is an obligation owed to humanity in order for humanity to perform a duty essential to its purpose.

In the end, if human rights do not originate from divine sanction, they become subject to popular majorities. John D. Inazu argues that "rights" language is an "important part of the check against majoritarian power and the ability of individuals to establish meaning apart from government orthodoxy."[42] The present conditions of liberal democracy, however, evidence a tenuous "rights" regime, since the substance of rights and their origin are being continually severed from their original grounding within a Christian worldview. History speaks of the collateral damage done when human rights, dignity, and worth are held without divine warrant.[43] Those violating human rights are not only doing damage to human dignity but also transgressing the laws of God. Human rights are best served by a theistic formulation because with it comes divine warrant, foundation, and accountability.

Is Religious Liberty a Human "Right"?

Carl F. H. Henry has argued that religious liberty is "not only a fundamental human right, but it shelters also the whole broad spectrum of human rights."[44] He argues that freedom is grounded, ultimately, in God.[45] A 2004 document by the National Association of Evangelicals echoes this: "Because God created human beings in his image, we are endowed with rights and responsibilities. In order to carry out these responsibilities, human beings need the freedom to form associations, formulate and express beliefs, and act on conscientiously held commitments."[46]

The NAE document establishes the rights of the conscience by grounding such rights in the image of God. The statement also declares, however, that the image of God carries responsibility and freedom to exercise the conscience. But how ought religious liberty be understood as a human right that follows from humanity being made in God's image? It is important to consider that it was the Christian religion that first posited any notion of religious freedom. In the words of the early church father Tertullian, "It is a human right (*humani iuris*) and inborn capacity (*naturlis potestatis*) that one should worship whatever he intends; the religious practice of one neither harms nor helps another. It is no part of religion to coerce religious practice, for it is by free choice and not coercion that we should be led to religion."[47]

In his *Apology*, Tertullian first recorded the phrase "religious freedom" (*libertatem religionis*).[48] That Tertullian framed his remarks on religious liberty in the context of "rights" (*ius*) language is not insignificant.[49] Timothy Samuel Shah observes that Tertullian's framing is important because it presents religious freedom not as a "tactical plea for forbearance" but rather as a "principled doctrine" of *libertatem religionis*, which implies protection and application to all religions.[50] Such a statement indicates that religious liberty is not merely a social construct but an issue of theological warrant necessary for authentic belief. From the earliest origins of Christianity, this new, marginalized sect of Jewish and Greek Christians posited a universalized understanding of religious freedom as an inherent grant of God to humanity. Church historian Robert Louis Wilken argues that Tertullian's language signifies the power of individual choice to arrive at an understanding of religious truth and obligation: "This 'right' precedes and is independent of any action by the ruling authorities; it is not a benefaction of the state."[51]

Critically, however, Tertullian and, later, Lactantius argued for religious liberty on the grounds of humanity's status as image bearers. The "natural capacity" that Tertullian describes derives from the "dignity and worth" of every human being. Tertullian cites Genesis 1:26–27 as evidence that humanity possesses reason and is "animated with divine life."[52] "Man was created by God as free," argues Tertullian, "with power to choose and power to act. . . . There is no clearer indication in him of God's image and similitude than this."[53]

An important caveat is necessary. We must establish "rights" in a way that does not damage the biblical text by overlaying it with classically liberal or Enlightenment ideas. "Rights" in biblical language come in the form of duty. A person's duty toward their Creator, themselves, and others is grounded in divinely mandated obligation. According to Charles, "Rights and duties are reciprocal in nature. If I have a fundamental right to something, others have the duty to guard and protect that right."[54] If an obligation is placed on humanity, and if the obligation is to seek God with all one's heart, soul, strength, and mind, then the ability to execute one's duty becomes sacred, which is synonymous with a right. Henry observes that "the Bible does not teach that human beings simply on the basis of existence have inherent or *a priori* rights." Instead, "the Bible has a doctrine of divinely imposed duties; what moderns call human rights are the contingent flipside of those duties."[55] Our duty to God posits a right to worship God as God demands to be worshiped. Protecting one's worship is the location of that "right."

In contemporary settings, David VanDrunen provides, once again, a helpful foundation for understanding how religious liberty is a human right. According to VanDrunen, human beings have no ultimate religious freedom before God, but they do before each other and the institutions of society.[56] This means, practically, that a right to religious freedom issues from the reality of humans bearing the image of God, but bearing that image in a fallen capacity. God does not hold his image bearers guiltless for exercising their reason imperfectly, but the gifts of their creative endowment (reason, freedom, moral agency, etc.) prevent institutions from excluding, repressing, or mediating religious belief on behalf of another image bearer or coercing an image bearer into belief. Because there is no temporal penalty for erring or false religious belief as there is for acts of injustice that humans commit against each other, a "right" to religious liberty is someone's negative right to have their pathway of religious belief unhindered. In the words of VanDrunen, "As part of the natural order sustained in the covenant with Noah, God has granted to each human being in the present age the common blessings of participating in the life of human society, without religious qualification, and thus each person may claim, against any fellow human beings who would seek to add such a qualification, the unhindered right to this participation."[57]

Earlier I argued that the Noahic covenant establishes a creational "right" to religious liberty, since false worship is not listed as a basis for any type of retributive justice in a postdiluvian world. The Noahic covenant is primarily preservative since it aims to address intrahuman wrongs. Wrong worship was not given to humanity to redress. Though it is not explicit in the text, there is a deducible "right" to religious liberty insofar as prohibiting idolatry is not given to human jurisdiction. Humanity thus has a right to search for God and to live out the duties imposed on them by their grasp of God and God's commands. In a postdiluvian world, humanity's search for God is assumed to be an uninterrupted pursuit. "Rights" as duty, in this instance, means for an image bearer that they have a right to have the pathway of religious pursuit open and unhindered.

This right, VanDrunen believes, is "penultimate" and "granted by God."[58] So a "right" to religious liberty is grounded in the fact that humanity bears God's image, is inherently religious because of this image, and cannot be restricted from acting on religious belief by human institutions, despite whatever inaccuracies subsist in the conclusions that are reached. Jeremy Waldron also observes that an emphasis on human rights implies a right to religious freedom: "Our lives need to be ruled in respect of God and worship; our natural impulse to neglect God our Creator in favor of mundane concerns needs to be mastered and suppressed. But *imago Dei* implies that we are actually the sort of beings that can master themselves in this way. We can be trusted in these matters. We are capable of the appropriate kind of self-regarding dominion in respect of these momentous matters. We do not need rule imposed from the outside."[59]

The right to religious freedom centers on the fact that humans' responsibilities to God are bedrock, which means that humans must be free to act on and fulfill these responsibilities. Religious liberty is thus a "moral absolute," an ethically consequential term.[60] Or, as Carrillo de Albornoz asserts, "religious freedom, although a human right, is nevertheless on a higher plane than other human rights, as it is based directly upon the absolute relation of man to God."[61] A right to religious liberty is the "first freedom" in that it is the foundation on which all other rights rest. A proper relationship with God is the foundation on which the rest of a person's life is ordered. The idea of humanity's individual responsibility before God promulgates immense dignity, intelligibility, and significance to the development of human rights doctrine.[62]

The image of God renders all persons equal before one another and before God. Because all humans are equal partakers in creation, each has the same right to religious liberty. There is no qualification to that statement: religious liberty implies total equality or else religious liberty as a principled doctrine falls apart. According to Duke, "All people bear the same image of the divine, to the same degree; therefore, all have equal status before God."[63] Indeed, the image of God has an "equalizing tendency"; no individual has more image-bearing rights than any other.[64] The Christian concept of dignity, built on the idea of personhood, demands liberty and equality.[65]

The image of God makes for an attractive foundation for religious liberty, because it secures religious liberty as an inviolable right. To wit, if religious liberty is a right conferred on humanity by virtue of its creational status, then religious liberty is an inalienable right. The image of God gives "theological substance" to a principle that modern rights are aimlessly questing after without theistic or confessional elements.[66] Inviolability denotes a sacredness that demands recognition.[67] The notion of "rights" denotes an "objective moral authority to which individuals could appeal."[68]

Wood argues that "religious liberty is biblically rooted in man's nature and in his inalienable right to respond freely to God's revelation."[69] If religious liberty is indeed inviolable, then religious liberty is something innate to personal integrity. Government does not grant those rights but protects them, ensuring that society treats its rights bearers equally. Religious liberty is "rooted in the inviolable sacredness of the human conscience. Man has juridical rights because he has certain inalienable moral rights as a person."[70] Religious liberty is said to be a "right of the individual" and not a "gift" of the state, because for the Christian, "the divinely ordered nature of man, as revealed in the Scriptures, constitutes the basis for all human rights and civil liberties."[71]

If Religion Is a Choice, Why Is It a "Right"?

There is a critique against religious liberty that goes like this: Religion is a matter of personal choice, so why protect religious freedom as a constitutional right? This is a criticism usually made by secularists who want to weaken the value of religion and its historical protections.

We should note one important assumption in this criticism— that religion is just a mere choice or preference that one can take or leave. Unless we address how religion functions in a person's life, much misunderstanding will follow regarding why it is worth protecting.

So is religion merely a matter of personal preference or choice? The answer is no. Thomas Jefferson wrote in the preamble of the Virginia Statute of Religious Freedom, "The opinions and belief of men depend not on their own will, but follow involuntarily the evidence proposed to their own minds."[72] Here Jefferson argues that convictions—religious or not—do not arise haphazardly. The love that a father has for his child is not the same type of conviction that the same father has for his favorite soft drink. People arrive at their deepest convictions by these convictions being impressed upon them by their conscience. A person does not casually choose to live their life following path A; rather, following path B becomes simply impossible. Path B could not be lived without great fragmentation and the violation of personal integrity. If path A is the path of liberty and authenticity, path B is the path of coercion and dishonesty.

Religion, according to Matthew J. Franck, "is not so much chosen as it is accepted, as a truth one has discovered or has learned."[73] Religion is not a "choice" as though one prefers Coke to Pepsi.

Religion and the constitutional protections historically afforded it are entailments that follow from someone apprehending the deepest truths and convictions about ultimate reality so completely that they cannot help but live faithfully. People do not sacrifice their lives for preferences. They do, however, for their convictions—religious or otherwise (think of the bravery of a soldier as well as that of a religious martyr).

The genius of the American experiment is that our founders understood that government should voluntarily restrict itself from adjudicating whether a person's convictions, arrived at by deliberation, are right or wrong (unless, of course, harm to civil society ensues). This is why the protections afforded to speech and religion are in the First Amendment. The founders understood that a free society requires allowing citizens to live in accordance with the truths impressed upon their conscience—not their mere "choices."

Religious Liberty and Caesar's Coin

Matthew 22:15–22 is often cited to support a doctrine of religious liberty. It is a locus classicus for denying the all-consuming authority of the state. The disputation between Jesus and the Pharisees is commonly marshaled to defend the authority the state has over certain affairs, which it does insofar as the issue of taxation is concerned. But the disputation is a revealing episode of theological score settling, one relevant to the image of God and religious liberty.

It is a contest of conflicting loyalties. Will Jesus affirm the use of a coin for taxation that bears Caesar's image even though Caesar claims divine status for himself? If he affirms the use of the coin, then Jesus will be seen as betraying God, but if he denies the use, then he will be seen as a subversive revolutionary. Jesus, however, affirms that Jews can pay taxes while "honoring the superiority of God's sovereignty."[74] Rebecca C. Mathis argues that this episode does not provide enough for a full theory of church-state separation but rather reveals a "tension" in which God's people find themselves. They live in an earthly kingdom and God's kingdom. As Mathis observes, "Jesus neither defines the church and state as one and the same nor portrays them as isolated institutions having no effect on one another."[75] Rather, Jesus makes a deeper inquiry: What belongs to Caesar and what belongs to God? Sometimes the answers are not in tension; other times they are. However, Jesus urges his followers to measure the limited claims of the state against the total claims of God. Jesus's emphasis on the coin's imprint is important: "The denarius, bearing the likeness of Caesar, belongs to Caesar; therefore humanity, bearing the likeness of God, belongs to God."[76] Genesis 1 sheds light on the fullness of this passage. Humans owe their ultimate allegiance to God. Jesus grounds this allegiance in their being made in the image and likeness of God. If each person bears the image of God, then their entire self—their rationality, their freedom, their moral agency—is responsible to God.

Conclusion

The argument of this chapter and the preceding one has been that biblical anthropology—the idea that humans have special significance because they have been made in the image of God—furnishes an anthropological framework for religious liberty. And secondarily, religious liberty is unsecured apart from humans' special status as image bearers. Religious liberty is grounded in the reality that humans are neither phantoms nor impersonal cogs but reasoning persons with intellects, wills, emotions, and desires. Religious liberty is not simply a question about how to order political communities. It is a reality that precedes the immediate authority of government and that sorts out how an individual's grasp and execution of their freedom, reason, and moral duty coordinate to promote human flourishing and divine accountability.

More fundamentally, religious liberty is about understanding the essential nature of the individual as a creative being made in the image of God. Religious freedom means responding freely to the God who made humanity in his image and who is redeeming humanity through Jesus Christ, the image of God. All humans are made by their Creator to worship him. All humans are made to find their satisfaction in him. All humans are made to know God. Everyone, however, must reach this destiny of their own accord with the freedom they possess as an image bearer. Persons made in the image of God will reach wrong conclusions, even damnable conclusions. But those conclusions are sincere conclusions based on their understanding of duty, the conscience, and divine revelation. All persons are owed the respect and dignity to reach the proper conclusion for themselves.

PART 3

MISSIOLOGY

6

Religious Liberty as Christian Mission

HELPING IGNITE A CONTEMPORARY mission emphasis in Reformed evangelical circles, pastor John Piper wrote in a now famous declaration, "Missions is not the ultimate goal of the church. Worship is. Missions exists because worship does not. Worship is ultimate, not missions, because God is ultimate, not man."[1] Lest there be confusion over the importance ascribed to religious liberty in this chapter, the following bears remembering: Religious liberty is not an ultimate goal or eternal ethic. Worship of the Lord Jesus Christ is. As I have argued, there is no *ultimate* right to religious liberty. It is an interim social ethic originating from God's common grace. It is a *penultimate* right granted to individuals so they can be free to seek after God. To say that religious liberty does not, in itself, have eternal merit is neither to denigrate it theologically nor to undermine its importance to Christian social ethics in a secular age. Rather, to situate religious liberty correctly is to see it as a temporal good meant to advance God's glory and God's kingdom.

Religious liberty is vital because worship is more vital. We give room to false worship in hopes that it becomes true worship. True worship requires voluntary faith. Worship is ultimate, not religious liberty, because God is ultimate, not humanity. Religious liberty has a missional significance for the church's witness because religious liberty helps "bring about the obedience of faith for the sake of his name among all the nations" (Rom. 1:5).

The purpose of any doctrine of religious liberty, from the vantage point of Christian social ethics, is to advance God's kingdom. Religious liberty exists, is intelligible, and is ultimately purposeful on the basis that it functions as a distinctly Christian social ethic designed to facilitate uncoerced and unobstructed access to humankind's greatest need—salvation in Jesus Christ. Religious liberty promotes the economy of salvation, and where religious liberty is threatened, one's salvation is not so much in view as is the legal and political conditions that shape the response to the call of obedience. As this chapter will argue, the internal logic of the gospel recognizes and even demands religious liberty, since only authentic faith freely grasped and freely acted on can be genuine faith.

Thus, religious liberty is integral to the advancement of the gospel; it is a missiological ethic used for the sake of the church's mission in society. It exists within a penultimate secular age to allow fallen consciences to respond, genuinely, to the truth that "there is no other name under heaven given among men by which we must be saved" (Acts 4:12). Christianity does not countenance religious liberty for its own end but so that a person, as an image bearer of God whose chief purpose is conformity to Christ (Rom. 8:29), can exercise their faculties toward their properly ordered end. The purpose of this chapter is to argue that the mission of God and religious liberty intersect in this age because religious liberty is an interim ethic meant to advance God's kingdom on earth.

The Mission of God in Biblical Theology

Biblical theology portrays God's mission as dynamic, reconciliatory, and participatory: God has a mission to sum up all things in Christ, and Christians are commanded to take part in God's mission.[2] The centerpiece of Christian mission is the biblical witness of God actively intervening through human history to accomplish his divine plan.[3] As Christopher J. H. Wright observes, mission is "a major key that unlocks the whole grand narrative of the canon of Scripture."[4] Moreover, unlocking the Bible's understanding of mission is critical to determining the relationship between the church and the world, which is pivotal in determining the church's mission. According to David J. Bosch, the biblical record reveals how "Christian mission gives expression to the dynamic relationship between God and the world, particularly as this was portrayed, first, in the story of the covenant people of Israel and then, supremely, in the birth, life, death, resurrection, and exaltation of Jesus."[5]

At the same time, everything cannot be collapsed into mission. As Christopher Wright and John Stott argue, rightly, "mission" cannot be a stand-in to "cover everything God is doing in the world."[6] God's providence and common grace, for example, are evidence that God is maintaining the world, yet common grace and providence are not coterminous with mission. Mission, rather, concerns God's redeeming actions and the vehicles through which he accomplishes them. In the brief sections below, I offer a framework for understanding the mission of God that explores the various planes through which mission ought to be conceived. I offer these categories in hopes that religious liberty is seen not as an addendum to mission but as an underlying component in how mission radiates outward in our personal lives and in our participation in culture. At no juncture in our understanding of mission is religious liberty's logic not implicated for consideration and priority. Where proclamation, piety, evangelism, congregational life, and moral witness converge is at the point of each requiring the necessary freedoms to engage in each. Unhindered proclamation, free response, and cultural influence in society all assume the presence of religious liberty, in whatever embryonic form it appears.

Christic

The mission of God is of inestimable importance in determining the full scope of God's plan for the cosmos.[7] At the center of that mission is the unfolding of the Christic drama—a "mystery"—to "unite all things in him, things in heaven and things on earth" (Eph. 1:9–10). God's mission is his plan to sum up all things in Jesus Christ and for Christ to rule over the cosmos as the appointed "heir of all things" (Heb. 1:2).[8] Jesus Christ is the Alpha and the Omega (Rev. 22:13); he is the telos of history. Even humanity's redemption is patterned after God's "firstborn," so that participating in God's mission includes more clearly reflecting the image of Jesus Christ (Rom. 8:29). The drama of Scripture, from creation and proceeding through all subsequent covenants, is guided by God's intention to magnify the Lord Jesus through his ascension to the throne as "King of kings and Lord of lords" (Rev. 19:16).

In this way, the Christic element of mission is cosmic; it encompasses all of the created order. Mission is understood as God's redeeming of all that he has created through an act of Christic rescue and restoration. God's mission in Christ is thus as wide as the cosmos he created, which he promises to redeem in perfection at the appointed time.

Ecclesial

God's mission established a church, and the church is the exclusive vehicle appointed to announce the good news of the gospel. The Second Vatican Council is right to state that "the church on earth is by its very nature missionary."[9] Though debates persist about the exact calling of the universal church in this era, most Christians agree that Jesus Christ's life, death, and resurrection are essential components of the gospel message.[10]

The church is God's outpost on the earth bearing institutional witness to God's mission in the world. The church is confident about its mission because Jesus promises that "the gates of hell shall not prevail against it" (Matt. 16:18). The church of Jesus Christ marches onward toward a heavenly city, where "the world will one day be the kingdom of God."[11] As Michael W. Goheen and Craig G. Bartholomew write, "The good news that Jesus announces and enacts and that the church is commissioned to embody and make known, is the gospel of the kingdom."[12]

Personal

The Son sent by God sends out individual heralds of the kingdom (John 17:18; 20:21). Jesus Christ commands his followers to "make disciples of all the nations" (Matt. 28:19). He gives this missionary command according to his own authority (28:18). Christians are called to display personal commitment to advancing God's kingdom in their lives by sharing their faith so that others may enter God's kingdom (Col. 1:13). God's mission is participatory in that God uses the means of the gathered and scattered church to fulfill his mission.[13] Christians are therefore evangelistic in their missionary efforts and utterances.

Cultural-Political

The gospel is announced as a kingdom, a term with overt political connotations. Jesus points to the reigning political paradigm to explain the significance of his own kingdom. Though not using the term "kingdom" in a directly political manner, the gospel has cultural and political ramifications as it takes root in regenerated persons united within a common culture.

On the one hand, Christians should expect the gospel to have cultural-political repercussions, as the requirements for Christian conceptions of humaneness and justice proclaim judgment on the world. As Carl F. H. Henry asserts, the church must "declare the criteria by which nations will ultimately be judged, and the divine standards to which man and society must conform if civilization is to endure."[14] While political dominance is not the object of Christian mission, it is a consequence of the gospel's success in forming the consciences of those within a political community. That the Christian gospel is "good news" means that Christianity must reckon with the fact that the good news it heralds has massive significance for how Christians order their lives and for summoning the rest of society to follow and obey God's law.

On the other hand, announcing that the gospel has political implications is categorically different from positing that the gospel's aim is political. The mission of God can rightly subvert an empire with God's own empire—but this is done through the transformation of consciences, not through a top-down initiative to make Christianity a political program. The kingdom of God threatens worldly powers who would be tempted to view themselves as sovereign and unaccountable. Regardless of how one chooses to regard the cultural and political implications of Christian mission, Christian mission is always situated within a historical-cultural milieu, where attitudes toward religious liberty may vary and which will invariably shape the nature of the church's mission in that context. The purpose of that mission is timeless because the "gospel is an announcement about where God is moving the history of the whole world."[15] That movement of history is accomplished through a mission that began in a garden and will be fulfilled in a city (Gen. 2:8; Rev. 21:2).[16]

If any point has been strenuously argued in this book, it is that Jesus Christ—as both king and the true image of God—centers reflection on the substance and purpose of religious liberty. This is no less true in the context of Christian mission and what God is accomplishing through mission—namely, the enlargement of Jesus's kingdom. All of the above dimensions that define the scope of Christian mission are aided by the possibility of unhindered proclamation and the free response of humans as the means for the mission of God to advance in society. Religious liberty is therefore a central fixture in supplementing how that mission is accomplished.

The Mission of God and Religious Liberty: Understanding the Soteriological Nexus

Before leaving on his missionary journey to India, William Carey, one of the architects of the modern mission movement, told his friend Andrew Fuller, "I will go down, if you will hold the ropes."[17] Fuller, of course, helped raise the funds to build the institutions that made mission possible. Holding the ropes is an apt metaphor for the relationship between religious liberty and mission: religious liberty facilitates mission by giving space and fostering the ideal conditions for the mission of Christ to continue. The mission of God does not wholly depend on Western ideals of religious liberty inasmuch as it is aided where religious liberty exists. Asked in the reverse, What Christian would want to create obstacles for the announcement of the gospel? No one, of course.

To "hold the ropes," so to speak, is to facilitate mission. This runs contrary to much of modern Christian discourse that seems to lust after martyrdom status, insisting that any demands for "rights" such as religious liberty run contrary to the witness of Christ, who forsook his rights and died on a cross. When Christians feign sanctimony about discarding "rights," they reveal a facile understanding of the common good and its connection to an ethic of reciprocity for all citizens, Christian and non-Christian alike. Since religious liberty is ordered to the common good, it is never about special pleas for one group but about identifying one's liberty as bound up in the broader political community's exercise of those same equally distributed rights. Those who criticize defenders of religious liberty for making it a culture-war issue and possessing martyr envy will likely someday learn that were ancient Christians to choose between Rome and America, they would have chosen the First Amendment.

While martyrs witness powerfully to the paradoxical nature of the kingdom's advancement through weakness, this witness does not elide Christians' responsibility to make their context ripe for gospel acceptance. It is one thing to accept an increasingly marginalized status within a society; it is another to seek it out, believing that social isolation and ostracization are required for faithfulness. Oliver O'Donovan has criticized Stanley Hauerwas and John Howard Yoder for idealizing "catacomb consciousness," the idea that only a church on the margins can retain purity and distinctiveness.[18] For O'Donovan, there is no inherent virtue in the church being driven to the margins. Yes, the church can do excellent work when removed from the center of power, but to romanticize marginalization is to invite a degree of persecution that most Christians in history would have wanted to avoid. To say that Scripture promises persecution is neither to invite it nor to bask in it but to accept it as a part of faithfulness. We should caution against valorizing marginalization as an exclusive measure of faith. Historically, persecution can root out religion, but the mustard seed metaphor in Scripture also suggests that growth can be faithful (Matt. 13:31–32).

Living the "peaceful," "quiet," and "dignified" lives that religious liberty makes possible is not in tension with God's desire that "all people . . . be saved and . . . come to the knowledge of the truth" (1 Tim. 2:2, 4). In fact, they seem to be complementary. We pray for political tranquility for the sake of gospel advance. To be sure, Christ promises to build his church (Matt. 16:18–19), so we can be confident that no barrier will stand in its path, but wanting to remove barriers is not contrary to this New Testament teaching.

There is no virtue in embracing a martyr complex that impedes the gospel's advance and jeopardizes the work of ministry by inviting hardship. Consider Paul. A Roman citizen, Paul did not shy away from asserting his rights as a citizen (Acts 22). Instead of seeking out a martyr's death so that the purity of the gospel could be realized, Paul appealed to his political context and the legitimacy of political rule to ensure the gospel's spread. He did so in particular by appealing to his Roman citizenship and to the political rulers of his day. For Paul, appeals to earthly citizenship were not in opposition to his heavenly citizenship. The former is subordinate to the latter. Paul's life testifies to the legitimacy of political rule, and also to the need to constructively relate to political authority in such a way that it is not in opposition to the advance of the gospel.

It would seem that a state limited in its scope makes the enlargement of God's kingdom more possible. A government that refuses to totalize its jurisdiction and works within its limited confines is acting justly. By refusing to amass or aggrandize power that does not belong to it, it more ably allows for the mission of Christ to succeed. Thus, a limited state is not merely within the province of a much-hackneyed political conservatism but is a faithful steward of the authority that derives from God (Rom. 13:1–7). Governments that allow religious freedom to prosper, whether consciously or not, are at least indirect participants in the unfolding drama of redemption. One hopes that a government, even a pagan one, "would maintain conditions appropriate for believers leading a specifically godly life in government supported civic-peace."[19] We should hope all government provides the conditions where a fruitful Christian life can be lived without political consequence or threat. In not allying itself with any one religion in particular, and by not impeding the mission of the church, the state is ordered in accord with the service it is to render to God as his "servant" (Rom. 13:4). A government that puts as few obstacles as possible in the way of its citizens being able to freely respond to the call of salvation is doing what God intended the state to do. Advocacy for religious liberty, especially via lobbying and petitioning government, must be seen as a rope-holding activity that ensures that ministry can occur within a given political community.

To use another metaphor, religious liberty is like brush clearing. Untamed terrain needs to be cleared in order for it to be properly cultivated and brought to order. Religious liberty clears a path so that the work of ministry can go forth. In this sense, religious liberty is a context-specific tool that catalyzes mission. To clear brush for a missionary to function as they ought is to cooperate in the mission of God. All of this activity is directed toward living God-honoring lives in every domain of life and advancing the message of salvation.

Where the nexus of religious liberty meets mission and soteriology is the concern for impending judgment. According to Stott and Wright, "The God who is Lord of history is also the Judge of history."[20] From this sentence arises an urgency, since the current era in which the church finds itself is not eternal. A coming judgment over this era awaits. The reality of this future judgment serves as the backdrop for why religious liberty connects with mission. According to Baptist theologian Jason G. Duesing, "As those living in an era of religious liberty between the time of Christ's ascension and his certain return, the knowledge of what awaits us on the last day should serve as a warning to all outside of Christ that the freedom to worship other gods without the judgment of the one true God will come to an end."[21]

Even more foundationally, a focus on the theological underpinnings of religious liberty and the mission of God fosters a greater awareness of the church's own rationale for advancing religious liberty in society: humanity's destined judgment. As I have sought to make clear throughout this book, it is eschatological judgment and our reason-using and truth-seeking nature that make religious liberty intelligible from a Christian perspective. The promise of judgment and the accountability of the person before God make sense only within a horizon of mission and the attainment of salvation. Christians insist on the necessity of religious liberty so that persons untainted by coercion can make voluntary professions of faith. It is correct to infer that religious liberty is not an end in itself. Instead, it is a means and a tool that the church utilizes to accomplish its mission with efficiency and effectiveness for the sake of the gospel.

This is why religious liberty is an urgent task of Christian ethics. As a social ethic, it informs a critical nexus that conceives of religious liberty as both useful and necessary for mission. An ethic of religious liberty is intrinsic to mission. Religious liberty is therefore foundational to the church's public theology since it serves as a firmament to the gospel's advance. It is, as it were, a grand corallary to Christian ministry in the present era. Christianity prioritizes religious liberty as an evangelistic tool. Where Christianity has any influence in society, a milieu of religious liberty ought to follow from Christian teaching when Christians apply their doctrine to society and seek to influence it.

Those heralding the gospel will exercise every tool at their disposal to see the mission of God advance. Moreover, the "historical situation" that Henry references is consequential to understanding that Christian mission is always historically situated, and "situatedness" is not a missionally insignificant category. Christians should desire to inhabit contexts that make gospel proclamation and evangelistic efforts more fluid and reject circumstances that create obstacles to gospel advancement. We should wish this not only for ourselves but also for Christians around the globe.

If Christians care about mission, they should seek to elevate religious liberty in their public theology. Christians should do this not because Christian mission is *necessarily* contingent on religious liberty but because religious liberty aids Christian mission in its ultimate task of seeing individuals reconciled and redeemed.

Understood through an evangelistic lens, religious liberty is appreciated by those who seek to advance the gospel for its utility but not its ultimate necessity.

Religious liberty is not simply a political doctrine that Western Christians enjoy while living in liberal democracies. It is not merely a construct designed to aid religious difference. Religious liberty is a principle that Christians from all corners of the world should prioritize, because it impacts gospel advancement and social tranquility; it forges a connection between the urgent task of mission and the opportunity to take that mission outward.

Most foundationally, however, religious liberty understood from the interior of biblical logic is a principle integral and internal to the gospel itself and essential for the church's mission in society. According to Barrett Duke, "The doctrine of salvation itself contributes to our understanding of God's design for religious liberty."[22] The soteriological moment is an individual event, and faith cannot be coerced. The gospel hinges on a free response. This is not to say that salvation is individualistic. We are saved *into* a community. But entry into that community comes from individual assent. Thus, an authentic faith assumes an uncoerced faith.[23] A Christian account of religious liberty as mission thus assumes a doctrine of justification by faith alone, insisting that individuals enter God's kingdom individually and conscientiously self-aware of an expressed faith. No one can attain someone else's salvation for them, and neither can someone's salvation be negated by another.

Christian advocacy for religious liberty in society is not pursued primarily to shore up or preserve the reigning political order. It is not pursued under the auspices of "rights," as important as rights are. Religious liberty must be imbued with theological gravitas. As Michael Hanby argues, concern for only the juridical or political benefits of religious liberty as a social practice neglects the "deeper freedom opened up by the transcendent horizon of

Christ's resurrection."[24] From this vantage point, religious liberty goes beyond the horizons of law and culture to the awakening of our world to the reality of the ascendant Christ. Hanby says that an outsized focus on the political import of religious liberty leads us to neglect its purpose in light of mission.

> If we cannot see beyond the juridical meaning of religious freedom to the freedom that the truth itself gives, how then can we expect to exercise this more fundamental freedom when our juridical freedom is denied? Too often we are content to accept the absolutism of liberal order, which consists in its capacity to establish *itself* as the ultimate horizon, to remake everything within that horizon in its own image, and to establish itself as the highest good and the condition of possibility for the pursuit of all other goods—including religious freedom.[25]

In other words, the church does not take its marching orders from protections afforded it only by the procedural rules of liberal democracy. The locus of Christian advocacy for religious liberty is the advancement of Christian mission, followed only then by its constitutional legitimacy. The practice of religious liberty is the expression of the church's mission under the sovereignty of God. In that, the church possesses a freedom of its own constitution. The church, by definition, ought to be a free society living in response to the call of God.

This focus on mission is not meant to undercut or devalue the political and social benefits that accrue when religious liberty graces society (the next chapter argues that Christian advocacy for religious liberty should result in practical social benefits). But implications that follow from Christianity's primary justification for religious liberty should not blur nor erase the urgency with which Christians advocate for its centrality in Christian social ethics and public theology—the advancement of God's kingdom resulting in the salvation of sinners.

Religious liberty exists because it issues from a place of sincere urgency, emanating from sober conviction about the judgment awaiting humanity. Any practice of religion that fails to uphold liberty as a critical element of its doctrinal system only pretends to be authentic. Halfhearted religion works as a "kind of inoculation or prevention against sincere religion."[26] Only religions so adamant about the judgment of God will seek the freedoms to advance that message for the sake of humankind.[27] Heartfelt convictions will always seek the liberty to be proclaimed.

Religious Liberty and Mission as Eschatological Judgment

Christians advocate for religious liberty because such a social ethic aids gospel proclamation. As argued previously, because Jesus Christ is the ultimate Lord over the conscience, a Christian understanding of religious liberty begins with affirming that Christ alone possesses the ability to execute judgment over the conscience (Acts 17:30–31). Because Christ has the exclusive right and authority to ultimately judge erring consciences, the institutions and ordinances of creation (family, state) do not. Religious liberty exists because of the forbearance of God. Whatever other themes constitute religious liberty, all of these find their intelligibility in reference to the lordship of Jesus Christ as the appointed judge over humanity (John 5:22; Heb. 9:27).

This reality that Jesus Christ is king over the conscience and possesses sole authority to execute judgment over the conscience is ground zero for a Christian understanding of religious liberty. Though debate exists about his orthodoxy, John Locke was correct to note that "only the Supreme Judge of all men" possesses the wisdom for "the chastisement of the erroneous" on religious matters.[28] This reality is also the firmament for religious liberty's social relevance. Christians should desire a society in which human institutions do not act as judges over the conscience. As I have argued previously, the domain of the conscience is outside the sphere of the state or other human institutions. That is not to say, however, that the actions that follow from the conscience are beyond scrutiny or limitation (hence the persistent need to determine where a government's compelling interest is when needing to restrict someone's liberty).

According to Acts 17:30–31, "The times of ignorance God overlooked, but now he commands all people everywhere to repent, because he has fixed a day on which he will judge the world in righteousness by a man whom he has appointed; and of this he has given assurance to all by raising him from the dead." These verses have functioned as a sort of lodestar to this book's thesis, since Paul's declaration in this setting encompasses so many of the underlying themes of this book. According to Paul, God is going to judge the world through Jesus. Paul's declaration comes at the Areopagus, "Mars Hill," a public venue that featured wide-ranging philosophical debates (Acts 17:21).

Future eschatological judgment punctuates the rationale for Paul's proclamation (Acts 17:30–31; Rom. 2:12–16; 2 Cor. 5:10). At the Areopagus in particular, the nature of that proclamation has a current or ecology underneath it that makes public proclamation urgently necessary. The nature and opportunity of Paul's address being public assume some type of latitude or open posture toward a person's ability to publicly proclaim the gospel. Religious liberty, then, is more than simply a vehicle of transmission, though it is never less than that. Religious liberty understood from its most critical interior makes possible the public declaration of future eschatological judgment. If religious liberty aids in pronouncement, the substance of that pronouncement is facilitated by the liberty to proclaim it.

Religious Liberty and Mission as Eschatological Blessing

But religious liberty is not just about the ability to pronounce judgment. Religious liberty is also essential to Christian mission's promise of blessing. Let's revisit Acts 17: Verse 34 reveals that "some men joined [Paul] and believed" in the resurrection that he proclaimed. Paul's proclamation resulted in persons believing the gospel. Proclamation facilitated by religious liberty allows persons to enter into the blessings of salvation. Religious liberty facilitates how a person receives eschatological blessing—both, again, in terms of how they accept the gospel freely and authentically and in terms of how they encounter the message itself.

Understood as a means through which an individual encounters the gospel and responds freely and authentically, religious liberty is critical to persons experiencing salvation. The logic of the gospel (proclamation, free response, authentic belief) assumes mechanisms that are tied to religious liberty because religious liberty is aided by open proclamation and a free response. Individuals experience the blessings of salvation as a result of hearing the gospel. The means of how the gospel reaches those individuals is not insignificant. Religious liberty is thus critical to mission because it is the means by which individuals experience the down payment of eschatological blessing in the present (Eph. 1:3–14). Gospel proclamation results in a divine "transference" by which an unbeliever is shuttled from the "domain of darkness" to the "kingdom of his beloved Son" (Col. 1:13). That "transference" requires the liberty to do so.

Religious Liberty and Evangelism

It is common to hear religious liberty advanced under the banner of the "free market of ideas." While we should exercise caution in reducing evangelism to ideas associated with mere choice and consumption, there is an important truth here: if the gospel is true, the gospel does not need government preference. Why? Because in the scope of history, truth wins. That is not to say that truth is always victorious, but that in the fullness of time truth will overcome error just as goodness will triumph over evil. Truth needs nothing other than itself for persuasion. John Milton, in his *Areopagitica*, stated that truth is its best offense and defense. Milton wrote that "though all the winds of doctrine were let loose to play upon the earth, so Truth be in the field, we do injuriously, by licensing and prohibiting, to misdoubt her strength. Let her and Falsehood grapple; who ever knew Truth put to the worse, in a free and open encounter?" He added that this truth "needs no policies, nor stratagems, nor licensings to make her victorious; those are the shifts and the defences that error uses against her power. Give her but room."[29]

What Milton speaks of in terms of "Truth," Christians speak of as their understanding of their doctrinal convictions. Baptist statesman John Leland states, "It is error, and error alone, that needs human support; and whenever men fly to the law or sword to protect their system of religion, and force it upon others, it is evident that they have something in their system that will not bear the light, and stand upon the basis of truth upon it."[30]

Thus, for a Christian, religious liberty expresses confidence in the gospel. The gospel needs no accomplices. It is independent from artificial supports that would attempt to bolster its credibility. The gospel needs not the bejeweled trappings of salesmanship or a sword-drawn threat. Those with ears to hear will hear (Matt. 11:15). Humanity is not under compulsion to accept the blessings of Christ. The rich young ruler's rejection of Christ was not met with earthly punishment (Luke 18:18–30). As one commentator observes, "God as disclosed in Jesus Christ is neither arbitrary nor coercive. It is an essential characteristic of the Gospel that God himself did not use force to win our allegiance."[31]

Paul did not fear a free market of ideas but used such a context to spread the gospel. Indeed, the apostolic witness of the New Testament asserts the priority of the conscience against the claims and protestations of government authorities in order to proclaim the gospel (Acts 5:29). Paul never backed away from the strange claim that God raised Jesus from the dead. He used persuasion, argument, and an appeal to the conscience to advance the gospel. The gospel advances in only convicted, not coerced, consciences. In the biblical text, "reason" (discussion and conversation aimed at persuading individuals) is consistent with evangelism (Acts 17:7; 18:4; 19:8–9; 24:25). The methods of evangelism in Scripture assume principles constitutive of religious liberty.

Persuasion, reason, proclamation, and free response are at the heart of evangelism in pluralistic settings.[32] For Paul, a pluralistic setting was not an obstacle to making an exclusivist claim concerning soteriology. Paul explicitly invoked Jesus and the resurrection to his hearers, doing so by exploiting their assumptions and directing them to see how Christ fulfilled their own metaphysical views. According to J. Daryl Charles, Paul "contrasts pagan inclusivity with Christian exclusivity."[33] Rather than watering down the exclusive claims to service the needs of an enlightened audience, Paul reinforced the starkness of the gospel by summoning all to its dawning. That is instructive for missiology because it demonstrates that religious liberty operates according to sincerity of conviction and that Christianity's messengers need not downplay the strength of their message for it to be received.

Religious Liberty, Natural Law, and the Gospel

For mission to proceed, and for religious liberty to play its proper role in facilitating mission, an account of natural law will have to enter into consideration.[34] Whatever we want to call it, whether natural law or general revelation, recalling our earlier definition, making intelligible propositions that persons are called on to grasp and order their lives around requires a confidence in the structure of creation that makes communication comprehensible. General revelation is what makes communicating the gospel intelligible between persons. Greg Forster notes how the "Bible does not at any point present a philosophical argument that there is such a thing as right and wrong." Instead, "the Bible consistently assumes that the reader is already aware of right and wrong without needing the Bible to establish that distinction."[35] This assumption speaks to the reality of an indemonstrable witness that makes communication about the knowledge of moral order possible. As C. S. Lewis wrote, "If nothing is self-evident, nothing can be proved. If nothing is obligatory for its own sake, nothing is obligatory at all."[36]

Speaking of moral consensus and the knowledge of moral law that makes individuals culpable before God, Charles rightfully argues that a doctrine of natural law is essential to an understanding of religious liberty. "Apart from natural law, which expresses general—that is to say, indirect—revelation to which all are held accountable, fulfilling this mandate is impossible. General revelation furnishes the basis on which Christians and non-Christians relate to one another."[37] It is an appeal to general revelation through which the apostle Paul says his audience is "without excuse" in knowing the one true God (Rom. 1:20). Religious liberty understood as the expressed ability to bear witness to the gospel assumes a ground of intelligibility between Christians and non-Christians. Religious liberty, then, assumes a doctrine of general revelation that makes rational communication possible.

Whatever differences may arise between "natural law" and "general revelation," Charles's point is important: the ability to communicate the gospel without external coercion assumes a communicative intelligibility wherein persons understand their guilt and freely respond to the gospel. Again, Charles states, "While general revelation is insufficient to justify humans before their Creator, it does give all people a minimal knowledge of the Creator as well as the moral standard to which all will be held accountable."[38] For the gospel to take root, an individual must be able to know right from wrong, which then inspires repentance and faith.

General revelation is not insignificant in what it avails religious liberty. An emphasis on religious liberty will animate a focus on general revelation because general revelation provides the epistemological, communicative, and moral grammar prerequisite to repentance and salvation.

At the same time, the relationship between natural law and religious liberty is of significance to not only communication, but epistemological awareness of the conscience's culpability. One is accustomed to reading of the "law . . . written on their hearts" (Rom. 2:15), scriptural evidence that God has implanted in the heart a moral order and moral goods that acts of reason can discover and be acted upon to fulfill their obtainment. At the same time, that sinful agents "by their unrighteousness suppress the truth" (Rom. 1:18) puts into question whether a sufficient account of morality obtains within the human agent such that the natural law can be of real value as a moral theory.

The crossroads of the natural law's existence and its continued knowability prompt us to explore how the gospel illumines our understanding of the natural law. The heart of the gospel is that Jesus Christ died and rose to save sinners. In our wretched state, the Bible declares, enough of the moral law obtains in our conscience that our suppression of God's authority renders us "without excuse" (Rom. 1:20; cf. 1:32). In other words, the Bible insists that it is our knowledge of the moral law and our violation of God's moral law that hold us culpable for judgment. Our violations of natural law are violations of eternal law. In other words, we are not transgressing law but, ultimately, God. That we are "without excuse" means there is at least a sufficient account of morality within each of us to know we have done wrong. Our conscience is pricked when we lie, cheat, steal, and lust. Our conscience is there to tell us when our actions go awry from what is right. But from where does that overriding sense of shame and guilt originate? The existence of such a law points to the existence of a divine Lawgiver. Morality is either theistic, evolutionary, or conventional. But the last two cannot explain an absolute duty to morality. This harkens back to Aquinas's famous maxim that "law is an ordinance of reason, by the proper authority, for the common good, and promulgated."[39] Christians believe that a divine Creator, one with rightful authority, has ordered a universal common good and promulgated that good through a natural law in "the things that have been made" (Rom. 1:20).

It would seem, then, that the natural law is the backdrop for the gospel's indictment of our plight. Our awareness of our violation of the natural law is rooted in the eternal law—what renders us guilty before a holy God. We have all sinned against God and his law that he has written on our hearts. In the Bible's depiction of humanity, each person knows this to be confirmed at their conscience's deepest level, even those persisting in unbelief. The Bible has no account of atheism. It only accounts for those who suppress what is self-evident by nature. Conversion thus requires recognizing the binding authority of that moral law, so much so that it indicts us and points us to our need for a Savior.

Those of us who are Christians came to know Christ not in our triumph but in a state of self-recognized misery. Some may have come to Christ through intellectual pursuits, but the intellectuals I know who have submitted to Christ have done so out of an aching sense of their insufficiency and personal disarray. The pangs of our conscience made each of us realize our pitiful lot. Yet we sinned not against the law as a mere abstraction but against a lawgiver who became incarnate (John 1:1–3; Col. 1:15–17). Christ, we read, "is the end of the law" (Rom. 10:4). Christ calls himself "the way, and the truth, and the life" (John 14:6). The foundation of the universe is not an impersonal force but is wisdom and law personified. Natural law, then, is Christotelic. Christ upholds the natural law and is its terminus (Rom. 10:4).

Paul declares in Acts 17:30–31 that "the times of ignorance God overlooked, but now he commands all people everywhere to repent, because he has fixed a day on which he will judge the world in righteousness by a man whom he has appointed; and of this he has given assurance to all by raising him from the dead." Paul is not excusing unbelief or allowing ignorance to go unchecked. Instead, Paul's sermon to his pagan audience is a call for them to worship in full knowledge of what Paul insists is their vain worship of an "unknown God." Acts 17 is Paul's manifesto that the providential upkeep of the world is held together by an incarnate Logos. Such is the same in our day where people are no less religious than in Paul's day but only redirect their worship to secularism's approved outlets.

The awareness of our sinful estate is an act of affection and cognition. Our understanding of the gospel is more than intellectual, but it is undoubtedly never less than propositional, meaning that acts of intelligible communication are a product of general revelation. An appreciation for the general-revelation aspects of natural law is essential if we are to take the gospel to the world. It is a foundation for gospel witness that sinners come to encounter their awareness of a need for a Savior. The natural law is an essential pillar in a Christian ethic that hopes to be faithful to the gospel in its public witness. The natural law allows us to communicate the standards of God's righteous judgment.

In my childhood Baptist church, we sang "He Paid a Debt He Did Not Owe," by Ellis J. Crumb, at the end of our services. Little was I aware at the time that I was witnessing to a truth about the natural law. The imbalance of the universe borne witness in my conscience made me aware that things were not as they ought to be and ultimately pointed me to Jesus Christ. Even at a young age and into adolescence, when I was truly converted, the world that made sense to me and which my soul would mimic was a world of both order and chaos but that in Christ found resolution.

The chapters of Scripture most often appealed to for the existence of the natural law and our culpability before it (Rom. 1–2) are one chapter away from the declaration of what God has done for us in Christ to vindicate both: "[All] are justified by his grace as a gift, through the redemption that is in Christ Jesus, whom God put forward as a propitiation by his blood, to be received by faith" (3:24–25). The natural law cannot ultimately save us. No natural lawyer I know of would believe it could. On its own, natural law is the remnant morality that exists because of God's common grace. May it be that we come to understand it—for it points us to saving grace.

The Ethical Horizon of Evangelism and Religious Liberty

Religious liberty is thus essential for grasping how personal ethics relate to the task of evangelism. How so? Because wrongdoing, or *sinning*, is what establishes the ground of our need for redemption by God. To discuss what sin is, then, is to immediately begin a discussion about right conduct and wrong conduct. What is a sin? It is a violation of a divine standard that human beings are obligated to obey (1 John 3:4). To put it another way, a sin is anything for which Christ needed to die to redeem a person.

Were each of us in a state of perfection in our day-to-day obedience, we would have no need of redemption. Considering that we are not, this means that ethics—the task of how we go about living our lives in accordance with God's holy nature—are not only relevant but also absolutely necessary to an understanding of evangelism. Understanding wrongdoing and sin is essential to understanding our accountability before a holy God, our deserved judgment for sinning against God, and how the sinlessness of Jesus can atone for our rebellion.

167

Evangelism is about more than ethics, but never less, especially if ethics means calling people to repentance for their sin against a holy God. In effect, our ethics condemn us, and Jesus's ethics make possible our salvation. Let's unpack all of this by using an example.

I recently watched the documentary *One Child Nation*, which exposes in graphic detail the horrific policy of the Chinese government allowing only one child per household, designed to protect against the concerns of overpopulation, such as starvation. To pursue this policy, the Chinese government oversaw a campaign of forced sterilization and abortion. The producer interviewed a family-planning official who delivered children, sterilized women, and aborted children. The number of children this official said she killed was upward of forty to fifty thousand. That is a staggering number that words fail to accurately comprehend. How could one person live with so much death and guilt on their hands? The official was deeply conflicted with an agonized conscience. She knew what she had done in killing so many babies was wrong, but it was what her job and the officials above her required. She has since made a pact with an impersonal force in the universe to try to act charitably and mercifully to all women and children in the aftermath, hoping that her good actions will outweigh her bad actions.

In essence, this woman is trying to atone for her sins by looking to herself for redemption. She is trying to save herself, which is the tendency of every self-justifying yet condemned person. In the movie, there is no gospel, there is no offer of Christ to whom she can look for atonement, redemption, and forgiveness. Instead, she is left to herself and her conscience and the fear besetting an individual who knows they are guilty and feels judged by some cosmic standard, even if they do not quite grasp that the cosmic standard is the triune God. She is involved in a vain pursuit of self-reckoning that will only bring further condemnation.

What was apparent from the documentary was that it was the woman's corrupt actions, *her ethics*, that led her to this place of unremitting despair. This means, in turn, that the gospel could reach her by contrasting her sinfulness with the sinlessness of Christ, the one who was qualified to obtain her salvation by his perfect life (2 Cor. 5:21). Such are the similar circumstances of a story we all know well: Jesus's interactions with the woman at the well (John 4). The woman told others, "Come, see a man who told me all that I ever did" (4:29). Jesus named her actions for what they truly were—sin—and the woman was awakened to the reality of her sin and her need for redemption, which she immediately recognized was available in Christ.

In sharing the good news and love of Christ, we must understand that people come to know Christ through the judgment they know they deserve and the redemption they know they cannot find in or by themselves. This means that evangelism requires telling people that their sin is wrong and is worthy of judgment because of God's holiness but that Christ offers the promise of forgiveness because his life is what saves us.

To love our neighbor as God intends means to see them as God sees them: as condemned but never outside Christ's reach. To love our neighbor is to proclaim to them the moral obligations owed to God and the truth that their nature is ordered toward and fulfilled by him. It is to tell them of forewarned judgment and doom.

There are likely two realities that follow from engaging the topic of ethics in relationship to evangelism. One possibility is that the person who hears of their rebellion and need for repentance will respond with scoffing dismissal, even rage. For this person, the awakening of their conscience to divine accountability brings anger. This is because at their conscience level they know they stand condemned before God, and their reflex is further self-justification. Even still, the reality of moral law stands, and we wait in patience, hoping that God's kindness will bring them to repentance (Rom. 2:4).

The other possibility is that the person who hears of their sin will respond with enthusiastic joy to the knowledge that their rebellion can be atoned for and forgiven at no cost to themselves but to Christ, who died for them. For this person, the call of Christ means casting their burdens on him, whose yoke is easy and whose offer of redemption brings rest to their soul (Matt. 11:28–30).

To say that "all have sinned and fall short of the glory of God" (Rom. 3:23) is to proclaim to people that they have sinned. They have failed to live for God's glory. They have rebelled. The good news of the gospel comes through recognizing the bad news of our sin. The good news, though, is not self-earned. The next verses in Romans remind us how we obtain the atonement, forgiveness, and reconciliation our souls are thirsting after: "justified by his grace as a gift, through the redemption that is in Christ Jesus, whom God put forward as a propitiation by his blood, to be received by faith" (3:24–25).

Salvation requires repentance of our sin. Conversion requires a turning away from our sin. It is clear, then, that the interior logic of the gospel is inseparable from a strong foundation in ethics and the pursuit of evangelism aided by the freedom to carry it out unhindered.

Religious Liberty and the Church's Mission in Society

God's mission for the church is to proclaim the message of the gospel and make disciples. The mission of the church incorporates religious liberty into a portfolio of concerns because, according to James E. Wood, "the ultimate concern of the Christian for religious freedom is that the Church may be the church."[40] A. F. Carrillo de Albornoz notes that the church's exercise of religious liberty is part of its "responsibility" as being the church. He continues, "The first main duty of the responsible church concerning religious liberty is to practice it, to proclaim it and to be its herald before society."[41] This means that religious liberty is at the heart of the church's mission. From proclamation to tangible acts of ministry in the community, the church will capture a vision for religious liberty inasmuch as it obeys God's purpose for the church's mission.[42] Capturing how the church's mission relates to religious liberty, Wood observes, "The very integrity of the Church is rooted in religious freedom which points not simply to a free Church but, more importantly, to a true Church as God's agent of reconciliation which is seeking in his name and in his spirit to bring all men to God. The Church seeks to be free, not for its own sake, but in order to be God's servant in the world, remembering always that Jesus said: 'When I am lifted up from the earth, I will draw all men to me'—words rooted in love and freedom."[43]

Jim Spivey argues that the church must reject the temptation to allow the church's mission to be subsumed under the state's authority. "In order for true religion to convince seekers that the gospel is credible," argues Spivey, "it must compete in the marketplace of ideas without artificial help from the state."[44]

While medieval Christendom treated membership in the church and membership in the state as one and the same, the prospect of a voluntary church consisting only of those with expressed faith in Jesus Christ makes possible the critical division necessary to identify the church as something distinct from the world and to identify the church's mission to the world. A flourishing church is a church that understands its distinctiveness and its calling to be an outpost of the kingdom of God. A free church operating in a free state may pursue its mission of evangelization and disciple-making most freely. A church made up only of those with professed faith in Christ is possible when government does not see the church as a useful appendage to enforce cultural, religious, or political conformity.

Furthermore, a trust in the state for assistance in the church's mission reveals a lack of trust in God to fulfill his mission. As Spivey asserts, allying with state power amounts to "blasphemy by arrogating to itself a pretended power which Christ himself never claimed. In fact, true religion separates itself from worldly power."[45] The church, by refusing the temptation of worldly power and the possibility of using coercive dominance in society, and by emptying itself of worldly power, is more able to channel divine power and the divine mandate that birthed it. An authentic church will rely on the power of the Spirit animating it and not an amassed power to privilege it. The church that chooses to operate from a position of social equality granted to it by religious liberty will see religious liberty as an opportunity to carry forth its message rightly and boldly.

A church that embraces religious liberty without the attending privileges of state empowerment is a church that more accurately perceives its own understanding of mission in the world. To understand that the church's authority and commission come from God—and from nowhere else—is to understand the unique status of the church and to live out the scandalous mission to which it is called. Great miseries have resulted from the church forming compacts and allegiances with governments, kings, and legislatures.[46] The church cannot look at history and see itself as guiltless regarding the tragedies that followed from the church and the state being united. As argued previously, the seeds of religious liberty are unique to Christian history and present from its beginning, but the failure of religious liberty is a mark of the church's imperfection and inconsistency. As Matthew J. Franck notes, "The story of religious freedom is, in some sense, a tale of Christianity purifying itself."[47]

As Spivey further argues, religious liberty animates Christian mission: "By removing the impediments of establishmentarianism, separation of church and state unleashes the full power of the gospel to accomplish genuine evangelism."[48] Furthermore, the very nature of the church as a gathered body distinct from the world and the state implies the freedom to clearly demarcate what constitutes faithfulness. Advancing mission, thus, requires the church to differentiate itself.[49]

Conclusion

Behind the mission of the church is an implied doctrine of religious liberty. This chapter has sought to make explicit the various lineaments of religious liberty that aid in the church's mission. At every juncture of the church's mission, religious liberty is implicated. Whether the church is proclaiming the gospel, receiving the gospel, or living out the gospel, religious liberty is a critical blueprint to its mission.

Religious liberty speaks to the confidence the church has in its gospel—that because the gospel is true, it requires neither force nor privilege. The gospel calls for the church to be prophetically separate from the institutions of society that would subjugate it for exploitative ends. Prophetic separation understands that the uniqueness of the gospel's message makes it incompatible with bland nominalism. Rather than propping up the social order, prophetic separation insists that the church is gathered under its own banner and institutional legitimacy, not the culture's or the state's. The liberty that comes from separation allows a pure message untainted by worldly influence and corruptions to call to repentance individuals within society ensnared in immorality and stoking injustice. True reform comes from true preaching. A church smitten with its own power and privilege will be deaf and blind to the possibility of internal reform. Stanley Hauerwas is right to observe the temptation that can come not only from established religion but also from the failure to use religious freedom in a Christian manner. According to Hauerwas, "The question is not whether the church has the freedom to preach the gospel in America, but rather whether the church in America preaches gospel as the truth."[50] A church can possess all the requisite freedoms it desires and still not preach a true gospel. A doctrine of religious liberty frees the church to be the church that God is calling it to be in society *for* the sake of the world.

173

7

Moral Ecology and Christian Mission

THE LAST CHAPTER ARGUED that religious liberty participates in the economy of salvation as a missiological device within a secular era. While the last chapter focused on how the logic of religious liberty helps advance the gospel, the present chapter examines how religious liberty is a missiological tool that aids in establishing a pluralistic and contestable era that allows the force of Christian proclamation to be brought to bear in society for the church's good, and society's as well.

A Christian social ethic of religious liberty sees religious pluralism and contestability as normative realities in a penultimate age that give shape to how the church understands itself in this era. Normative pluralism shapes the posture of Christian witness in a secular age. Witnessing to the diversity of our age, religious liberty serves not only the church's interests but also society's. In society's embrace of religious liberty, it opens itself up to the claims made upon it by religion in general and the gospel in particular.

In a reverse application of Jeremiah 29:7, in the church's welfare, society's general well-being is enhanced as well. This is because an *ethic* of liberty promotes a particular ecology in the broader society. As an application of the Golden Rule and the command to love one's neighbor on a social scale, religious liberty is a dispensation of common grace and civil tranquility that allows deeply divergent societies to organize themselves peacefully. Religious liberty is oriented to the common good by promoting civil tranquility within a given community.

Engaging in public argument assumes the necessary freedom, or *agency*, to enter an arena where the exchange of ideas can occur. Religious liberty serves the common good by forcing society to reckon with the reformational aspects of the gospel. The moral witness of the gospel requires agency. Call this mere liberty or free speech, but if Christian mission cares about the shape and tenor of society—a "moral ecology"—it will utilize the space, made available by religious liberty, to influence society in a more just and humane direction. In this, religious liberty is an ingredient for Christian influence and, as Christianity influences society, religious liberty ought to be a mark of this influence.

Religious liberty is thus inextricably tied up with the individual and collective moral witness that Christians—and the church—hope to offer society. The freedom to believe requires the freedom to proclaim and act on those beliefs. Religious liberty, then, not only facilitates relationship between God and humanity but also allows the moral witness of the gospel to be made in society. But since religiously grounded arguments are met with skepticism within liberal democracy, overcoming secular objection to religious argument requires learning how religious argument works in a pluralistic setting.

Since a Christian social ethic of religious liberty is motivated by a concern for the ability of free consciences to authentically respond to the gospel and to live out the gospel's ethical implications in society, this ethic will hopefully produce a moral and social ecology within a secular era that aids in the promotion of civil tranquility and Christian moral witness. The common grace offerings of a Christian understanding of religious liberty promote the common good.

Pluralism and Christian Mission

Pluralism is a bogeyman in Christian circles. It is a term sullied by liberalizing forces that downplay confessional boundaries. The so-called problem of pluralism is not only that it is undesirable (would not religious agreement be ideal?) but that, Christianly speaking, it is misunderstood.

Religious difference exists because of Adam and Eve's rebellion (Rom. 5:12). In the garden of Eden, pluralism did not exist. And there will not be religious pluralism in the new creation. But nowhere in the interim era of the New Testament age is government tasked with the responsibility of upholding Christian orthodoxy, or any religious orthodoxy, as a way to mitigate the effects of sin, moral disagreement, and religious pluralism. Whereas the state is called to a minimalist justice ethic that seeks to order society in accordance with natural law, the church proclaims the deeper righteousness of the law such that individuals are awakened to their need for the gospel. As Jim Spivey notes, this is observed even in the life of Christ, who "refused to sit as a judge in secular matters, resisting the temptation to seize worldly power, and fled from those who would have crowned him king."[1] Christ, who could have conquered by force, defined his ministry less by power and more by persuasion and proclamation.

Socially speaking, pluralism is a social arrangement wherein diverse people of different religious or ideological persuasion occupy a shared social space. Of course, pluralism does not imply moral skepticism, for it is a requirement that ordered societies determine legitimate grounds for participation and banishment. One cannot steal and kill under the canopy of pluralism. On a political level, pluralism is an admission that a principle of equality among religions in society means abandoning a partnership between church and state. Pluralism follows from an understanding that, in the words of Carl F. H. Henry, "it is not the role of government to judge between rival systems of metaphysics and to legislate one among others. Government's role is to protect and preserve a free course for its constitutional guarantees."[2] This fact is significant because it signifies a theologically informed principle of separation and the admission that government does not act as a theological referee amid religious diversity.[3]

Theologically speaking, pluralism is a reality from living within a penultimate age. According to Oliver O'Donovan, pluralism is a "metaphysic of society, at once a way of reading the world and a way of reacting to it."[4] To accept pluralism is to accept that not all has been brought under the reign of Christ. According to Dallas Willard, "Pluralism simply means that social or political force is not to be used to suppress the freedom of thought and expression of any citizen, or even the practice that flows from it, insofar as that practice is not morally wrong."[5] Pluralism does not treat truth claims as relative but equal in their opportunity to be made without fear of reprisal. Playing by the ground rules of pluralism invites humility: because your fellow citizen may believe differently than you, you must find yourself possessed with a willingness to default to respect, especially where no moral line has been crossed. In places of deep, irreconcilable disagreement, because pluralism means that debates are settled using nonviolent means, discourse—rather than force—is the modus operandi of society.

But the question remains as to whether the reality of pluralism bears any intrinsic connection to soteriological concerns. John Piper, echoing a point I made earlier, argues that Jesus as the judge over the conscience is the ground of religious tolerance and, by implication, religious liberty. He argues that Jesus's kingship supplies Christianity with a normative and *principled* account of societal pluralism. Piper frames his answer to the question of pluralism's intelligibility by asking, "So, how do we express a passion for God's supremacy in a pluralistic world where most people do not recognize God as an important part of their lives, let alone an important part of government or education or business or industry or art or recreation or entertainment?" Part of his answer is that we do so "by making clear that God himself is the foundation for our commitment to a pluralistic democratic order—not because pluralism is his ultimate ideal, but because in a fallen world, legal coercion will not produce the kingdom of God. Christians agree to make room for non-Christian faiths (including naturalistic, materialistic faiths), not because commitment to God's supremacy is unimportant, but because it must be voluntary, or it is worthless." He concludes, "We believe this tolerance is rooted in the very nature of the gospel of Christ. In one sense, tolerance is pragmatic: freedom and democracy seem to be the best political order humans have conceived. But for Christians it is not purely pragmatic: the spiritual, relational nature of God's kingdom is the ground of our endorsement of pluralism, until Christ comes with rights and authority that we do not have."[6]

Thus, far from being solely a pragmatic doctrine that relativizes religious difference, religious liberty as a reality of pluralism is a prerequisite of freedom that facilitates stable political order and the authentic realization of Christ's lordship. In addition, Piper's argument that coercion does not produce faith is an insight into evangelism's relationship to the inner logic of the gospel: mission advances when faith is freely received. A pluralistic order, then, is simply a response to the lordship of Jesus Christ not fully enacted in the present.

To again cite S. M. Hutchens, a Christian doctrine of pluralism amounts to God's "forbearance and patience."[7] Hutchens prefers

179

this terminology because it offers a critical assessment of other religions. Arguments for pluralism based on divine judgment and forbearance, rather than a concession to the demands of liberal democracy, offer a more attractive theological and christological foundation for pluralism. Pluralism is thus a patient response to God's promise of future judgment, or as Christian theologian and ethicist Richard J. Mouw writes, "Christian civility will display the patience that comes from knowing that the final accounting belongs to God."[8] Because God promises to bring pluralism to an end, Christians cannot. The reality that pluralism and religious difference will not last into eternity is a catalyst for the church to use the mechanisms of a pluralistic society to announce that salvation is found in Jesus Christ alone (John 14:6; Acts 4:12).

Moreover, pluralism is an outgrowth of Christian reflection on human diversity done through successive eras of history as the church ministers in society while awaiting promised judgment. Pluralism is the textured reality of a secular age. According to Mouw and Sander Griffioen, "Disagreement about fundamental human issues is an inescapable fact of life under present conditions. If there were no other reason for orthodox Christians to endorse some version of pluralism, this alone would be sufficient to cause us to do so. When it comes to the issues of belief and unbelief, the Bible calls our attention to at least one basic plurality: the division within the human community between those who worship the true God and those who persist in their apostasy."[9]

I have asserted that secularism is fitting for the era of time between the resurrection and the second coming. Larry Siedentop likewise argues that secularism as an outgrowth of Christian social thinking was one of "Europe's noblest achievements," because it contributed to an atmosphere in which "different religious beliefs continue to contend for followers."[10] Pluralism understood as a product of secularism is a way of making room for non-Christians to become Christians without coercion or reprisal. Sylvie Avakian argues that a Christian doctrine of secularism, which grounds pluralism, allows for genuine Christian faith to flourish: "Only in a secular society, where unbelief is a possibility, has the individual the freedom either to take upon oneself the claims of Christian faith, or reject them. Further, it is only through a responsible taking upon oneself the claims of faith that Christian faith might become one's own. I propose that this is the culmination of Reformation and it is this that secularization evokes."[11]

Thus, a pluralistic order can actually deepen faith, since one must make a deep-seated choice about who God is on their own terms. Pluralism ought to invite civility, dialogue, and tolerance in a social context. If no one religion can claim particular privilege over another, a level playing field exists where religious actors are given equal footing and are less apt to engage in retributive acts of hostility that come from religious intolerance. Pluralism enables the free exchange of competing ideas, one that grounds an individual's search for meaning, purpose, and truth. In one of the most illuminating quotations on the nature of truth and pluralism, Catholic philosopher Jacques Maritain argues:

> There is real and genuine tolerance only when a man is firmly and absolutely convinced of a truth, or of what he holds to be truth, and when he at the same time recognizes the right of those who deny this truth to exist, and to contradict him, and to speak their own mind, not because they are free from truth but because they seek truth in their own way, and because he respects in them human nature and human dignity and those very resources and living springs of the intellect and of conscience which make them potentially capable of attaining the truth he loves, if someday they happen to see it.[12]

A pluralistic environment ought to be one of the most intellectually capacious environments. Pluralism leaves open the possibility for genuine conversion. Pluralism is not concerned with diversity for diversity's sake but with the ability for rigorous debate to occur among people with diverse perspectives in order that truth may be found. As Abraham Kuyper wrote, "Christianity itself needs this constant dueling with champions from other camps and must prove its moral superiority by triumphing in a strictly spiritual battle."[13] Only in a society committed to the vigorous pursuit of truth, where those conclusions are held humbly yet firmly, will there be religious liberty.

Much about a Christian paradigm of pluralism understands that society is diverse organically. The givenness of difference is a Kuyperian theme, one that understands that the organic nature of society demands "mutual recognition" and an "absence of coercion or persecution."[14] Christians thus see a pluralistic society as an open invitation for Christian mission to participate. Christians accommodate pluralism because they see debate and contestability as a "friend of the gospel" that "paves the way" for the gospel's advancement.[15] It is also critical to see that the opposite of pluralism, where some type of formal or even informal church-state establishment exists, deadens Christian mission by drawing incorrect lines or blurring lines around what constitutes faithfulness.

In the interest of clearly demarcating what is and is not authentic Christianity, Christians should embrace a pluralistic context that leaves the church free to clearly understand itself and its mission in society. Pluralism is thus a purifying element of Christian mission that allows the church to be confident of its own mission without the need of false supports or corrupting power alliances.

Real pluralism strives for social tranquility by agreeing to live peaceably, kindly, and respectfully despite deeply held and irreconcilable beliefs about who God is, how God calls us to live, and how we attain a relationship with God. We do no service to our neighbors by weakening the claims of our religion in order to serve a greater social good. The common good is better served when honest brokers approach one another within a society that pledges to foster religious liberty by giving each equal space in the public square—not in spite of deep difference, but because of it. This means that true pluralism entails religious liberty. Only an environment committed to treating religions with respect and equal freedom can hope to be a social environment where disagreement is resolved without recourse to violence and social unrest.

Contestability and the Common Good

More must be said about the social conditions that pluralism fosters. Chapter 3 argued that the twin pillars of illiberalism surrounding religion and society are secularism ("seculocracy") and theocracy. In each of these iterations, there is a dominating force. In seculocracy, a dismissal of religion robs civil society of religious norms. In theocracy, destructive political forces wed to religion undermine civil society by crippling religious liberty. A better paradigm involves what legal philosopher Steven D. Smith calls the "principle of contestation."[16] Contestability is a normative claim on society wherein society understands that various ideologies and religions compete with one another as the primary social imaginary within a society. As a political matter, contestation is the reality that in free societies "winners are provisional winners only."[17] As a nation's mood swings, so too do its religions and politics. Contestability reflects the contingencies of history; culture evolves and develops over times. The evolution and development of a society can be positive or negative. In similar fashion, orthodoxies come and go in an imperfect society governed by fallen individuals. A free society will and must be marked by vigorous debate; at times, Christian influence may decline, but it is better to ensure mechanisms that promote debate than mechanisms that give long-standing entrenchment to tyranny.

The good news is that in a pluralist society, losing may only be temporary.[18] Facing such a reality may be unsettling, but Christian mission must be governed by the sober-minded reality that in given contexts, Christianity's influence waxes and wanes. As of the writing of this book, the long-term prospects for the continued influence of Christianity in America are discouraging. But whatever hardships may come for Christianity, a commitment to pluralism that allows the Christian message to be freely expressed may be one of its greatest long-term strategies for continued presence and activity in the public square. Contestability should be one of Christianity's most cherished principles as its influence wanes, as it allows for continued dialogue and public Christian witness. To be sure, the challenge and paradox to pluralism presented here is that in the absence of a Christian conception of pluralism, pluralism will wither under the weight of growing illiberalism and soft tyranny.

Contestability is underwritten by a theological principle that Christian social hegemony will not be totalized in a given age. Whatever social consensus may exist, there will always be dissent. According to Robert A. Markus, "Tension, conflict, insecurity are woven into the texture of human existence in its sinful state and draw narrow limits to the responsibilities and the efficacy of public authorities."[19] The church sits at the center of this conflict. Furthermore, according to Markus's reading of Augustine, "The agencies and institutions of society cannot serve to promote man's ultimate good; they serve only as a means to turn human ferocity itself to the fostering of a precarious order, some basic cohesion which Augustine called the earthly peace."[20]

A statement like this calls for radically reconfiguring the assumptions about our shared lives. If we truly grasp the radical nature of our fallenness, we should expect, rather than substantive social agreements, a minimum standard of decency. This does not negate a concept like the common good, but it does suggest that attainment of the common good will be won on modest grounds as opposed to thick moral commitments. We ought to be chastened for expecting agreement on deep moral matters. When a society commits itself to basic ideas such as human dignity and when the rule of law around such freedoms as speech, religion, and association is respected, built on top of those foundations will be much moral disagreement. This is why the US Constitution is ingenious: it ensures that disagreement can be dealt with among the citizenry using nonviolent means while protecting certain liberties regardless of what majorities determine is popular. The Constitution is designed to accommodate the proclivities of human nature.

This does not mean agnosticism about the common good. Under common grace, the moral faculties inherent in the *imago Dei* and the moral content inherent in the natural law are constitutive aspects of attaining the common good. Whether they can provide the substantive goods that lead to a robust common good is debatable. Both offer an attractive framework to debate morality, but in a fallen world, both will be continually bombarded by humanity, "who by their unrighteousness suppress the truth" (Rom. 1:18).

What is the common good? To start, it is better to speak of a pluralized common good. What is determined as the common good is a reflection of individual, familial, religious, and national identities, which are shaped by customs, traditions, and laws. The family has a common good—to obtain the conditions where parents care for and raise children into adulthood. A business has a common good—to coordinate its operations for the production of goods that result in commercial benefit and profit. The church has a common good—to make disciples for the sake of building up God's kingdom. When each of these institutions functions as it ought, the common good is realized. The common good of all is thus the common good of each. The *Catechism of the Catholic Church* defines the common good as "the sum total of social conditions which allow people, either as groups or as individuals, to reach their fulfillment more fully and easily."[21] George Duke similarly defines it as a "state of affairs in which each individual within a political community and the political community as a whole are flourishing."[22] In these definitions, the common good is both a means and an end. As a means, at the macro level, the common good is a temporal state of affairs that provides the cooperating institutions of society a peaceable horizon to realize their respective ends. In this, the common good is a conduit that facilitates individual and social flourishing. It does so by protecting the agency rights of various institutions to live out their respective duties. The common good, as such, allows mediating institutions to cooperate toward the advancement of the just society freely. As an end, the common good realizes a state of affairs where institutions are properly ordered and human flourishing is present. The common good is not coterminous with justice but facilitates the advancement and realization of justice. Yet the common good will never be realized void of justice.

This means that the common good is more substantive or better realized in proportion to the depth of the relationship in which a particular good is experienced. A family's understanding of its common good will be distinct from (but not necessarily contradictory to) the common good of the political community. As we work our way outward, we should expect the common good to be more minimally apprehended by citizens within the political community. Citizens may not agree on all moral claims, but they can agree to a baseline of moral obligations. This means that we should expect to share little in common, except for a basic adherence to the natural law, with strangers who differ from us on more granular matters of religion and politics. What we can agree on, however, is a system that allows for differences to play out without coercion or violence.

The common good can be refined by the norms of a political community as it revises and improves on previous errors. Thus, a commitment to deliberative government is one common good. Common goods, however, are primarily those ends around which people direct and coordinate their individual and collective lives, such things as such things as life, health, family, integrity, knowledge, friendship, play, skillfulness, aesthetic experience, authenticity, practical reasonableness, and religion.[23] Each of these is realized in unique ways within its unique setting. A Christian conceptualization of the common good will have much in common with natural law simply by virtue of Christianity's belief in an enduring creation order.

This thinking reshapes the reality of what is achievable while living in a penultimate era. It means, theologically speaking, that a Christian expectation of social dominance is a form of overrealized eschatology. If popularity and acceptance—rather than faithfulness for faithfulness's sake—are the expectation for Christian mission, Christians will be setting themselves up for disappointment. Nowhere in the New Testament is faithfulness measured by cultural dominance or cultural acceptance. And nowhere in the New Testament is a government's legitimacy associated with the government acknowledging true religion. Government is held accountable for its judgments, but its judgments are judged according to the contours of divine justice and natural law, not right confession.

Regarding missional concerns, the pretense of an overrealized or triumphalist hegemony is one of the most catastrophic effects undermining authentic Christian mission. This does not mean that Christianity may never become a majority religion in society (we should hope it does) or that Christianity should not influence a society's norms (it certainly should); rather, it means rejecting a version of Christianity that is championed primarily for the benefits it accrues to society instead of its radical commitment to Christ and the Word of God. This paradigm need not imply a moral agnosticism about society's need for moral consensus. Rather, contestability calls for heightened suspicion of civil religion and reshapes expectations about how religion encounters culture and civilization. Contestability understands that while influencing society is legitimate, faithfulness matters more than the attainment of a common culture, for the tempting veneer of civil religion is an inoculating counterfeit to biblical Christianity.[24] Augustine realized that expecting the full Christianization of a social order apart from the eschaton is futile and a "dangerous delusion." According to Markus, Augustine came to see that "conflict over the ultimate purpose [of society] would be a permanent feature of society."[25] This means that a proper understanding of Christian mission requires understanding the time in which the church's mission is operating: a time of pluralism and contestability.

Ecology of Mission: Religious Liberty as Common Grace for the Common Good

A by-product of religious liberty is its benefit for the common good of society. Religious liberty is evidence of God's common grace toward humanity in allowing for a modicum of social stability to continue amid the multitude of diversity in society. Any social cooperation whatsoever in a fallen social order is an expression of God's common grace. It should not be a surprise, then, that religious liberty has often been labeled an "article of peace" for what it avails society.[26] This means that one practical consequence of religious liberty as a Christian social ethic is its transformational and common-grace benefits for society.

Common grace refers to the Reformed doctrine that God restrains the full effect of sin on society while also allowing positive civil cooperation to occur in culture that benefits human civilization.[27] At a deeper level, however, common grace is evidence of God's patient calling of a wayward creation to salvation in Jesus Christ. God has not wiped away the earth in final judgment, and the grace allowed by our continued existence in creation allows for salvation to be obtained. That God continues to uphold the structures of creation is a promise that the general nature of his providence is making possible the way of salvation.

Practical results of Christianity's focus on religious liberty, understood as helping facilitate its mission in society, are the social benefits that accrue to society more broadly. There is an obverse reality to my broader point: apart from Christianity's influence, the long-term prognosis of liberty in a society will hang in the balance. How can I make the argument that (1) government should be, as a matter of theological requirement, disestablished from religion and (2) Christianity should resist the tendency to become a civil religion while (3) warning that without Christianity's influence religious liberty will recede? We are, admittedly, on tenuous grounds. Christianity, it should be said, need not become a civil religion in order for it to be influential. What I propose is an orthodox Christianity concerned with public justice and the common good in keeping with the transcendental foundations of natural law. An impassioned, orthodox Christianity concerned for the world around it will always be concerned with value systems. Because Christians espouse a belief in God and objective morality, they can speak prophetically to society. We must be actors of prophetic faithfulness. That faithfulness is born not of a confidence that all of society will become Christian but of a concern that the world live in alignment with how God has ordered it.

Religious liberty, as I am arguing, is an expression of Christian faithfulness that will benefit society insofar as Christianity bears any social consequence at all. The perennial theopolitical question is whether a civilization can hope to survive without an appreciation for religion informing its moral ecology. My judgment is that it cannot—or, at least, that it cannot for long. The forces of human sin will erode freedom and justice. This is not to say, however, that non-Christian societies are incapable of religious liberty. But it does mean that they will be robbed of a principled account of religious liberty. It does mean that a society without the influence of Christianity will acquire a form of religious liberty easily defenestrated. As argued previously, this is because Christianity places judgment in the realm of the eternal. If secular ideologies that reject transcendence believe themselves capable of achieving a just society on their own terms, there is no principle that would grant liberty to dissidents of that vision. In contrast, Christianity produces a moral ecology of liberty and social tranquility beneficial to society at large.

Religious liberty is not just about the freedom to believe in transcendent truths (though it is never about less than that). Building once again on the theme of contestability, religious liberty is a fundamental principle that ties together the principles that underwrite free societies and allows differences of opinion the space to compete. Societies that allow for free speech, free association, and free assembly are the types of societies that understand that citizens have beliefs and obligations that precede the demands and obligations of the state and civil society. This is why religious liberty is so central to building societies that not only are free but also understand that with freedom come the corresponding reciprocities of pluralism, respect, civility, kindness, and a commitment to diversity that allow freedom's continued existence. Debate and the free exchange of ideas can only occur in contexts that cultivate respect and a commitment to nonviolence. To see these gifts as anything less than valuable assets to be deployed and welcomed in society for the sake of Christian mission is to possess a malnourished understanding of social mission and religious liberty. A commitment to religious liberty is thus a commitment to the principles that make life together as a diverse people possible.

As part of their commitment to upholding the integrity of social order, Christians are to be resolutely committed to the common good. But Christianity is not committed to the common good out of generic principles such as solidarity or equality, as noble and necessary as both are. For Christians, the deepest commitments about advocacy for religious liberty and love of neighbor come from one essential angle: because Jesus is Lord, there can be true freedom of conscience and religious liberty on the basis of an enduring theological principle.[28] This means that Christianity offers a principled account of religious liberty.

Other worldviews do not regard this principle as inalienable or inviolable. Even Christianity can get it wrong. "Error has no rights," a refrain of Catholicism, was and is a stain on the Christian tradition's understanding of religious difference.[29] If religious liberty is not grounded in transcendence, or if Christianity arrogates for itself political power, then religious liberty becomes a tool of convenience that can easily be denied when those in power decide to do away with dissent.

Nature abhors a vacuum, as the saying goes. No less is that true concerning religious liberty. If Jesus Christ is not recognized as Lord, then something else will attempt to masquerade in this role. Idolatrous ideologies that lack the promise of future judgment have no principled reason to respect religious freedom of conscience as something inviolable. If religious liberty is denied, the "common good" easily becomes the domain of whatever worldview has a majority stake in defining what the "good" is. This is why it is necessary for Christians to advocate for religious liberty in the public square. Christianity must not advocate for religious liberty just for Christians as a majoritarian political doctrine but with the conviction that true freedom means allowing fellow citizens the right to freely exercise their beliefs with dignity—even when Christians think non-Christians are wrong and eternal judgment is at stake.

How, practically, ought religious liberty as mission be understood as a benefit for the common good and a gift of God's common grace? Religious liberty benefits society by creating good neighbors.

The founder of Philadelphia, William Penn, named the city the "City of Brotherly Love" due to his conviction that religious liberty is an ethic grounded in the Golden Rule. He explicitly cited Matthew 7:12 in his argument.[30] The Golden Rule of religious liberty practiced in the context of loving one's neighbor is a simple principle: if an individual wants religious liberty for himself or herself, that person must be willing to extend the same liberty to others. This principle of self-constituting one's religious life is pivotal for persons to engage freely in society. According to ethicist J. Daryl

Charles, "Religious freedom, issuing out of human dignity, benefits all members and segments of society—private and familial, public and social—and not merely those of religious conviction."[31] Charles's emphasis on human dignity is particularly important, since the image of God is the basis of religious liberty's inherent application to all persons. Religious liberty is therefore one critical juncture where the image of God and neighbor love form a critical nexus. According to John David Hughey, "True concern for the welfare of others leads to religious liberty. The Golden Rule forbids the oppression of anyone for his religious beliefs or practices or the lack of them. . . . It is unethical, and therefore unchristian, to demand a right for oneself if one would not be willing under different circumstances to grant the same right to others."[32] Or as Christian legal scholars Robert P. George and David French argue, religious liberty is the "legal corollary" to the Golden Rule.[33] If religious liberty is to have any social value, it must be reciprocal and applicable to all persons without qualification.[34]

Religious liberty as neighbor love has two manifestations. First, religious liberty is a form of *civil* neighbor love. Allowing a person to live earnestly with their convictions, even in a state of error, respects the integrity of their religious faculties and the sincerity with which their convictions manifest themselves. For example, a Christian can respect the freedom of a Jewish person to live an authentically Jewish life if those convictions arise authentically, even while pleading with this person to accept Christ. A person may be sincerely wrong, but we must love the person as an image bearer of God by respecting their religious faculties.

Second, religious liberty is neighbor love in that it advances the mission of the gospel by allowing one's neighbor to freely move toward the possibility of receiving the gospel.[35] This goes beyond the practice of mere reciprocity by insisting that love itself is rooted in free responses to the gospel. Thus, a person can truly love their neighbor in an ultimate sense of Christian love only by allowing them to respond freely to the gospel and not coercing them to believe or penalizing them for false belief. O'Donovan writes, "True neighborliness requires the recognition of the supreme goods simply in order that we may see the neighbor for what he is."[36] Here the emphasis on the *imago Dei* undergirds O'Donovan's argument. Truly loving one's neighbor means understanding that they were made for God. Truly loving one's neighbor means optimizing the conditions in which a free response to the gospel is possible. James K. A. Smith writes, "If we truly love our neighbors, we will bear witness to the fullness to which they are called. If we truly desire their welfare, we should proclaim the thickness of moral obligations that God commands as the gifts to channel us into flourishing, and labor in hope that these might become laws of the land, though with appropriate levels of expectation."[37]

Smith likewise frames how practicing neighbor love leads to fostering conditions in which those "moral obligations" are grasped authentically. By being allowed their religious liberty, individuals come to understand the uncoerced nature of the gospel. Religious liberty as neighbor love hinges on the affirmation that one's neighbor is made in the image of God and is made to know their Creator.

Rebecca C. Mathis similarly argues that a Christian understanding of religious liberty is rooted in the very principle of Christian love.

> Baptist advocacy to extend religious liberty to all people serves as a faithful response to God's ethical standards. God reminds God's people to treat aliens as citizens; in modern America this principle requires extension of equal religious freedom to all. Honoring the faith of another, whether a fellow citizen or foreigner, serves as a powerful act of godly love. God's commands surpass mere toleration. Offering love to one's neighbor means offering friendship, radical hospitality, and the hope of Christ in every situation. To love

as God loves requires extending grace and mercy to the unlovable, to the undeserving, and to the most despicable.[38]

This principle of love is bound up, intricately, with religious liberty as fostering relational justice between the Christian and the non-Christian within a secular society.

Moral Witness as Christian Mission

Religious liberty is essential to advancing the church's moral witness. Because religion informs ethics, religious arguments must find appropriate means of translation or communication to advance their persuasiveness in society. Religious liberty supplies the justification for proclaiming repentance, catalyzing personal moral reformation, and making moral proclamations.

First, religious liberty allows a person to call for repentance. To call for repentance is to proclaim a moral reckoning. It is to tell hearers of their need to bring their lives under the lordship of Jesus Christ. But the idea of calling someone to repentance presupposes the ability of the one making the call to do so. Second, religious liberty allows the one who has responded to the gospel to reorder their life accordingly. Religious liberty protects the exercise of moral instincts that people come to grasp and order their lives around. Third, religious liberty protects the ability to make Christian moral arguments in the public square. Moral witness assumes an outward posture of action. Christian faith is not a mere abstraction but incarnational in the ethical demands it calls forth. The reality of Christian moral witness in society raises important issues about the communication and translation of Christian social values as part of advancing Christian mission. This means that Christian moral witness will seek the liberty and freedom to give witness in a diverse society in hopes that individuals will encounter the truth of Christianity and salvation in Jesus Christ.

Christian moral witness is not a proclamation of rules but of standards of judgment and righteousness that reflect the holiness of God. Essential to the task of personal evangelism is the reality of moral conviction, and intrinsic to the responsibility of Christian moral witness in society is bearing witness to the moral demands of the kingdom. A Christian enters the public arena with the mindset of seeing Christian ethical commitments advanced as part of Christianity's influence.

So much of Christian mission and evangelism assumes a moral grammar between parties, that ideas such as repentance, wrongdoing, and morally praiseworthy actions and choices are intelligible properties. Persuasion is thus part and parcel of religious transformation, and we come to rely on it whether we are conscious of its importance or not. A religion unable to make religious and moral arguments or that fails to appreciate how persuasion and missionary activity are essential to religious vitality will be a religion sequestered in its own moral ghetto. Christian mission requires a rationale or justification for its involvement in matters of law and public policy in order to advance the common good and social tranquility. Religious liberty, predicated on the idea of free and rational decision-making, supplies such a need.

It is impossible for there to be missionary activity that is not at the same time situated around advancing moral argument. All of this presumes the possibility of reasoned communication and intelligibility within an individual and social context. This means, fundamentally, that religious liberty becomes an important asset in moral appeals striking at the level of individual conscience. If general revelation makes possible the communication of Christian moral demands, religious liberty is central in giving the communication of these ethical criterion substantive force and the possibility of response.

On the social and political level, for Christians to attempt to proclaim the gospel in any environment, they must understand the moral grammar of the context and how religious arguments function. The possibility of moral persuasion means operating contextually. The ability to make religioethical arguments operates as a function of general revelation, which makes moral arguments intelligible in a fallen world. General revelation is what makes reception of the gospel intelligible.

Colonial Baptist and iconoclast Roger Williams addressed the coordination of Christian moral witness in a pluralistic setting. In his famous ship analogy, Williams likened the inherent diversity of society to a ship at sea with travelers from diverse religious backgrounds.[39] According to Williams, there are three rules the ship must uphold: first, not forcing those of one religion to join the prayers of another religion; second, not suppressing the rights of those of a religion to worship in their own way; and third, understanding and mutually consenting to the authority of the ship's captain for the purpose of executing justice properly so that the ship may fulfill its purpose of reaching its destination. Only persons who disturb the safety and undermine the operation of the ship are worthy of punishment. No person is prohibited from participating in common life by virtue of the shared similarity of all rational persons cooperating together.

While Williams's argument has its limits when overlaid on today's most fraught moral conflicts, especially those in which religious liberty conflicts with rival conceptions of human autonomy, his illustration demonstrates how a diverse society can attain "civil cooperation" through "mutual obligation," a peace and solidarity pact amid religious and moral pluralism.[40] According to Williams, natural law allows each religious adherent to ascertain, if even minimally, the necessary moral and ethical requirements for social stability. This idea is similar to John Rawls's "overlapping consensus" framework, which has subsequently dominated debate on the concept of moral discourse in pluralistic settings.[41] If anything, Williams's illustration demonstrates that Christians inhabit a "shared moral space" with individuals unlike them in their theological convictions but like them in possessing moral aptitude.[42]

Contra Rawls and to underscore Williams's point, individuals in the same moral space can uphold their "comprehensive doctrines" and yet live with a shared recognition of others' rights to make similar moral and religious liberty claims. The ability to live by one's comprehensive doctrines is part of one's ability to make contestable claims to another—not to "dominate" another but to lovingly persuade through moral discourse.[43] Religious liberty thus helps solve the dilemma of how diverse individuals can peaceably coexist amid differing moral claims without nullifying the reality that individuals, as religious creatures, are poised to make religious arguments, and that religious arguments are not inherently irrational or inapplicable to society since all persons possess, in the words of Williams, "civill and morall goodness."[44] This sense of commonality is where religious liberty, general revelation, and a concept of contestability central to advancing Christian moral witness come together. According to James Calvin Davis, Williams is instructive for modernity because his approach to religious liberty as a component of civil peace assumed contestability: "The hope for public moral conversation depends on mutual exchange, openness to the criticism and interpretation of the other, and an effort at sharedness that may include the approximate 'translation' of certain norms and values into language that conversation partners may understand, if not adopt."[45]

Thus, at the center of religious liberty is a reliance on debate. The church's mission is one of not only proclamation but also debate. In the throes of debate, when parties are equally open to being confronted with truth, the free exchange of ideas ensures a plane of civility and respect.

Christian mission cannot wall itself off. It must proactively engage with its surroundings. The question of translating religiously motivated moral discourse intersects with the challenge posed by

Rawlsian liberalism and "public reason"[46]—namely, its settled rejection of allowing "comprehensive doctrines" into political discourse.[47] Were Rawlsian liberalism to have its way, Christian moral discourse, the type that calls for repentance based on the moral demands of Christ's kingdom, would be rendered ineligible for participation, and, by default, Christianity's mission would be curtailed. The task of religious communication becomes an issue, fundamentally, of religious liberty. A view toward advancing mission must confront the challenge of secularism's and liberalism's objections to religious discourse. This, in effect, is a challenge to religious liberty and entails the question, Should Christians obey the demands of secularism and liberalism and renounce religious discourse and Christian moral argument in public debate? In the interest of furthering a vision of religious liberty that is true to the tenets of religious conviction, the answer should be no.

How Religion Functions in Public Argument

According to Harlan Beckley, "The freedom to agree to a public conception of justice does not prevent Christians (or others) from advocating their beliefs and accompanying way of life to other persons, individually or collectively, as long as they do not attempt to enforce that way of life through the basic structure of society."[48] While it is certainly the case that persons in society will contest what is "just," this does not elide the justificatory grounds for religious argument. It invites outward reasoned deliberation based on internalized religious premises. A commitment to public discourse that is publicly accessible does not negate the possibility of distinctly Christian argument in the public square. This raises an important question: How, in the paradigm explained here, does Christian moral discourse deliberate and operate in the public square so that the work of mission and moral argument can occur?

No topic is more fraught in American life than the relationship between religion and politics. Someone's understanding of the American experiment often hinges upon their understanding of how the two relate: Is America a mostly secular nation that should eschew religious influence? Or, does religion play an important role in America's legacy in terms of its values and national identity?

Thinkers such as President John Adams and philosopher Alexis de Tocqueville argued that religion is central to the American experiment of ordered liberty. But that raises the question of how religion is to function. There are two primary ways: (1) Religion provides a system of morality necessary to teach virtue and re-strain vice among its people, making self-government possible; (2) religion provides a metaphysical account of moral norms that government looks to in order to make sense of its authority, pur-pose, and obligations. Hence, the Declaration of Independence speaks of mankind's "unalienable rights" being "endowed by their Creator." Religion plays a vital role in making sense of the political community we live in, the values we hold dear, and the type of society and culture we hope to foster.

But this raises an important question: How should religion function in a public argument? Does a Christian legislator have the grounds to argue for a policy by citing a Bible verse? Properly understood, yes. But behind this question is the issue of authority. Considering that America does not have an established religion, it means there is a range of competing authorities to determine what moral norms are binding on policy making. Christians do not accept the dictates of Islam, and Muslims do not believe in Christian Scripture. Moreover, we do not want laws that are intel-ligible to or agreed on only by members of one religion. But this raises the issue of how religious presupposition can influence or inform political and policy debates: Insofar as the issue at stake is something that is foundational, intelligible, applicable, and neces-sary to the ordering of a just society for all persons, it is perfectly fine for religion to play a part in our public and political discourse. Differing premises or moral foundations that result in a shared conclusion testify to the natural law. Law is meant to advance a rational purpose and conform actions to its standards *for all*. So how can religion play an important part in shaping public debate if Americans have differing accounts of how moral authority originates when it comes to law and policy?

Matthew J. Franck argues positively for the rights and abilities of people—even public officials—to make religious arguments when advocating for a specific policy. Religious adherents, he argues, need to explain how their religiously informed ethics relates not only to morality but to policy as well. Franck writes,

> There is no compelling reason in principle for religious citizens to refrain from employing religious discourse in the public square. They must, of course, reason together with their fellow citizens in order to persuade others of their policy views. But if their major premises, so to speak, are theological, there is no harm done, so long as their policy conclusions can be reasonably embraced by others who have different commitments.
>
> The attribution of a "strictly religious" motivation to a policy view offers an incomplete account of how people actually reason in political life. Beliefs that may be called "strictly" religious or theological typically supply only a major premise for a policy conclusion. The minor premise will usually be supplied by other considerations—of cost, of prudence or practicality, of justice to others, of forbearance toward those same others. Even "thou shalt not kill," for instance, is not a principle that by itself can lead straight to anything in public policy—not even a coherent homicide law—without intervening minor premises that will tell us when, how, and with regard to whom the principle will be applied.[49]

According to Franck, the blunt use of religion to bring about a specific policy in itself is not immediately intelligible, because, in a diverse country like America, it is not only possible but even likely that someone will disagree with your account of who God is and how God has been revealed. But different understandings of who God is do not prohibit overt references to religion; rather, as Franck argues, this merely reveals the need for an act of translation to occur.

He uses the Sixth Commandment as an example. The Sixth Commandment (Ex. 20:13), in Christian moral thought, not only prohibits murder but also commands Christians to act in ways that prosper and protect life. The idea that life is worth preserving and safeguarding to such a degree that prohibiting murder and establishing penalties for murder seems, on the surface, intelligible and rational. It may not be provable, but human experience would suggest that acting in ways that foster rather than harm life is praiseworthy. Not all moral principles are provable since they are underived and self-evident. To stay with this example, one need not be a Christian to understand that murder is wrong (Rom. 2:14–15).

What the Sixth Commandment teaches in the broadest possible application is that we should act in ways and codify laws that reflect a fundamental good of human nature: it is better to live than to be dead. So, a moral principle is on the immediate horizon, followed by application to a particular law or policy enacted to uphold the principle. The moral principle is that life is good, so act in ways that cause people to flourish. But, if we want to move from moral principle to public policy, we must decipher how moral abstractions can become particularized in law. This process is why, in American contexts, we have legal distinctions between first-degree murder, second-degree murder, third-degree murder, and manslaughter to recognize variations in intentionality and culpability. Law is deduced and specified based on the underlying moral principle. What this means is that simply saying "The Sixth Commandment should be a law" gives minimal specificity as to how to apply the underlying moral principle in particular cases. We need to utilize wisdom and prudence to apply the broad principle of the Sixth Commandment in specific cases.

We could repeat this logic for innumerable policy considerations: property law, contract law, family law, and political authority among them. When we talk about the application of religion to politics, it does not mean that laws on marriage, for example, are designed with the intention to explicitly honor Genesis 1–2 because everyone in America accepts Genesis 1–2 as authoritative. That surely is not the case, given the diversity of perspectives in America. But from the interior perspective of Christianity, when a nation's laws get marriage right, we say so because Christians believe that the picture of marriage in Genesis 1–2 is creational. We believe that principles of natural law, derived from and compatible with the Christian moral tradition, are relevant to all political communities and are essential properties for the just ordering of society and the common good.

The idea of natural law ethics is that there are binding moral principles, governed by reason and attested to in nature, that all persons, regardless of whether they are Christians or not, are obligated to obey for their own sake and God's. Marriage in Scripture bears witness to a creational reality. And that's the context where most discussions of how Christians relate to the political sphere begin: the portrait of reality given in creation is not "Christian reality" but reality as it truly is.

Thus, when Christians insist on laws upholding the dignity of the unborn or seeking justice for victims of human trafficking, we do so because concepts like dignity reflect a principle of morality that is binding on all persons. Christians believe this is true regardless of whether a person accepts the specific teaching that humans are made in God's image. Every person possesses innate dignity and should have that dignity recognized and protected by the law. Someone may agree with this by appeal to revelation, or they may assert the same idea on other grounds, or they may reject the idea altogether. This is because the existence of human dignity is either true for all or false for everyone. Furthermore, because we believe that God's common grace gives all persons an ineradicable sense of right and wrong, we believe that society can attain a reasonable morality to allow for its continued existence.

Public policy, from the perspective of Christian thought, incorporates themes of Christian ethics at the broadest possible level. To say that Christians should care about public policy and make arguments *as* Christians in the public square is not to say that Levitical laws on sacrifices or Deuteronomic civil laws are going to make their way into federal statute. Nor should they, as Levitical laws foreshadow Christ and Deuteronomic laws dissolved with the passing of the Israelite theocracy. No, only those moral principles of broadest application to the public square are relevant to public policy, and then particularized to meet the needs of those living within a political community. It means we have a duty to explain and articulate the inner workings of Christian moral thought and how they relate to an issue of public significance.

So do not be fooled. Banal, oft-quoted statements such as "You cannot legislate morality" are meant to intimidate religious persons while smuggling in nonneutral secular morality. Far from being "neutral," such arguments unfairly tilt public discourse in the direction of the nonbeliever, which violates the spirit of the First Amendment. The secularist and religious believer have just as much say in making their arguments in the public square. Those with the best, most persuasive arguments deserve to win out on matters of public concern.

Faith is not opposed to reason in matters of moral claims but is simply antecedent. It is the responsibility of the religious actor to demonstrate why any ethical claim is sensible in the realm of culture and public policy. Whether religious or nonreligious, all possess a moral aptitude. The use of religious presuppositions in moral debate does not mean that an argument is futile or groundless or that the argument is untrue. For example, a religious argument for proving the Trinity in public debate is not the same type of argument as one supporting or opposing capital punishment on religious grounds. Prudential and principled deliberation about the application of religious argument is obviously necessary, and so nothing about a religious argument qua religion is necessarily illegitimate. An argument will strike at the level of reason and instinct in its persuasiveness regardless of whether the argument is religious in nature. Furthermore, the pursuit of religious neutrality in public argument says more about the person requiring debate on such grounds than it does about the merits of a religiously originated argument. The claim that public reason or "neutrality" can attain a perfect common ground is as unattainable as it is unreasonable.

According to Nicholas Wolterstorff, "No comprehensive vision—be it religious or not, be it of God and the good, or only of the good—no comprehensive vision can properly serve as the basis of public reason on fundamental political questions."[50] Wolterstorff's argument is that public reason is an idealized view of society that does not reconcile with people's experiences regarding how moral conclusions are reached.[51] There is no universalized political grammar that can adequately capture the complexity of how humans actually argue and experience life. He is surely correct to see public reason as its own form of overrealized political eschatology. The requirement that moral debate occur within artificially imposed and religiously sanitized constraints such as "neutrality" does not do justice to the moral deliberation of humans, whose reason is more often than not informed by the authority of transcendence and contexts that shape the moral imagination. What, then, comes of Christians making moral arguments in the public square? The duty of Christians becomes explaining in earnest the contours and contents of their beliefs and moral conclusions in hopes that their interlocutor will be open to understanding, if not persuasion.

The call for Christian moral argument in the public square is not a call exclusively to natural law. It can never be less than an appeal to natural law or reason, but it must be more if it is an ethic that is truly Christian. The backing of Christian moral witness in the public square must be grounded on an authority outside mere reason, not because Christian morality is irrational but because individuals are capable of responding to transcendence as much as they are to reason. According to the witness of the apostle Paul, every individual, even those who would call themselves atheists, recognizes some aspect of transcendence, regardless of whether such transcendence is ever admitted (Rom. 1:18–32).

The task of Christian moral witness, strengthened by a liberty to bear such a witness, serves to advance Christian mission by opening up society to the realities of Christian truth. As James K. A. Smith writes, "The public task of the church is not just to remind the world of what it (allegedly) already knows (by 'natural' reason) but to proclaim what it couldn't otherwise know—and to do so as a public service for the sake of the common good."[52]

Thus, Christian social witness is under no obligation to surrender its message in order to play by the rules of public reason. The state and society need the comprehensive doctrines issuing from religious claims in order to prevent the state from enacting a perverse form of secular orthodoxy.[53]

Engaging in moral deliberation in a pluralist society requires two tasks. First, the Christian must profess—honestly—what they believe on any given matter. Second, they must be committed to explaining, as well as possible, the grounds of that belief and to translating how the religious grounds of an ethical conviction relate to the non-Christian.

Christians can find great opportunity for witness among the procedural rules of liberal democracy if they will courageously wield the freedoms it provides and call foul when the system is rigged with nonneutral biases. We should not be so naive to believe that proponents of liberal democracy are without their smuggled-in biases. Christian accounts of modernity or liberal democracy that make it an enemy of Christianity fail to acknowledge that Christianity's own participation in liberal democracy is an extension of its commitment to its mission. This is the catch-22 of liberal democracy's critics: they are criticizing a system of government that maintains and invites the freedom to criticize it by placing burdens on the state, not religion, to justify its actions. Participating in liberal democracy is not a surrender to sanitized notions of moral discourse. For citizens of a shared political order, a commitment to proclamation is a commitment to upholding the political order that makes proclamation possible, even if it means, at times, transgressing the so-called neutral boundaries imposed by liberal democracy in order for liberal democracy to be the best version of itself. According to Richard John Neuhaus,

> It means quite simply that the Church proclaims its message of salvation to all but that it also feels morally bound to uphold the consensus on which civilized public order is built. To endorse a shared loyalty which falls short of a Christian's loyalty to the gospel is not a betrayal and does not imply thinking of society in amoral, quasi-mechanical, terms as being driven by "internal dynamics rather than led by moral purposes." It is to deny only the kind of claims commonly made by upholders of the ideal of "Christendom," implicitly affirming a Christian duty to seek to shape society and political forms.[54]

Social Stability as Christian Mission

A nation that fosters religious liberty will be a nation open to religious proclamation that is practiced peaceably. There will be a commitment to settling debates through nonviolent means. From this vantage point, religious liberty is an expression of God's common grace because it allows religious difference in society to attain a minimal account of social harmony and tranquility. This social tranquility enables individuals to pursue the actions sustainable to human flourishing. Religious liberty "opens up the space in which individuals can pursue the spiritual life as they understand it."[55] As a tool of Christian mission applied to society more broadly, religious liberty enhances social tranquility by fostering the conditions of equality, justice, and civility.

Appealing to book 19, chapter 17 of Augustine's *City of God* as a heuristic device, we can see that an ethic of religious liberty as mission ought to take advantage of a nation's stability to advance the mission of Christ.[56] This passage may be one of the most important nonbiblical arguments for understanding religious liberty as an ethic of mission.[57] The focus of chapter 17 is on what produces peace and discord between the city of God and the earthly city.

According to Augustine, the earthly city strives after a temporal earthly peace in order that society might prosper, what Augustine calls an "ordered concord of civic obedience and rule in order to secure a kind of cooperation of men's wills for the sake of things which belong to this moral life."[58] Those belonging to the city of God strive after an earthly peace while also knowing that their eternal hope is secured in Christ. The city of God makes use of the laws of the earthly city for its own benefit—a shared peace and tranquility—but for different ends.[59] This shared peace secures "a common sense of membership for Christian and unbeliever alike."[60] The secular state is not the "neutral state" but merely a peaceful state. Neutrality as a theological principle is untenable. When the city of God and the earthly city strive toward mutual peace, "a harmony is preserved between them" pertaining to the conditions of life in a fallen world.[61]

Augustine acknowledges that the earthly city is marked by great divergence as to religion. Crucially, he then observes that because of the diversity within a penultimate secular era, "it has not been possible for the Heavenly City to have laws of religion in common with the earthly city."[62] This is not to say that a nation's laws are precluded from aligning with God's moral law; rather, it is to acknowledge that the earthly city's purpose in enacting law precludes it from prescribing laws directing humanity toward its ultimate religious end, since pronouncing what constitutes the religious end of humanity is outside a government's jurisdiction.

At times, the city of God must dissent from the customs of the earthly city, which may disturb the peace and provoke persecution. The city of God, in Augustine's framework, continues to advocate for social harmony and prosperity to every length possible insofar as the laws do not "impede the religion by which we are taught that the one supreme and true God is to be worshipped."[63] Here Augustine upholds the importance of the city of God's free exercise. The city of God upholds the worthwhileness of social tranquility in whatever its context, striving after earthly peace. But for what end is the earthly peace ordered? "Indeed, she directed that earthly peace toward heavenly peace: towards the peace which is so truly such that—at least so far as rational creatures are concerned—only it can really be held to be peace and called such. For this peace is perfectly ordered and perfectly harmonious fellowship in the enjoyment of God, and of one another in God."[64]

According to Augustine, then, Christians make use of laws that benefit the mass of fallen society in order to facilitate humanity toward its ultimate end—fellowship with God. Augustine operates on two planes simultaneously. He understands the integrity and purposefulness of earthly law, for its own sake, for the prosperity and peace it offers inhabitants. Yet a deeper motive undergirds Augustine's appreciation for the stability of law—namely, that Christians can leverage social harmony and social tranquility for eternal purpose. Augustine believes that earthly cooperation and the maintenance of civil order that law provides should be stewarded toward humanity's ultimate end: salvation.

Augustine's view of social cooperation is instrumental and, in that sense, penultimate. Christians take advantage of the context in which they live in order to advance that context and ecosystem toward redemption. As I wrote earlier, the state plays an indirect role in helping citizens obtain spiritual good. It promotes access to the common good only and offers a horizon to its citizens to obtain the spiritual and ultimate good (as they grasp it). The state removes obstacles to the pursuit of the spiritual good by upholding access to the common good (1 Tim. 2:1–2). We are to care about just laws, but for the sake of using just laws to point people toward their ultimate telos. This happens while occupying the same saeculum, or secular age. How so? According to Markus, "For the citizen of the heavenly city, concern for the saeculum is the temporal dimension of his concern for the eternal city."[65] We use temporal laws for the heavenly city's benefit. This means, in effect, that Christians are to "recognize penultimate convergence even where there is ultimate divergence."[66] Christians are to cooperate in seeing just laws established while recognizing that the loyalties of the earthly city and the city of God are at odds. When Jesus says his kingdom is not of this world, such an antithesis should remind us of the ultimate divergence between the earthly city and the city of God but also of the possibility of penultimate convergence. As both seek the common good, the common good facilitates access to the spiritual good. A Christian politics, then, ought to be more focused on the common good than seeing the order radically transformed. Social orders do not get saved; they get influenced. The former is a politics of incremental, specific realism; the latter is a politics of ambiguous, utopian triumph.

We cannot pursue a political Gnosticism that holds that there is a platonic ideal to politics that does not require engaging the kingdoms of this world for what they fundamentally are: worldly, fallen, and temporal, but also creational ordinances ordained by God for achieving proximate justice. Such political realism does not mean Christians can enter the political arena like everyone else, acting as bullies, charlatans, or hacks. It means that political orders, as such, do not care about or recognize our primary heavenly citizenship. Our heavenly citizenship, of course, is the truest reality that reconfigures our orientation to political matters, but it does not alleviate us of the responsibilities of statecraft. A Christian politics is one of subordinating the powers, not repudiating their legitimate, temporal, and preservationist rule. A Christian politics refuses to ascribe to the political orders a power that is not theirs to begin with. Even still, the city of God acts amid the earthly city where an ultimate divergence of loves and loyalties still allows for a temporal and penultimate convergence of justice.

Those with an awareness of ultimate divergence do not cordon off the state and its policy makers from the claims of the gospel. They confront both, asking policy makers to craft policies and rule on the basis of justice. While an entailment of this chapter is that governments should not be religiously confessional, this does not omit the reality that legislators and policy makers bring their own religious and ideological commitments to the task of governing, commitments that are far from neutral. According to Lesslie Newbigin, "It is the duty of the church to ask what those beliefs and commitments are and to expose them to the light of the gospel."[67] Government is always occupied by persons who are accountable to God and who therefore are open to the claims of the gospel. This means that government leaders and legal systems are within the purview of Christian mission. Christian mission may achieve success insofar as transformed consciences pass laws that are just and righteous (1 Kings 3:28). This can happen without formal "establishment" occurring.

Furthermore, Augustine's ethic sees a church living by faith in a fallen society but hoping that fallen society can attain a justly ordered peace whereby the means of transmitting the gospel are all the more free: "This peace the Heavenly City possesses in faith while on its pilgrimage, and by this faith it lives righteously, directing towards the attainment of that peace every good act which it performs either for God, or—since the city's life is inevitably a social one—for neighbor."[68]

How does Augustine's reflection inform religious liberty as mission in society? Christians care about utilizing religious liberty for the ultimate purpose of humanity's salvation while prioritizing it as an essential element for common life within the earthly city. Society is fractured, according to Augustine, but laws exist that provide for tranquility and the ability of the church to capitalize on these laws for divine purposes. In the view of Augustine, an eschatological division in both the era of time and who the people of God are does not inhibit, but actually animates, the activity of mission in society. Much like Jeremiah in his admonition to exiled Israelites to "seek the welfare of the city," Augustine grounds participation in the social order on the basis of social order itself yet with the possibility of the social order itself unwittingly participating in the mission of God by opening itself up to the gospel. The openness of society to religious truth means that "religion can remind us all of a good that encompasses and then transcends political life. Only religion can remind us that the temporal ultimately answers to the eternal."[69] All of this means that a Christian view of religious liberty sees the liberty to engage in Christian mission as one mediated through public discourse and political debate "without threatening the autonomy of the secular."[70]

Conclusion

Religious liberty is a necessary component for the unhindered advance of the gospel. To be sure, the gospel finds fertile soil wherever the Spirit of God moves, even in authoritarian contexts. But there is no virtue in seeking out persecution. If persecution comes, let it come, and let those who follow Christ receive it with honor (Acts 5). But the reality of persecution does not nullify the need for religious freedom; it intensifies it.

The gospel is never disconnected from the means through which the gospel advances. In 2 Corinthians, Paul is clear: he is pleading for his audience to be reconciled with God (5:17–21). May that be the church's declaration too. When the church understands what is at stake in how the gospel is advanced, it should want to remove every obstacle to making new disciples and new creations in Christ.

To believe one's convictions authentically without fear of reprisal, one needs a social context that views the conscience as an inviolable force for integrated human fulfillment. To live out one's faith, one needs a social context that caters to religious freedom. To advance the gospel, one needs a social context that is not threatened by religion.

A proper understanding of the relationship between the kingdom of God and the image of God culminates in a paradigm that sees religious liberty as a critical ingredient to the advance of human happiness, social tranquility, and, supremely, God's mission on earth.

Conclusion

Retrieving a Tradition for the Common Good

The Future of Statecraft and Religious Liberty

Elevating the significance of religious liberty means that it must become a foundational pillar of our engagement. It means that Christians who live in a particular national context—who inhabit a location and citizenship on earth while also claiming that their truest political authority is Jesus Christ and their truest membership is within the body of Christ (Acts 17:6–7; 1 Tim. 3:15)—should desire that their neighbors inhabit a nation-state that promotes human rights, human dignity, and just order in accordance with God's moral law and creation ordinances.

Christians should desire such things in hopes of securing what the founders referred to as the ideals of "domestic tranquility" and the "general welfare." This phrase testifies to a broader, deeper biblical principle that rulers are "to punish those who do evil and to praise those who do good" (1 Pet. 2:14). A Christian social ethic desires to ennoble that which is "good" in keeping with the rule

213

written on the heart (Rom. 2:14–15). This means that indifference or hostility toward the political environments and outcomes that impact our global neighbors is an abdication of Christian social responsibility for one's neighbor. Surely, Jesus's response to the question "Who is my neighbor?" (Luke 10:29) beckons the Christian to a sober-minded concern for the nation-state on the global stage. The love of one's neighbor can never be divorced from the political realities and implications that produce either loving or unloving results.

Within the Christian political tradition, the state is a divine ordinance (Rom. 13:1–7), necessary even in a sinless state. The state is meant for the good of its people, and thus the social situatedness that Christians find themselves in means that there is a responsibility and a stewardship to see good and justice instantiated. The reality of the state is a call to vigilance, gratitude, and responsibility under the umbrella of God's providence. A socially responsible Christian ethic understands that the ordinance of the state—even in a fallen world—calls for prophetic scrutiny in hopes that the state will be brought more and more in alignment with civic and moral righteousness.

We are living in a time when citizens of nearly every country in the world are turning inward and growing suspicious of international order. But Christians must recognize that while we have an earthly citizenship, the solidarity of Christian community means that citizens of a heavenly kingdom (Phil. 3:20) transcend the natural limits of the nation-state while also working within the parameters of the nation-state on one another's behalf. This is a tension in which God calls Christians to live. In lobbying for a more just nation-state for others, I am doing what I hope my Christian brothers and sisters would do for me in the context of their own nation-states (Matt. 7:12). We all have a role to play. The job of the missionary is to proclaim and share the gospel, and it is the job of the lawyer and ethicist to till the soil of the political environment so that conditions allow the gospel to be spread without hindrance or obstacle. While Christians dutifully insist that God's gospel will go forward with his providential decree, it is right to see ourselves as instruments of his will who will fight for values within the nation-state that call the nation-state to the best, most just form of itself.

A Final Word

On a cold, rainy Friday a few years ago, my wife and I and a few friends from church gathered for a night of worship sponsored by a Christian organization that works with local Christian artists in our former town. At the end of the evening, the individual emceeing the night closed with an impassioned prayer in which he expressed gratitude to God for the liberty to join together with other believers to worship Christ without fear of government harassment. There was palpable gratitude in this man's voice for the freedom to worship.

This gathering did not have to be registered with the government, which is tragically the case in other countries. We entered and left in peace without a hint of fear of whether we would be "exposed" as Christians. Upon leaving, I knew I would be free to utilize social media to share the event's details without fear of censorship. Moreover, that weekend I would be free to go to church and hear a sermon on why Christians should seek to influence their culture, whether related to the sanctity of life, racial reconciliation, or any other issue of ethical controversy in the culture. While I am accustomed to sermons and prayers in which gratitude to worship freely is expressed, hearing a prayer that gave God praise for religious liberty while writing this book struck me anew, and it dawned on me that this book was not just a rote academic exercise.

Something pivotal about my existence as a Christian and my participation in a local body is bound up with the liberty to live faithfully in accord with God's call on my life and my family's life. Religious liberty is not the gospel. That night, however, I was reminded that my experience of the gospel assumes a freedom I so often ignore and even neglect to be thankful for. Religious liberty fans the flames of personal holiness and proclamation. It gives breath to the life of a local congregation gathering together every Sunday to declare that Jesus Christ is king.

I was reminded and convicted that night of how trite, routine, and domesticated religious liberty is in my own mind—as an American, I know nothing other than religious liberty. That is one of the challenges to religious liberty in an American context—Americans are so accustomed to it that they may not recognize when its pillars are slowly eroding.

But why this book? Because the task of Christian thought includes both retrieval and proclamation. Christian reflection on religious liberty is as old as Christianity itself. But unless it is rehearsed and given fresh expression and articulation in new contexts, it can fall by the wayside. Karl Marx was believed to have said, "Take away a people's roots, and they can easily be moved."[1] This book has been an exercise is exposing the roots of freedom found in Christianity. Christians need to be presented with arguments for the defense of their own liberty but also the liberty of others—for securing the liberty of others ensures the security of our own. This need for ethical apologetics is true of every age.

At this writing, religious liberty in America is entering a new age beset with challenges and opposition that call into question a once-sacred consensus. By grounding religious liberty in eschatology, anthropology, and missiology, I hope that this contribution to the field of Christian social ethics can be but one resource that helps to usher in a new era of Christian preoccupation with religious liberty.

May the Christian church return to its first love, a primal fortitude that allows us to turn the other cheek and confidently, under pressure, insist that no worldly scheme can push back the onward advance of Christ's invasion—for Christianity needs neither the state nor the culture for its truthfulness and efficacy. The liberty Christians seek, and the liberty Christians use, is a liberty to seek a city that is not yet and to allow those in the church's midst to join it in the promise of its coming (Heb. 13:14).

Any claim or pursuit of religious liberty must always point to its telos: the advancement of God's kingdom. In the spirit of our missionary faith, let each of us, like the apostle Paul, go about "proclaiming the kingdom of God and teaching about the Lord Jesus Christ with all boldness and without hindrance" (Acts 28:31).

Epilogue

Liberal Democracy
and Religious Liberty

Does Religious Liberty Require Liberal Democracy?

One of the necessary questions that follows from this book's argument is whether liberal democracy is the ideal political arrangement for religious liberty. This question is particularly relevant because a large swath of religious conservatives—Catholic and Protestant alike—are calling into question the origins and continued viability and legitimacy of liberal democracy.

If a person accepts the reality of pluralism within a secular age and the theologically legitimate separation of church and state, they would be right to conclude that something *like* liberal democracy would emerge from the paradigm put forth in this book. I say this exercising great caution, fearing that I may be interpreted as making liberal democracy *biblical*. My intention is not to baptize liberal democracy but rather to state that when forms of government emerge that create a strict institutional distinction between a religious body and a government, such arrangements are just and biblically ordered. This does not mean that religious liberty is always properly manifested. Take, for example, England, with its established church. England would surely be considered a part of the liberal democratic order, yet its legacy is one of religious establishment. The reference to "liberal democracy" is a distraction from the larger, tectonic aspects of my argument.

When liberal democracy promotes, rather than hinders, a system of laws that allows for a robust conception of religious liberty to flourish, liberal democracy is acting in accord with biblical sanction. This is not to say that liberal democracy is the imagined ideal of Scripture or what Scripture portends. I would be satisfied with a host of hypothetical political arrangements, were those arrangements to ably allow individuals to exercise their faith apart from arbitrary government interference. Rather, because the Bible demands no particular *form* of government other than one that understands itself as limited, wherever the principles of religious liberty emerge that are consistent with the preceding chapters' arguments, that government is acting justly and biblically.

I say this out of an abundance of prudence with an eye looking backward and forward. History documents torrid harms that resulted when government was overly cozy with religion. Politicized Christianity can result in hypocritical Christianity, and government-backed religion deadens vibrant faith by domesticating it and reconciling it to the needs of regime and culture. To be candid, I cannot look back nostalgically at any arrangement in America's past and see it without error. Such is the paradoxical reality of living in fallen social orders. So-called golden ages are nostalgic myths. At its Judeo-Christian zenith, America's record on race was nothing short of an abysmal tragedy. And as America secularizes, new waves of Christian vibrancy are finding creative ways to thrive as a counter-polis. As of this writing, a postliberal spirit is enveloping many religious conservatives with the luster of social cohesion. Behind much of this spirit is a wish for government to offer a more rich and robust conception of the common good, to have religion at the center of society's life. I do not disagree that religion is urgent and vital to protect the project of liberal democracy; what I want to warn against is that the adoption of a policy that serves a Christian interest today can just as easily be turned against Christianity tomorrow. It is better, prudentially speaking, to be a provisional loser today while appealing to constitutional democracy than be an indefinite political prisoner tomorrow. The freedoms now exploited by some continue to be the same freedoms that allow—at least for the foreseeable future—individuals, families, and churches to pursue the religious goods that bring meaning to their lives. It is undeniable that a militant secularism wishes to narrow the plane where those religious goods are pursued. In response, I simply suggest that we make better and more beautiful arguments—to speak with intoned passion against illiberalism while at the same time embodying in our communities of contrast the ideals we hope to see others embody as well. Liberty will not be enhanced 280 characters at a time on Twitter; it will be enhanced when unlikely partners of goodwill work together to push for a society that is more honest, more civil, and, at times, yes, more willing to expose the most virulent illiberal forces in society.

Make Liberal Democracy Christian Again?

But a question hangs in the background: Whose liberal democracy? The vision for liberal democracy envisioned in this book is one owing to the moral capital of Christianity's transcendent truth claims—a vision for government anchored in the ideal of limited government, human dignity, and a commitment to ordered liberty. The best of liberal democracy allows communities of persons to be free to live lives of virtue apart from arbitrary government edict. Such a vision stands in stark contrast to criticisms of liberal democracy that depict it as cruelly contractarian, obsessed with maximized and autonomized "rights" that stand against the bonds of community and religiously grounded morality.

Today, liberal democracy affords the best framework available for the principles contained in this book. There are no better achievable alternatives on the horizon, especially not those that would severely undermine religious freedom (postliberalism, secularism, fundamentalist Islam), that seem capable of brokering the level of social tranquility that liberal democracy obtains, even as liberal democracy convulses from its transcendent origins being whittled away.

Even still, this does not mean that liberal democracy contains the seeds within its own philosophy to prevent abuse and the abandonment of its own principles—for example, "rights" becoming subjectively defined as whatever the reigning moral zeitgeist deems acceptable ("right to abortion," "right to die," etc.). Liberal democracy is precarious and delicate and must be nourished by the ideas of mediating institutions, like Christianity, that were the seedbeds of the best forms of liberal democracy, forms emphasizing ordered liberty, virtue, natural law, the rule of law, and constitutional democracy. The late Roger Scruton described the freedoms wrought through the Christian-influenced Enlightenment as "fragile" and "threatened" and averred that their continued success "depended upon a cultural base that it [the Enlightenment] could not itself guarantee. Only if people are held together by stronger bonds than the bond of free choice can free choice be raised to the prominence that the new political order promised. And those stronger bonds are buried deep in the community, woven by custom, ceremony, language and religious need. Political order, in short, requires cultural unity, something that politics itself can never provide."[1]

Scruton is doubtlessly right. "Choice" is not sufficient to sustain a political community, and when liberal democracy is defined as a philosophy designed to maximize debauchery and cast off the restrains of tradition, family, and religion, liberal democracy will not survive. Though the number of issues we hope to achieve a consensus on may be modest, if we all work together in goodwill to be more patient, more civil, and even more kind, we might create the "cultural unity" necessary for a free society. So by all means vote, but practice the virtues necessary for the attainment of liberty for all.

If liberal democracy succeeds in securing liberty and freedom, it will be the result of these Christian virtues. Where it collapses into moral anarchy and justificatory license, it will collapse into illiberalism. If liberal democracy is eclipsed, it will be the result of forces inimical to its foundations. Echoing Scruton, apart from the lasting influence of Christianity in a given ecosystem such as liberal democracy, I do not hold out long-term hope for religious liberty's continued viability. As of this writing, a militant, secular progressivism continues apace with a very clear intention of challenging and subjugating the moral claims of Christianity. To the extent that America embraces secular progressivism, it will turn its back on all forms of liberty except where voices in authority and the ballot box can restrain it.

How do religious conservatives persist in this climate? We continue to make arguments, hoping that persuasion is still possible. I want those who disagree with me to come into agreement with me on all matters of religion, morality, and politics. But knowing full well that the views of Christians are disfavored, I will accept the consolation of agreeing on political goals that allow the sorting out of differences to occur under law, not through violence. We hope for goodwill from our neighbors, and we should lobby and advocate for the types of political leaders that understand the connection between religious vitality and political freedom. If we do not, liberal democracy will recede, as would any political system unable to restrain the effects of sin's hold on the world.

Because I believe in a world marked by radical divergence, I can hope for and work to build a peaceable society that allows for modest conceptions of the common good to flourish without full agreement about society's metaphysical foundations. This is an accommodation I not only am willing to endure but also expect due to the reality of pluralism in society. Yet even with intractable disputes about when life begins or what constitutes a marriage, I believe enough in the image of God, the ineradicability of common grace, and the enduring existence of natural law to accept that a modicum of social stability is possible without every cast and character in society agreeing on the theological premises of these ideas. Insofar as natural law, justice, and religious liberty can be realized in society—even where imperfectly realized—there will be a sufficient account of morality, authority, and freedom necessary for social order.

I might find others' arguments about justice, morality, and liberty lacking in substantive coherence. I might even find them relying on the borrowed capital of a Christian moral grammar. But I am happy to indulge the inconsistencies of their worldviews if it means the furtherance of a society that is nonviolent, peaceable, and willing to open itself up to viewpoints it disagrees with presently yet may in the future be persuaded by. Such is a risk, but it is a trade-off I am willing to live with if my neighbor's freedom to live and believe differently is bound up with my own freedom to live and believe differently about life's ultimate questions.

Such an idea does not run contrary to political unity but rather lives with the reality that any given society comprises a "politics of multiple communities" within one larger umbrella community held together by a loosely developed conception of the common good.[2] Legal scholar John D. Inazu refers to this as shedding our expectation for deeply held moral agreement and grouping ourselves around "many-ness."[3] The ever elusive common good is attainable in society. It is attainable and realizable by any community of persons in society who commit themselves to transcendental foundations of the natural law. One can believe in a concept of the common good for civil society without government enforcing every last contour of it. Perhaps this is as it ought to be—the common good is a concept of subsidiarity, and the goods are recognized more densely the tighter one's community becomes. We need to understand that the very nature of human society means that voluntarist communities of home, church, and neighborhood will have richer conceptions of the common good than the broader political community. It is possible to pursue and fulfill the common good without government offering a heavy-handed declaration of all the finer points of what the common good must be. And I am glad about that, because I do not agree with what our government considers the common good. Government should never be in opposition to the common good, but it is also unable in itself to offer a heavy-handed definition that will resolve the diversity in its midst without doing more policing and damage as a result.

Members of a functioning and just society need not agree on premises or rationales for all policy measures in order for a modicum of justice to be realized. Individual persons might have different reasons for reaching the same conclusion about an important matter of policy. We should strive for an overlapping consensus on conclusions while hoping that agreement on the premises remains possible. Even still, the argument here does not solve the truly intractable disputes facing fractured political communities. The best that can be hoped for in such situations is a commitment to free speech, civility, and procedural norms that allow differences to be settled at ballot boxes, not in boxing rings.

This is why I continue to hold out the promise of natural law discourse as a form of engagement and communication with non-Christians that does not require Christians to abandon the foundations of their moral claims but instead merely requires them to make them publicly accessible. Short of accepting the reality of religious, moral, and political disagreement, Christians will find themselves in perpetual gridlock, with building resentment toward a society that fails to believe as it should. What we must internalize is that we do not need a confessional state in order to have a moral nation. The sooner we realize that, the sooner we will relieve ourselves of the fool's errand of trying to immanentize the eschaton for the nation-state.

Appendix

How Religious Liberty
Made Me a Baptist

I AM A LITTLE EMBARRASSED to admit this considering I am a professor at a prominent Baptist seminary, but I came to be a passionate Baptist not because I thought baptism by immersion was the most compelling foundation but because Baptist ecclesiology was the natural outcome of what I understood to be the correct theory and practice of religious liberty. That may sound confusing, so let me unpack it.

I grew up in central Illinois going to a Southern Baptist church. If you grew up outside the geographic South, you may have attended a Southern Baptist church without any real sense of it feeling explicitly Baptist. That is because in the North, at least in my experience, we did not understand ourselves as Baptist as much as just Bible-believing Christians. I remember going to the church we went to because, well, they believed the Bible without qualifying it a thousand times over with nuance and deference to our cultured despisers. In other words, they were not theological moderates or liberals. If you would have asked me as a teen if I were a Baptist, I would have answered yes, but only because I understood that I was not Catholic.

Feeling a call to ministry, I went to a Baptist college in southwest Missouri (Southwest Baptist University). Upon graduation, I went to the seminary where I now teach, the Southern Baptist Theological Seminary. At both institutions, I took Baptist history classes and became aware of our history and our theological distinctives, which I appreciated at the time but still did not feel overly zealous about. This was not the fault of the professors. In fact, looking back, I recall that my two Baptist history classes were well taught, and the professors were passionate about their subject. Perhaps owing to my general immaturity, ideas like regenerate church membership, believer's baptism, baptism by immersion, congregational authority, local church autonomy, and religious liberty did not really animate me. That does not mean I disagreed with them; I agreed with them because they seemed biblical. But ecclesiology was not front and center in my earlier theological angst. Questions about Calvinism, inerrancy, and the emergent church were front and center.

It was not until I "came of age" that my first jobs, incidentally, led me in a more fervently Baptist direction. My first jobs out of seminary were for think tank and advocacy organizations that focused on social conservative causes like the sanctity of life, marriage, and, well, *religious liberty*. Of course, I had heard of the issue, but at the time, I did not understand its urgency. What is now a token issue of concern for Christians was not so a decade ago. In 2008 to 2010, there was a different cultural climate. Many of the religious-liberty challenges we are encountering now were predicted, at the time, by documents like the Manhattan Declaration. This joint document of Catholic and Protestant luminaries declared in somber tones that were the government to continue its leftward lurch, a reassertion of religious-liberty rights would be necessary, as would the possibility of civil disobedience. I knew I was treading in deep, turbulent waters. I recall that as I was getting my feet beneath me careerwise, I was having to play catch-up on an issue that I was told was fundamental but was now threatened.

So I got to work in both Kentucky's capital and our nation's capital on, among other things, religious liberty. I was largely unfamiliar with it, aside from what little I had learned in my Baptist history classes. It certainly was not, at the time, the top-tier pillar or foundation to my public theology as it is now. I argued for it because, well, my job required me to. My work required me to read on the subject, and that is what I did. The heavy reading load in religious-liberty theory did not initially convince me of religious liberty's importance as much as my immersion into the advocacy world of social conservatism, which necessarily and rightly treated religious liberty as a lifeblood issue. Because I was enamored of the intersection of first principles, theology, and political philosophy, religious liberty afforded me the opportunity to merge topics I was already passionate about but on which my inchoate understanding still needed tuning.

As I would learn, the posture a state takes toward religion is one of the most decisive indicators of whether it will be broadly pluralistic and limited or tyrannical and coercive. I would also learn that unless you have the requisite liberties to act on your convictions, you cannot do much of anything, whether worship in your church or advocate in the public square. If one does not possess the freedom to act on one's most primary beliefs, one is not free in even the most basic sense of the word. The idea that persons are endowed with self-constituting capacities that endear them to religion made more and more sense. If religion informs morality, then morality in public life hinges on the doctrine of religious liberty. Life, I came to understand, entails various types of liberties (speech, association, religion) in order for it to be authentic, meaningful, and worthwhile. The presence of these liberties determines what type of life someone will have in their community. In short, religious liberty is deeply intertwined with human flourishing and the common good.

All of these questions about religion and society led to a flood of first-principle questions, among them the following:

- How does one understand what truth is?
- How does an individual come to grasp religious claims?
- What posture should the state take toward religion?
- How is one's quest to understand truth related to their personhood?
- What is the relationship between moral obligation and religious foundation?
- What are one's obligations to the state? To God?
- What are the jurisdictions and responsibilities of the state?
- What are the jurisdictions and responsibilities of the church?
- Who gets to decide who is right and wrong about such matters as religion and morality?
- What is the relationship between religious liberty and other liberties?

When I began to answer these questions, I was led to a distinctly Baptist ecclesiology. It was in the Baptist tradition, which had helped birth religious liberty in North America through the likes of Roger Williams and John Leland, that I saw the principles of religious liberty most fulsomely applied. How so? Because the questions above are best answered in light of key Baptist ecclesiastical distinctives that focus on the individual and the associations they form in life.

What I want to present is both a natural law case for religious liberty and its overlapping similarities with principles that emerge from Scripture. Like widening concentric circles, religious liberty is based on an understanding of (1) individual assent, (2) group association, and (3) institutional distinction. These are reflected in the practices of individual conversion and regenerate church membership, which entail a distinction between membership in the church and membership in society and between the institution of the gathered church and the institution of the state.

Individual Assent

As I began to understand religious liberty at its most philosophical core, I discovered an emphasis on the individual's stance before God: nothing is to stand between the individual and God, not the state or the family. Known as "soul competency," this was and is the most important principle of religious liberty from an anthropological perspective.

As free agents, individuals have to voluntarily accept religious truths based on their own grasp of those truths and their merits. Every individual, *on their own terms*, has to give an account of who they believe God to be. I cannot make that decision for others, nor can others make that decision by proxy for me. The reality of accountability and forewarning of judgment is baked into the idea of religious liberty. The New Testament speaks of a day of individual reckoning, and each person has to answer for their conscience (2 Cor. 5:10; Heb. 9:27). If God is the rightful judge, human institutions, on account of their own infallibility, cannot be. A person can be instructed and argued with, but their conclusion about who God is must be their own decision made with their own volition and will. A certain *individuality* punctuates religious liberty without devolving into *individualism*. Religious liberty implies a conversionary foundation, not religion by osmosis or absorption. Individuals have to arrive at conclusions consciously.

In my view, this means that forms of baptism and church membership that do not hinge on the individual's expressed faith are invalid. This is why Baptists emphasize the notion of being "born again" to enter the kingdom of God (John 3:3; 2 Cor. 5:17). Authentic faith is self-chosen and results in the growth of new affections. We do not merely shuttle between belief and unbelief. We believe a radical disjunction has occurred, for Christ has "delivered us from the domain of darkness and transferred us to the kingdom of his beloved Son" (Col. 1:13). This idea of conversionary primacy looms supreme in discussions on religious liberty because it understands both coercion and nominalism as coequal threats: If a religious body contains people who have not made the same profession of faith or who have made such a profession under false pretenses, how can I be sure that the community is composed of authentic believers united around the same truths and mission? This reality rules out any religious body that practices infant baptism, since infant baptism attempts to effectuate some type of covenant membership without individual assent even being possible. Baptism by immersion—which is what Baptists practice—reflects the conscious and conversionary nature of Christian identity.

Group Association

The necessity of justification on the basis of a personally believed faith led me to a very important conclusion in my ecclesiology: the best form of ecclesiology is one composed of only those individuals who have joined together under the same banner of explicit conviction and profession. Membership in the church is not just generic membership in a social organization. It involves a body of believers united around the same mission and purpose. Thus, only those believing the same truth about Jesus Christ should be baptized and recognized as members of the local church assembly. This is known as regenerate church membership and is the basis for believer's baptism, another key Baptist distinctive. Members who have not personally assented to Jesus's kingship and experienced regeneration are not true members of the church and not eligible for baptism. The church is not an exclusionary society, as salvation is available to all who call on Christ. It is, however, exclusive on the grounds that its makeup consists only of those sharing a commitment to common truths. Only those consciously expressing faith may be baptized, and they make up the true church. From there, regenerate church membership establishes the practice of church discipline, because it is only those members who are truly considered regenerate who are held accountable to the community's standards of sanctified fellowship.

The distinguishing marks of the church's essence and practices establish the need for religious liberty in order for the church to be true to its calling before God and humanity. The church has a separate authorization and separate practices from the society around it and the government above it. Christians intermingle with the rest of society while understanding themselves as sojourners and exiles.

Institutional Distinctions

Regenerate church membership implies that the church is not simply synonymous or coterminous with the state or society around it. One is not a Christian just because they live in a country influenced by Christianity. Rather, to be a Christian is to be part of a called-out body, the church, which is distinct from other types of associations and autonomous, another Baptist distinctive. The church, being an institution of professed faith marked by believer's baptism, exists by right of its own authorization, not because the state allows it or calls it into existence. The church and the state are both divinely authorized, but with distinct callings and jurisdictions. The church is on mission in society and is concerned with the eternal destiny of humanity; the state is concerned with temporal affairs, such as making sure that wrongdoing is punished and that laws exist that make society inhabitable. In past arrangements, in which the church and the state overlapped or were formally united, with one reinforcing and intermingling with the other, Christianity was conformed to the culture around it and used as a prop for social uniformity.

If someone were to ask me how to destroy a vibrant church, my answer would be to use a combination of infant baptism and church-state union. These, together, would unravel religious liberty by unraveling the cohesiveness of regenerate Christian identity and ecclesial distinction. In such cases, cultural preferences are deemed sufficient to make someone think they are a Christian, while church membership is diluted down to membership in society. One of the greatest arguments against the union of church and state is the history of the union of church and state, which produced dead churches and pseudo-Christians.

Conclusion

For fear of being misunderstood, I am not arguing that other ecclesiastical arrangements are hostile to religious liberty. I am thankful for godly Presbyterians, Lutherans, and others who stand for religious liberty. My argument is, rather, that a rightly ordered account of religious liberty bears the richest fruit within a Baptist ecclesiology.

Religious liberty implies a recognition that individuals make conscientious decisions to participate in group associations that have different requirements and different callings than the rest of society and the state. In my view, these truths lead one inside the walls of a Baptist church.

Notes

Acknowledgments

1. *True Detective*, season 1, episode 4, "Who Goes There," directed by Cary Joji Fukunaga, aired February 9, 2014, on HBO.

Introduction You Get to Decide What to Worship, Not Whether to Worship

1. David Foster Wallace, "This Is Water" (commencement address, Kenyon College, Gambier, OH, May 21, 2005, https://fs.blog/2012/04/david-foster-wallace-this-is-water/).

2. Wallace, "This Is Water."

Chapter 1 Religious Liberty as a Christian Social Ethic

1. Oliver O'Donovan, *Resurrection and Moral Order: An Outline for Evangelical Ethics* (Grand Rapids: Eerdmans, 1994), 12.

2. The popular misconception that religious liberty is first an issue of statecraft and secondarily a theological and ethical matter is represented in, for example, the declaration of Christian ethicist J. Philip Wogaman that "religious liberty is distinctively a political problem, however much it depends upon theological insight for principled solution." J. Philip Wogaman, *Protestant Faith and Religious Liberty* (Nashville: Abingdon, 1967), 148.

3. The two volumes that come closest to this endeavor are Os Guinness, *The Global Public Square: Religious Freedom and the Making of a World Safe for Diversity* (Downers Grove, IL: InterVarsity, 2013); and Jason G. Duesing, Thomas White, and Malcolm B. Yarnell III, eds., *First Freedom: The Beginning and End of Religious Liberty*, 2nd ed. (Nashville: B&H, 2016).

4. Thomas L. Pangle, "The Accommodation of Religion: A Tocquevillian Perspective," in *Religious Liberty in Western Thought*, ed. Noel B. Reynolds and W. Cole Durham (Grand Rapids: Eerdmans, 1996), 291.

5. Robert H. Mounce, *The New International Commentary on the New Testament: The Book of Revelation*, New International Commentary on the New Testament (Grand Rapids: Eerdmans, 1997), 251.

6. John David Hughey, "The Theological Frame of Religious Liberty," *Christian Century* 80, no. 45 (November 1963): 1365.

7. A. F. Carrillo de Albornoz, *The Basis of Religious Liberty* (New York: Association Press, 1963), 56.

8. Carrillo de Albornoz, *Basis of Religious Liberty*, 56.

9. Demonstrating how meager biblical and theological scholarship is surrounding religious liberty, I located only two volumes dedicated solely to religious liberty's theological and biblical underpinnings: Wogaman, *Protestant Faith and Religious Liberty*; and Carrillo de Albornoz, *Basis of Religious Liberty*. Both volumes were written in the 1960s, and neither author holds evangelical commitments to biblical authority and biblical inspiration. An edited volume by Baptist scholars explores different biblical facets of religious liberty but cannot be considered systematic or comprehensive. See Duesing, White, and Yarnell, *First Freedom*. Popular Christian author Os Guinness has contributed a volume to religious liberty, but the arguments contained therein are neither biblical nor theological in nature. Rather, Guinness situates religious liberty as a necessary component to uphold Western liberal order. See Guinness, *Global Public Square*. In addition, exhaustive searches have located only a handful of articles concerning biblical and theological foundations for religious liberty: Niels Søe, "The Theological Basis of Religious Liberty," *Ecumenical Review* 11, no. 1 (October 1958): 36–42; Hughey, "Theological Frame of Religious Liberty"; James E. Wood, "A Biblical View of Religious Liberty," *Ecumenical Review* 30, no. 1 (January 1978): 32–41; Amos Niven Wilder, "Eleutheria in the New Testament and Religious Liberty," *Ecumenical Review* 13, no. 4 (July 1961): 409–20; Rebecca C. Mathis, "The Roots of Religious Liberty in Scripture," *Sewanee Theological Review* 55, no. 4 (2012): 389–402; and Jim Spivey, "Separation No Myth: Religious Liberty's Biblical and Theological Bases," *Southwestern Journal of Theology* 36, no. 3 (1994): 10–16. One other additional resource is Barrett Duke's helpful chapter articulating the Christian basis for religious liberty. See Barrett Duke, "The Christian Doctrine of Religious Liberty," in *First Freedom: The Baptist Perspective on Religious Liberty*, ed. Thomas White, Jason G. Duesing, and Malcolm B. Yarnell III (Nashville: B&H, 2007), 83–110.

10. Wood, "Biblical View of Religious Liberty," 41.

11. Carl Emanuel Carlson, "Need for Study of the Biblical Basis of Religious Liberty," *Journal of Religious Thought* 16, no. 2 (1959): 141.

12. J. Budziszewski, ed., *Evangelicals in the Public Square: Four Formative Voices on Political Thought and Action* (Grand Rapids: Baker Books, 2006).

13. Budziszewski, *Evangelicals in the Public Square*, 18–19.

14. I am indebted to my doctoral supervisor, Russell D. Moore, for this insight.

15. For a scholarly look at Christianity's connection to human rights, see John Witte Jr. and Frank S. Alexander, eds., *Christianity and Human Rights: An Introduction* (Cambridge: Cambridge University Press, 2011); Kevin P. Lee, "Deeper Longings: The Relevance of Christian Theology for Contemporary Rights Theories," *Ave Maria Law Review* 3, no. 1 (2005): 289–302; Nicholas Wolterstorff, "Modern

Protestant Developments in Human Rights," in Witte and Alexander, *Christianity and Human Rights*, 155–72; and Nicholas Wolterstorff, *Justice: Rights and Wrongs* (Princeton: Princeton University Press, 2008).

16. Christopher Tollefsen, "Conscience, Religion and the State," *American Journal of Jurisprudence* 54, no. 1 (January 2009): 93–115.

17. Robert A. Markus, *Christianity and the Secular* (Notre Dame, IN: University of Notre Dame Press, 2006).

18. Carlson, "Need for Study of the Biblical Basis of Religious Liberty," 139.

19. Carl F. H. Henry, *Aspects of Christian Social Ethics* (Grand Rapids: Baker, 1964), 82.

Chapter 2 The Reign of Jesus Christ and Religious Liberty

1. George Eldon Ladd, *A Theology of the New Testament* (Grand Rapids: Eerdmans, 1993), 54.

2. George Eldon Ladd, *Gospel of the Kingdom: Scriptural Studies in the Kingdom of God* (Grand Rapids: Eerdmans, 1990), 19–20.

3. Ladd, *Gospel of the Kingdom*, 18.

4. Ladd, *Gospel of the Kingdom*, 19.

5. Ladd makes a helpful clarification: "The church is the people of the Kingdom but cannot be identified with the Kingdom." Ladd, *Gospel of the Kingdom*, 55.

6. For an in-depth study of the purpose and scope of state power in the New Testament, see Oscar Cullmann, *The State in the New Testament* (New York: Charles Scribner's Sons, 1956).

7. Carl F. H. Henry, *God, Revelation and Authority: God Who Speaks and Shows, Fifteen Theses*, vols. 2–4, 2nd ed. (Wheaton: Crossway, 1999), 4:612.

8. Russell D. Moore, *The Kingdom of Christ: The New Evangelical Perspective* (Wheaton: Crossway, 2004), 29.

9. I am indebted to my friend Jonathan Leeman for much of the preceding argument, which has come through personal conversation as well as Jonathan Leeman, *How the Nations Rage: Rethinking Politics in a Divided Age* (Nashville: Thomas Nelson, 2018); and Jonathan Leeman, *Political Church: The Local Assembly as Embassy of Christ's Rule* (Downers Grove, IL: InterVarsity, 2016).

10. Carl F. H. Henry, "An Ecumenical Bombshell," *Christianity Today*, September 15, 1967, 28.

11. Elisha Williams, "The Essential Right and Liberties of Protestants 1744," in *Political Sermons of the American Founding Era, 1730–1805*, ed. Sandoz Ellis, 2nd ed. (Indianapolis: Liberty Fund, 1998), 66.

12. Robert A. Markus, *Christianity and the Secular* (Notre Dame, IN: University of Notre Dame Press, 2006), 65.

13. Edmund P. Clowney, *The Church* (Downers Grove, IL: InterVarsity, 1995), 188.

14. John Piper, "Jesus Christ: The End and Ground of Tolerance," Desiring God, May 12, 2002, http://www.desiringgod.org/messages/jesus-christ-the-end-and-ground-of-tolerance.

15. Richard Mouw and Sander Griffioen make a similar argument in their taxonomy of pluralism. In commenting on what they call "directional pluralism," which

refers to the notion of diverse religions coexisting in society, they refer to the reality of judgment being in view when Christians discuss pluralism: "In emphasizing the importance of dialogue we do not mean to divert attention from the moral painful dimensions of directional pluralism. As we have already stated, a theocentric position treats all our human points of view as ultimately accountable to divine authority." Richard J. Mouw and Sander Griffioen, *Pluralisms and Horizons: An Essay in Christian Public Philosophy* (Grand Rapids: Eerdmans, 1993), 109.

16. John Piper, "Making Room for Atheism," Desiring God, August 10, 2005, http://www.desiringgod.org/articles/making-room-for-atheism.

17. S. M. Hutchens, "Toleration and Divine Forbearance," *Touchstone* 29, no. 4 (August 2016): 33–36.

18. Hutchens, "Toleration and Divine Forbearance," 33.

19. Hutchens, "Toleration and Divine Forbearance," 33.

20. Jason G. Duesing, "The End of Religious Liberty," in *First Freedom: The Beginning and End of Religious Liberty*, ed. Jason G. Duesing, Thomas White, and Malcolm B. Yarnell III, 2nd ed. (Nashville: B&H, 2016), 251.

21. Duesing, "End of Religious Liberty," 255.

22. Russell D. Moore, *Onward: Engaging the Culture without Losing the Gospel* (Nashville: B&H, 2015), 139.

23. Moore, *Onward*, 140–41.

24. Russell D. Moore, "Personal and Cosmic Eschatology," in *A Theology for the Church*, ed. Daniel L. Akin (Nashville: B&H Academic, 2007), 899.

25. According to Russell Moore, "Church/state separation means that the church does not bear Caesar's sword in enforcing the gospel, and that Caesar's sword is not to be wielded against the free consciences of persons made in the image of God" (Moore, *Onward*, 142). Undoubtedly, because the state does not have ultimate power but only subordinate power this side of the eschaton, widely divergent values will interface in the public square and the best one can hope for is a public square where ideas can compete. Interestingly, Glenn Moots makes a provocative argument that the theme of eschatology dictates every belief system's hospitality toward religious liberty. For more on this theme, see Glenn Moots, *Politics Reformed: The Anglo-American Legacy of Covenant Theology* (Columbia: University of Missouri Press, 2010), 10.

26. Moore, *Onward*, 145.

27. Evan Lenow, "Religious Liberty and the Gospel," in Duesing, White, and Yarnell, *First Freedom*, 115.

28. Paige Patterson, "Mutually Exclusive or Biblically Harmonious? Religious Liberty and Exclusivity of Salvation in Jesus Christ," in Duesing, White, and Yarnell, *First Freedom*, 36. On the use of the wheat and the tares parable in church history related to religious liberty and religious coercion, see E. Glenn Hinson, *Religious Liberty: The Christian Roots of Our Fundamental Freedoms* (Louisville: Glad River Publishing, 1991), 28–32.

29. For more on the parable of the wheat and the tares, see David L. Turner, *Matthew*, Baker Exegetical Commentary on the New Testament (Grand Rapids: Baker Books, 2008), 343–44; Leon Morris, *The Gospel according to Matthew*, Pillar

New Testament Commentary (Grand Rapids: Eerdmans, 1992), 355–58; Craig S. Keener, *A Commentary on the Gospel of Matthew* (Grand Rapids: Eerdmans, 1999), 385–90; and Craig L. Blomberg, *Matthew*, New American Commentary, vol. 22 (Nashville: Broadman, 1992), 218–20.

30. John Locke, *A Letter concerning Toleration*, ed. James H. Tully (Indianapolis: Hackett Publishing, 1983), 32.

31. Oliver O'Donovan, *The Desire of the Nations: Rediscovering the Roots of Political Theology* (New York: Cambridge University Press, 1999), 219.

32. O'Donovan, *Desire of the Nations*, 219.

33. The state is still making some type of moral commitment even if in a non-preferential way and without making an explicit religious commitment. For example, the state that permits abortion is meddling in divine matters by transgressing the moral law of God. A state can enact immoral policies, however, without committing itself, formally, to one religion.

34. I am indebted to the thought of Robert P. George for my insights on the natural law. For more, see the introduction of *Making Men Moral: Civil Liberties and Public Morality* (Oxford: Oxford University Press, 1993).

35. Carl F. H. Henry, *The Christian Mindset in a Secular Society: Promoting Evangelical Renewal and National Righteousness* (Portland, OR: Multnomah, 1984), 80.

36. Carl F. H. Henry, *Aspects of Christian Social Ethics* (Grand Rapids: Baker, 1964), 97–98. I am indebted to my friend and fellow Henryian Tim Walker for assistance with this insight.

37. Lenow, "Religious Liberty and the Gospel," 115.

38. John Leland, "The Rights of Conscience Inalienable," in *The Sacred Rights of Conscience: Selected Readings on Religious Liberty and Church-State Relations in the American Founding*, ed. Daniel Dreisbach and Mark David Hall (Indianapolis: Liberty Fund, 2010), 339.

39. Hendrikus Berkhof, *Christ and the Powers*, trans. John Howard Yoder, 2nd ed. (Scottdale, PA: Herald, 1977), 30.

40. Markus, *Christianity and the Secular*, 16.

41. This passage is a classic text often cited for giving limits to state power and legitimizing religious liberty. For examples, see Barrett Duke, "The Christian Doctrine of Religious Liberty," in *First Freedom: The Baptist Perspective on Religious Liberty*, ed. Thomas White, Jason G. Duesing, and Malcolm B. Yarnell III (Nashville: B&H, 2007), 103–4; and Steven D. Smith, *The Rise and Decline of American Religious Freedom* (Cambridge, MA: Harvard University Press, 2014), 21.

42. Francis J. Beckwith, *Politics for Christians: Statecraft as Soulcraft* (Downers Grove, IL: InterVarsity, 2010), 64.

43. Beckwith, *Politics for Christians*, 64.

44. Beckwith, *Politics for Christians*, 64.

45. Wayne A. Grudem, *Politics according to the Bible: A Comprehensive Resource for Understanding Modern Political Issues in Light of Scripture* (Grand Rapids: Zondervan, 2010), 25.

46. James K. A. Smith, *Awaiting the King: Reforming Public Theology* (Grand Rapids: Baker Academic, 2017), 76.

47. O'Donovan, *Desire of the Nations*, 92.

48. J. Smith, *Awaiting the King*, 76.

49. Cullmann, *State in the New Testament*, 18.

50. Cullmann, *State in the New Testament*, 37.

51. H. Richard Niebuhr, *Radical Monotheism and Western Culture: With Supplementary Essays* (San Francisco: Harper, 1960), 71.

52. O'Donovan, *Desire of the Nations*, 223.

53. Peter J. Leithart, *Against Christianity* (Moscow, ID: Canon Press, 2003), 136.

54. John Corvino, Ryan T. Anderson, and Sherif Girgis, *Debating Religious Liberty and Discrimination* (New York: Oxford University Press, 2017), 144.

55. Corvino, Anderson, and Girgis, *Debating Religious Liberty and Discrimination*, 144.

56. O'Donovan, *Desire of the Nations*, 219.

57. Duke, "Christian Doctrine of Religious Liberty," 100.

58. John David Hughey, "The Theological Frame of Religious Liberty," *Christian Century* 80, no. 45 (November 1963): 1365.

59. Leeman, *Political Church*, 374.

60. Hughey, "Theological Frame of Religious Liberty," 1365.

61. Duke, "Christian Doctrine of Religious Liberty," 95.

62. O'Donovan, *Desire of the Nations*, 140.

63. J. Philip Wogaman, *Protestant Faith and Religious Liberty* (Nashville: Abingdon, 1967), 64–65.

64. A. F. Carrillo de Albornoz, *The Basis of Religious Liberty* (New York: Association Press, 1963), 91.

65. James E. Wood, "A Biblical View of Religious Liberty," *Ecumenical Review* 30, no. 1 (January 1978): 40.

Chapter 3 Religious Liberty and Christian Secularism

1. O. Palmer Robertson, *The Christ of the Covenants* (Phillipsburg, NJ: Presbyterian and Reformed, 1980), 109–25.

2. Robertson, *Christ of the Covenants*, 111.

3. Robertson, *Christ of the Covenants*, 122.

4. For more on the Noahic covenant, see the helpful explanations in David VanDrunen, "The Two Kingdoms and the Social Order: Political and Legal Theory in Light of God's Covenant with Noah," *Journal of Markets and Morality* 14, no. 2 (Fall 2011): 445–62; and David VanDrunen, *Divine Covenants and Moral Order: A Biblical Theology of Natural Law* (Grand Rapids: Eerdmans, 2014), 95–132.

5. David VanDrunen, *Politics after Christendom: Political Theology in a Fractured World* (Grand Rapids: Zondervan, 2020), 186.

6. Jonathan Leeman, *Political Church: The Local Assembly as Embassy of Christ's Rule* (Downers Grove, IL: InterVarsity, 2016), 201.

7. VanDrunen, *Politics after Christendom*, 189.

8. VanDrunen, *Politics after Christendom*, 191.

9. Leeman, *Political Church*, 204.

10. VanDrunen, *Politics after Christendom*, 202.

11. "The institutional church, not the state, possesses the authority to formally distinguish true from false doctrine, and true believers from unbelievers. The church alone has the authority to formally name the things of God, whether doctrine or people." Leeman, *Political Church*, 372.

12. For a summary of VanDrunen's argument, see VanDrunen, *Divine Covenants and Moral Order*, 205, 480–87, 509.

13. VanDrunen, *Divine Covenants and Moral Order*, 131.

14. VanDrunen, *Divine Covenants and Moral Order*, 506.

15. VanDrunen, *Divine Covenants and Moral Order*, 506.

16. VanDrunen, *Divine Covenants and Moral Order*, 131–32.

17. VanDrunen, *Divine Covenants and Moral Order*, 508.

18. Citing Rom. 1:21–23, VanDrunen states, "These verses indicate that human beings have *no ultimate* natural law right to religious freedom *before God*. No human being can stand before God and claim the right to be religious or commune with the divine in whatever way she chooses. Rather, natural law requires each person to worship *the one true God*—the creator of heaven and earth—and to worship him properly" (VanDrunen, *Divine Covenants and Moral Order*, 506). This notion leads VanDrunen to criticize the work of natural lawyers such as Robert George, whom VanDrunen accuses of too cheerfully characterizing the contributions of other religions. Regarding George's work, VanDrunen rejects that natural law posits an irreducible good from the contributions of other religions. He states, "Natural law, in Romans, does not lead humanity down the road to spiritual enlightenment and nobility, but makes condemnation before God more plain" (507). Again, he writes, "I conclude that human beings do not have an *ultimate* natural law right to religious freedom *before God*. God holds all people accountable for serving him properly, and by the light of nature alone all people know who God is but respond to him sinfully, a condition rectified only through Christian faith" (507).

19. VanDrunen, *Divine Covenants and Moral Order*, 508.

20. VanDrunen, *Divine Covenants and Moral Order*, 508.

21. Oliver O'Donovan argues, "The Christian conception of the 'secularity' of political society arose directly out of this Jewish wrestling with unfulfilled promise. . . . Secularity is irreducibly an eschatological notion; it requires an eschatological faith to sustain it, a belief in a disclosure that is 'not yet.'" Oliver O'Donovan, *Common Objects of Love: Moral Reflection and the Shaping of Community* (Grand Rapids: Eerdmans, 2009), 24.

22. Luke Bretherton, *Christ and the Common Life: Political Theology and the Case for Democracy* (Grand Rapids: Eerdmans, 2019), 229.

23. Robert A. Markus, *Christianity and the Secular* (Notre Dame, IN: University of Notre Dame Press, 2006), 4–5.

24. For a discussion on the impact of secularist attempts to banish religion from public discourse, see Richard John Neuhaus, *The Naked Public Square: Religion and Democracy in America*, 2nd ed. (Grand Rapids: Eerdmans, 1988). See also Bretherton, *Christ and the Common Life*, 240–50.

25. Markus, *Christianity and the Secular*, 73.

26. VanDrunen, *Divine Covenants and Moral Order*, 515.

27. James K. A. Smith, *Awaiting the King: Reforming Public Theology* (Grand Rapids: Baker Academic, 2017).

28. Michael Horton, "The Time Between: Redefining the 'Secular' in Contemporary Debate," in *After Modernity? Secularity, Globalization, and the Re-Enchantment of the World*, ed. James K. A. Smith (Waco: Baylor University Press, 2008), 46.

29. Horton, "Time Between," 52.

30. Markus, *Christianity and the Secular*, 6.

31. Markus, *Christianity and the Secular*, 14. For an explanation of the impact of Christ's rule on present political regimes, see Oliver O'Donovan, *The Desire of the Nations: Rediscovering the Roots of Political Theology* (New York: Cambridge University Press, 1999), 211–12.

32. J. Smith, *Awaiting the King*, 32.

33. VanDrunen, *Divine Covenants and Moral Order*, 515.

34. Markus, *Christianity and the Secular*, 14.

35. Oscar Cullmann, *Christ and Time: The Primitive Christian Conception of Time* (Philadelphia: Westminster John Knox, 1964), 54–55.

36. O'Donovan, *Common Objects of Love*, 63.

37. Bretherton, *Christ and the Common Life*, 231.

38. Horton, "Time Between," 55–56.

39. J. Smith, *Awaiting the King*, 79.

40. O'Donovan, *Desire of the Nations*, 146.

41. Markus, *Christianity and the Secular*, 36. See also Augustine, *The City of God against the Pagans*, ed. R. W. Dyson, Cambridge Texts in the History of Political Thought (Cambridge: Cambridge University Press, 1998), 35.

42. VanDrunen, *Divine Covenants and Moral Order*, 515.

43. Robert P. George, *The Clash of Orthodoxies: Law, Religion, and Morality in Crisis* (Wilmington, DE: Intercollegiate Studies Institute, 2002).

44. Carl F. H. Henry, "An Ecumenical Bombshell," *Christianity Today*, September 15, 1967, 29.

45. Horton, "Time Between," 63.

46. Isaiah Berlin, *Two Concepts of Liberty* (Oxford: Oxford University Press, 1959), 171.

47. David VanDrunen, "The Importance of the Penultimate: Reformed Social Thought and the Contemporary Critiques of the Liberal Society," *Journal of Markets and Morality* 9, no. 2 (September 2006): 235–36.

48. Steven D. Smith, *The Rise and Decline of American Religious Freedom* (Cambridge, MA: Harvard University Press, 2014), 9.

49. Markus, *Christianity and the Secular*, 56.

50. For a discussion on the intersections of Christian political theory and the foundations and compatibility of liberal democracy, see Robert Song, *Christianity and Liberal Society* (Oxford: Oxford University Press, 2006); J. Caleb Clanton, ed., *The Ethics of Citizenship: Liberal Democracy and Religious Convictions* (Waco: Baylor University Press, 2009); Nicholas Wolterstorff, *John Locke and the Ethics of Belief* (Cambridge: Cambridge University Press, 1996); Nicholas Wolterstorff, *The Mighty and the Almighty: An Essay in Political Theology* (Cambridge: Cambridge

University Press, 2014); and Nicholas Wolterstorff, *Understanding Liberal Democracy: Essays in Political Philosophy*, ed. Terence Cuneo (Oxford: Oxford University Press, 2016).

51. Jeffrey Stout, *Ethics after Babel: The Languages of Morals and Their Discontents* (Princeton: Princeton University Press, 2001), 233–34.

52. Leeman, *Political Church*, 374–75.

53. O'Donovan, *Desire of the Nations*, 211–12.

54. Eric Voegelin, *The New Science of Politics: An Introduction* (Chicago: University of Chicago Press, 1952), 121.

55. John Murray Cuddihy, *No Offense: Civil Religion and Protestant Taste* (New York: Seabury, 1978), 108.

56. Richard John Neuhaus, "From Providence to Privacy: Religion and the Redefinition of America," in *Unsecular America*, ed. Richard John Neuhaus (Grand Rapids: Eerdmans, 1986), 63.

57. Henry R. Van Til, *The Calvinistic Concept of Culture*, 2nd ed. (Grand Rapids: Baker, 1959), 200.

58. G. K. Chesterton, "The Debate on Spiritualism," *London Illustrated News*, March 15, 1919.

59. Van Til, *Calvinistic Concept of Culture*, 39.

60. Glenn A. Moots, *Politics Reformed: The Anglo-American Legacy of Covenant Theology* (Columbia: University of Missouri, 2010), 10.

61. Jonathan Leeman, *How the Nations Rage: Rethinking Politics in a Divided Age* (Nashville: Thomas Nelson, 2018), 211. For a similar argument, see Horton, "Time Between," 45–65. See also Richard J. Mouw and Sander Griffioen, *Pluralisms and Horizons: An Essay in Christian Public Philosophy* (Grand Rapids: Eerdmans, 1993), 108.

62. Joseph Bottum, "Spiritual Shape of Political Ideas," *Weekly Standard* 40, no. 12 (December 1, 2014): 25.

63. Carl Schmitt, *Political Theology: Four Chapters on the Concept of Sovereignty* (Chicago: University of Chicago Press, 1985), 36.

64. Tom Wilson, "Irving Kristol's God," *First Things* 251 (March 2015): 21.

65. J. Smith, *Awaiting the King*, 23n10. See also Oliver O'Donovan, *The Ways of Judgment: The Bampton Lectures* (Grand Rapids: Eerdmans, 2005), 309–12.

66. "1776: Witherspoon, Dominion of Providence over the Passions of Men (Sermon)," Online Library of Liberty, https://oll.libertyfund.org/pages/1776-witherspoon-dominion-of-providence-over-the-passions-of-men-sermon.

67. Alexis de Tocqueville, *Democracy in America*, ed. Harvey Mansfield and Delba Winthrop (Chicago: University of Chicago Press, 2000), 282.

68. Thomas Smail, *The Forgotten Father* (Grand Rapids: Eerdmans, 1980), 16.

69. Robert A. Markus, *Saeculum: History and Society in the Theology of St Augustine*, 2nd ed. (Cambridge: Cambridge University Press, 1989), 171–72.

70. Markus, *Saeculum*, 173.

71. Dietrich Bonhoeffer, *Ethics*, ed. Clifford J. Green, vol. 6 of *Dietrich Bonhoeffer Works* (Minneapolis: Fortress, 2008), 84.

72. Mouw and Griffioen, *Pluralisms and Horizons*, 109.

Chapter 4 The *Imago Dei* and Religious Liberty

1. Frederick Douglass, *Narrative of the Life of Frederick Douglass, an American Slave* (Boston, MA: Anti-Slavery Office, 1849), 40–41, https://www.loc.gov/resource /lhbcb.25385/.

2. Augustine, *Confessions*, vol. 1, *Books 1–8*, trans. Carolyn J. B. Hammond, Loeb Classical Library (Cambridge, MA: Harvard University Press, 2014), 3.

3. Larry Siedentop, *Inventing the Individual: The Origins of Western Liberalism* (Cambridge, MA: Belknap, 2014).

4. Jeremy Waldron, "The Image of God: Rights, Reason, and Order," in *Christianity and Human Rights: An Introduction*, ed. John Witte Jr. and Frank S. Alexander (Cambridge: Cambridge University Press, 2012), 217.

5. For a review of literature concerning the doctrine of the image of God, see G. C. Berkouwer, *Man: The Image of God* (Grand Rapids: Eerdmans, 1952); Anthony A. Hoekema, *Created in God's Image* (Grand Rapids: Eerdmans, 1994); Philip Edcumbe Hughes, *The True Image: The Origin and Destiny of Man in Christ* (Grand Rapids: Eerdmans, 1989); Meredith G. Kline, *Images of the Spirit* (Eugene, OR: Wipf & Stock, 1999); John Laidlaw, *The Bible Doctrine of Man* (Edinburgh: T&T Clark, 1895); John Gresham Machen, *The Christian View of Man* (Edinburgh: Banner of Truth Trust, 1984); and Hugh Dermot McDonald, *The Christian View of Man* (Wheaton: Crossway, 1981).

6. John F. Kilner, *Dignity and Destiny: Humanity in the Image of God* (Grand Rapids: Eerdmans, 2015), 95.

7. Kilner, *Dignity and Destiny*, 39.

8. John M. Frame, "Men and Women in the Image of God," in *Recovering Biblical Manhood and Womanhood*, ed. John Piper and Wayne Grudem (Wheaton: Crossway, 2006), 225, 229.

9. Wayne Grudem, *Systematic Theology: An Introduction to Biblical Doctrine* (Grand Rapids: Zondervan), 442–43.

10. Kilner, *Dignity and Destiny*, 104.

11. Frame, "Men and Women in the Image of God," 225.

12. Grudem, *Systematic Theology*, 446–50.

13. Frame, "Men and Women in the Image of God," 230–31.

14. David C. Innes, *Christ and the Kingdoms of Man: Foundations of Political Life* (Phillipsburg, NJ: P&R, 2019), 10.

15. Hoekema, *Created in God's Image*, 13.

16. Hoekema, *Created in God's Image*, 73.

17. Millard J. Erickson, *Christian Theology*, 2nd ed. (Grand Rapids: Baker, 1998), 520–29.

18. Erickson, *Christian Theology*, 521.

19. Erickson, *Christian Theology*, 523–27.

20. Erickson, *Christian Theology*, 529.

21. David VanDrunen, *Politics after Christendom: Political Theology in a Fractured World* (Grand Rapids: Zondervan, 2020), 59.

22. Kilner, *Dignity and Destiny*, xi.

23. John Kilner states helpfully, "Christ, as both the standard and the source of humanity's renewal, breaks the power of sin and liberates people to resume their

God-intended development to become fully conformed to Christ—to God's image who is Christ. . . . Being in God's 'image' and 'glory' are what God intends humanity fundamentally to be. Their destiny involves becoming that, though at present they are only en route." Kilner, *Dignity and Destiny*, 92.

24. Siedentop, *Inventing the Individual*, 64.

25. Jim Spivey, "Separation No Myth: Religious Liberty's Biblical and Theological Bases," *Southwestern Journal of Theology* 36, no. 3 (1994): 10.

26. Matthew J. Franck, "Two Tales: Getting the Origins of Religious Liberty Right Matters," *Touchstone* 29, no. 4 (August 2016): 24.

27. James E. Wood, "A Biblical View of Religious Liberty," *Ecumenical Review* 30, no. 1 (January 1978): 32.

28. The Witherspoon Institute Task Force on International Religious Freedom, *Religious Freedom: Why Now? Defending an Embattled Human Right* (Princeton: Witherspoon Institute, 2012), 16.

29. I recommend Matthew Franck's essay on the competing origins of religious liberty. See Franck, "Two Tales," 19–26. See also Matthew J. Franck, "Christianity and Freedom in the American Founding," in *Christianity and Freedom*, vol. 1, *Historical Perspectives*, ed. Timothy Samuel Shah and Allen D. Hertzke, Cambridge Studies in Law and Christianity (New York: Cambridge University Press, 2016), 264–89.

30. Spivey, "Separation No Myth," 10.

31. Hoekema, *Created in God's Image*, 5–6.

32. Frame, "Men and Women in the Image of God," 225–26.

33. Waldron, "Image of God," 227.

34. For an overview and critique of Irenaeus's, Aquinas's, and Calvin's understandings of reason in relationship to the image of God, see Hoekema, *Created in God's Image*, 33–49. See also Kilner, *Dignity and Destiny*, 178.

35. Hoekema, *Created in God's Image*, 71.

36. Kilner, *Dignity and Destiny*, 181.

37. Kilner, *Dignity and Destiny*, 183.

38. Kilner, *Dignity and Destiny*, 228.

39. Carl F. H. Henry, *God, Revelation and Authority*, vol. 1, *God Who Speaks and Shows, Preliminary Considerations* (Wheaton: Crossway, 1999), 227.

40. John David Hughey, "The Theological Frame of Religious Liberty," *Christian Century* 80, no. 45 (November 1963): 1365.

41. Waldron, "Image of God," 227.

42. Alexander Hamilton, James Madison, and John Jay, *The Federalist Papers No. 10*, ed. Clinton Rossiter and Charles R. Kessler (New York: Penguin, 2003), 73.

43. I owe this insight to an essay on the philosophical underpinnings of the founding of America. See Robert R. Reilly, "For God and Country," *Claremont Review of Books* 17, no. 3 (Summer 2017): 46.

44. Waldron, "Image of God," 228.

45. Roger Ruston, *Human Rights and the Image of God* (London: SCM, 2004), 47.

46. Siedentop, *Inventing the Individual*, 64.

47. Wood, "Biblical View of Religious Liberty," 32. See also Spivey, "Separation No Myth," 10.

48. Planned Parenthood v. Casey, 505 U.S. 833 (1992).

49. Edmund Burke, *Reflections on the Revolution in France [1790]*, in *The Works of the Right Honourable Edmund Burke*, World's Classics (London: Oxford University Press, 1906), 4:105.

50. Amos Niven Wilder, "Eleutheria in the New Testament and Religious Liberty," *Ecumenical Review* 13, no. 4 (July 1961): 412.

51. A. F. Carrillo de Albornoz writes, "Man is liberated in Jesus Christ in order that he may live a life of obedience to God. In the freedom to which God has called him, man is to become God's fellow-worker in the fulfillment of this obedience. There is, then, in our due Christian obedience, a relationship between God and man which is based on freedom." A. F. Carrillo de Albornoz, *The Basis of Religious Liberty* (New York: Association Press, 1963), 78–79.

52. Wilder, "Eleutheria in the New Testament and Religious Liberty," 413.

53. Siedentop, *Inventing the Individual*, 69.

54. Wilder, "Eleutheria in the New Testament and Religious Liberty," 413.

55. J. Philip Wogaman, *Protestant Faith and Religious Liberty* (Nashville: Abingdon, 1967), 65.

56. Oliver O'Donovan, *Resurrection and Moral Order: An Outline for Evangelical Ethics* (Grand Rapids: Eerdmans, 1994), 25.

57. Wogaman, *Protestant Faith and Religious Liberty*, 35.

58. *Christian Statement on the Nature and Basis of Religious Liberty* (St. Andrews, Scotland: World Council of Churches, 1960), quoted in Carrillo de Albornoz, *Basis of Religious Liberty*, 66.

59. Carrillo de Albornoz, *Basis of Religious Liberty*, 147. He continues on the same page, noting, "This free response is compatible with God's judgment and with the teachings of the enslavement of man's will by sin and the mystery of election."

60. Wood, "Biblical View of Religious Liberty," 32.

61. On the rise of "dual jurisdictions" in Christian developments of religious liberty, see Steven D. Smith, *The Rise and Decline of American Religious Freedom* (Cambridge, MA: Harvard University Press, 2014), 37.

62. Carl F. H. Henry, *Twilight of a Great Civiliation: The Drift toward Neo-Paganism* (Westchester, IL: Crossway, 1988), 175.

63. John Finnis, *Natural Law and Natural Rights*, 2nd ed. (Oxford: Oxford University Press, 2011), 88.

64. Wood, "Biblical View of Religious Liberty," 33.

65. For more on the relationship between the incarnation and religious liberty, see James Davis's explication of Roger Williams's focus on the incarnation as evidence that God's kingdom comes not through political power but through a renewed covenant with humanity. James Calvin Davis, *The Moral Theology of Roger Williams: Christian Conviction and Public Ethics* (Louisville: Westminster John Knox, 2004), 22–29.

66. Niels Søe, "The Theological Basis of Religious Liberty," *Ecumenical Review* 11, no. 1 (October 1958): 40.

67. Wood, "Biblical View of Religious Liberty," 34.

68. Søren Kierkegaard, *Training in Christianity*, trans. Walter Lowrie (Princeton: Princeton University Press, 2015), 55.

69. Barrett Duke, "The Christian Doctrine of Religious Liberty," in *First Freedom: The Baptist Perspective on Religious Liberty*, ed. Thomas White, Jason G. Duesing, and Malcolm B. Yarnell III (Nashville: B&H, 2007), 95.

70. Wood, "Biblical View of Religious Liberty," 37.

71. Carl F. H. Henry, *Has Democracy Had Its Day?* (Nashville: ERLC, 1996), 48.

72. Robert Louis Wilken, "The Christian Roots of Religious Freedom," in Shah and Hertzke, *Historical Perspectives*, 69.

73. "Conscience includes the perception of the principles of morality (synderesis); their application in the given circumstances by practical discernment of reasons and goods; and finally, judgment about concrete acts yet to be performed or already performed. The truth about the moral good, stated in the law of reason, is recognized practically and concretely by the *prudent judgment* of conscience. We call that man prudent who chooses in conformity with this judgment." *Catechism of the Catholic Church*, Vatican, para. 1780, accessed September 14, 2020, http://www.vatican.va/archive/ccc_css/archive/catechism/p3s1c1a6.htm#I.

74. Carrillo de Albornoz, *Basis of Religious Liberty*, 29.

75. Charles Villa-Vicencio, "Christianity and Human Rights," *Journal of Law and Religion* 14, no. 2 (1999): 587.

76. Wilken, "Christian Roots of Religious Freedom," 69.

77. Gary T. Meadors, "Conscience," in *Evangelical Dictionary of Biblical Theology*, ed. Walter A. Elwell (Grand Rapids: Baker, 1996), 115.

78. Andrew David Naselli and J. D. Crowley, *Conscience: What It Is, How to Train It, and Loving Those Who Differ* (Wheaton: Crossway, 2016), 22.

79. Carl F. H. Henry, *Christian Personal Ethics* (Grand Rapids: Eerdmans, 1957), 151–52.

80. Christopher Tollefsen, "Conscience, Religion and the State," *American Journal of Jurisprudence* 54, no. 1 (January 2009): 95.

81. Wood, "Biblical View of Religious Liberty," 36.

82. For a recent Christian volume on the conscience, see Naselli and Crowley, *Conscience*.

83. Carl F. H. Henry, *The Christian Mindset in a Secular Society: Promoting Evangelical Renewal and National Righteousness* (Portland, OR: Multnomah, 1984), 72.

84. *Catechism of the Catholic Church*, para. 1783.

85. Tollefsen, "Conscience, Religion and the State," 100.

86. Senator Ben Sasse, a Christian and academic historian, offers a helpful statement on the relationships between "rights," the image of God, and noncoercion. "I want a public square where people who are created in the image of God with dignity can affirm everyone else's right of free assembly and free speech and freedom of religion and freedom of the press. And then engage robustly—lovingly, but robustly—and vigorously in the market place of ideas to try to persuade other people" (Ben Sasse, "Senator Sasse on the Importance of Religious Freedom in Society," *Light Magazine*, Summer 2016, 41). Consider also the words of the Witherspoon Institute Task Force on International Religious Freedom, *Religious Freedom*, 28:

> Human beings are noble agents—agents with high worth and dignity. An integral aspect of these characteristics is that all persons have the great

privilege and responsibility of freely forming their own judgments of reason and conscience about—and freely establishing their own relationship with—transcendent reality. They have an intrinsic interest in forming their characters and lives—constituting themselves—into integrated wholes that fully reflect the demands and implications of transcendent truth as they grasp it. Anything less than full religious freedom fails to respect the dignity of persons as free truth-seekers, duty-bound to respond to the truth (and only the truth) about the transcendent in accordance with their own judgments of conscience.

87. John Henry Newman, *Certain Difficulties Felt by Anglicans in Catholic Teaching Considered* (London: Longmans, Green, 1897), 250.

88. Daniel R. Heimbach, "Understanding the Difference between Religious Liberty and Religious Autonomy," in White, Duesing, and Yarnell, *First Freedom*, 133.

89. Heimbach, "Understanding the Difference between Religious Liberty and Religious Autonomy," 133. Heimbach helpfully contrasts this with an "Autonomous Liberty" paradigm that defines freedom as the absence of obligation.

90. Naselli and Crowley, *Conscience*, 25.

91. Carl F. H. Henry, *Twilight of a Great Civilization: The Drift toward Neo-Paganism* (Westchester, IL: Crossway, 1988), 150.

92. J. V. Fesko, *Reforming Apologetics: Retrieving the Classic Reformed Approach to Defending the Faith* (Grand Rapids: Baker Academic, 2019), 123.

93. Wilder, "Eleutheria in the New Testament and Religious Liberty," 413.

94. John Corvino, Ryan T. Anderson, and Sherif Girgis, *Debating Religious Liberty and Discrimination* (New York: Oxford University Press, 2017), 170.

95. Carrillo de Albornoz, *Basis of Religious Liberty*, 73.

96. Henry, *Christian Mindset in a Secular Society*, 72.

97. Henry, *Twilight of a Great Civilization*, 151.

98. For more on this argument, with which I agree and which has informed my thinking, see Rex Ahdar, "Is Freedom of Conscience Superior to Freedom of Religion?," *Oxford Journal of Law and Religion* 7, no. 1 (2018): 1–20.

Chapter 5 That They Should Seek God

1. This exchange occurs in chap. 5 of C. S. Lewis, *The Great Divorce* (New York: HarperCollins, 2001), 33–42.

2. Timothy Samuel Shah and Jack Friedman, eds., *Homo Religiosus? Exploring the Roots of Religion and Religious Freedom in Human Experience* (Cambridge: Cambridge University Press, 2018).

3. Alexander Schmemann, *For the Life of the World: Sacraments and Orthodoxy* (Crestwood, NY: St. Vladimir's Seminary Press, 1973), 118.

4. Barrett Duke, "The Christian Doctrine of Religious Liberty," in *First Freedom: The Baptist Perspective on Religious Liberty*, ed. Thomas White, Jason G. Duesing, and Malcolm B. Yarnell III (Nashville: B&H, 2007), 96.

5. Luke Timothy Johnson, "Religious Rights and Christian Texts," in *Religious Human Rights in Global Perspective*, ed. John Witte Jr. and Johan van der Vyver (The Hague: Martin Nijhoff, 1996), 87.

6. Augustine, *Confessions*, vol. 1, *Books 1–8*, trans. Carolyn J. B. Hammond, Loeb Classical Library (Cambridge, MA: Harvard University Press, 2014), 3.

7. The Witherspoon Institute Task Force on International Religious Freedom, *Religious Freedom: Why Now? Defending an Embattled Human Right* (Princeton: Witherspoon Institute, 2012), 12.

8. Christian Smith, *Moral, Believing Animals: Human Personhood and Culture* (New York: Oxford University Press, 2009).

9. Justin L. Barrett, *Why Would Anyone Believe in God?* (Walnut Creek, CA: AltaMira, 2004); and Jesse Bering, *The Belief Instinct: The Psychology of Souls, Destiny, and the Meaning of Life* (New York: Norton, 2012).

10. Steven D. Smith, *Pagans and Christians in the City: Culture Wars from the Tiber to the Potomac* (Grand Rapids: Eerdmans, 2018), 29.

11. Christopher Tollefsen, "Conscience, Religion and the State," *American Journal of Jurisprudence* 54, no. 1 (January 2009): 100.

12. Tollefsen, "Conscience, Religion and the State," 100.

13. The Witherspoon Institute Task Force on International Religious Freedom, *Religious Freedom*, 15.

14. The Witherspoon Institute Task Force on International Religious Freedom, *Religious Freedom*, 15.

15. Ronald Dworkin, *Religion without God* (Cambridge, MA: Harvard University Press, 2013).

16. J. Daryl Charles, *Natural Law and Religious Freedom: The Role of Moral First Things in Grounding and Protecting the First Freedom* (New York: Routledge, 2018), 27.

17. Benedict XVI, "44th World Day of Peace 2011, Religious Freedom, the Path to Peace," Vatican, January 1, 2011, http://w2.vatican.va/content/benedict-xvi/en/messages/peace/documents/hf_ben-xvi_mes_20101208_xliv-world-day-peace.html.

18. Sidney Greidanus, "Human Rights in Biblical Perspective," *Calvin Theological Journal* 19, no. 1 (April 1984): 29.

19. Charles, *Natural Law and Religious Freedom*, 24.

20. Ryan T. Anderson and Robert P. George, "The Baby and the Bathwater," *National Affairs* 41 (Fall 2019): 176–77.

21. Robert P. George, *Making Men Moral: Civil Liberties and Public Morality* (Oxford: Oxford University Press, 1993), 191–92.

22. George, *Making Men Moral*, 220–21.

23. I am indebted to Robert P. George for this concept.

24. John Henry Newman, *Certain Difficulties Felt by Anglicans in Catholic Teaching Considered* (London: Longmans, Green, 1897), 250.

25. Tollefsen, "Conscience, Religion and the State," 96.

26. Charles Taylor, *A Secular Age* (Cambridge, MA: Belknap, 2007), 171–72. See also Taylor, *Modern Social Imaginaries* (Durham, NC: Duke University Press, 2004).

27. Carl Trueman, *The Rise and Triumph of the Modern Self: Cultural Amnesia, Expressive Individualism, and the Road to Sexual Revolution* (Wheaton: Crossway, 2020), 37.

28. On this theme, see Dworkin, *Religion without God*.

29. Leo Strauss, *Persecution and the Art of Writing* (Glencoe, IL: Free Press, 1952), 37.

30. James Madison, "A Memorial and Remonstrance against Religious Assessment (1785)," in *The Sacred Rights of Conscience: Selected Readings on Religious Liberty and Church-State Relations in the American Founding*, ed. Daniel Dreisbach and Mark David Hall (Indianapolis: Liberty Fund, 2010), 309.

31. H. Richard Niebuhr, *Radical Monotheism and Western Culture* (New York: Harper & Brothers, 1960), 25.

32. For example, see Article 18 of the United Nations' Declaration on Human Rights, available at https://www.un.org/en/universal-declaration-human-rights/.

33. Charles, *Natural Law and Religious Freedom*.

34. Carl F. H. Henry, *The Christian Mindset in a Secular Society: Promoting Evangelical Renewal and National Righteousness* (Portland, OR: Multnomah, 1984), 66.

35. This statement begs qualification since it would be irresponsible to consider "human rights" solely causative as the result of Christian ethical and theological reflection. Charles Villa-Vicencio observes, "The history of the emergence of human rights within the Western Christian tradition recognizes that religions develop in interaction with other social and cultural forces in society" (Charles Villa-Vicencio, "Christianity and Human Rights," *Journal of Law and Religion* 14, no. 2 [1999]: 579). For more on the development of human rights in the context of Christian ethical and theological thinking, see Harold J. Berman, *Faith and Order: The Reconciliation of Law and Religion* (Grand Rapids: Eerdmans, 1993); Harold J. Berman, *Law and Revolution: The Formation of the Western Legal Tradition* (Cambridge, MA: Harvard University Press, 1983); Harold J. Berman, *Law and Revolution II: The Impact of the Protestant Reformations on the Western Legal Tradition* (Cambridge, MA: Belknap, 2006); and Brian Tierney, *The Idea of Natural Rights: Studies on Natural Rights, Natural Law, and Church Law, 1150–1625*, Emory University Studies in Law and Religion, no. 5 (Grand Rapids: Eerdmans, 1997).

36. T. B. Maston, *The Bible and Race*, 3rd ed. (Nashville: Broadman, 1959), 13.

37. For more on the relationship between the image of God and human rights, see Nicholas Wolterstorff, *Justice: Rights and Wrongs* (Princeton: Princeton University Press, 2008), 342–61; and Robert P. Kraynak, *Christian Faith and Modern Democracy: God and Politics in the Fallen World* (Notre Dame, IN: University of Notre Dame Press, 2001), 107–64.

38. Carl F. H. Henry, *Twilight of a Great Civilization: The Drift toward Neo-Paganism* (Westchester, IL: Crossway, 1988), 145.

39. R. Albert Mohler Jr., *The Gathering Storm: Religious Liberty and the Right to Be Christian* (Louisville: SBTS Press, 2017), 43.

40. Kevin P. Lee, "Deeper Longings: The Relevance of Christian Theology for Contemporary Rights Theories," *Ave Maria Law Review* 3, no. 1 (2005): 294.

41. Robert P. George, "Natural Law, God and Human Dignity," in *The Cambridge Companion to Natural Law Jurisprudence*, ed. George Duke and Robert P. George (Cambridge: Cambridge University Press, 2017), 60–61.

42. John D. Inazu, *Confident Pluralism: Surviving and Thriving through Deep Difference* (Chicago: University of Chicago Press, 2016), 26.

43. This is an important point worth stressing. Human convention is not a firm foundation on which to secure the rights of humans. Consider the Universal Declaration of Human Rights (1948), which attempts to string together a universal understanding of rights (among them, religious freedom). Carl F. H. Henry observes that the statement "wholly ignores the subject of the ultimate source and sanction of rights and does not even obligate states to enact the stipulated rights." Henry, *Twilight of a Great Civilization*, 149.

44. Henry, *Christian Mindset in a Secular Society*, 72. For a chapter-length treatment on the connection between human rights and religious liberty, see A. F. Carrillo de Albornoz, *The Basis of Religious Liberty* (New York: Association Press, 1963), 33–41.

45. Henry, *Christian Mindset in a Secular Society*, 73.

46. National Association of Evangelicals, "For the Health of the Nation: An Evangelical Call to Civic Responsibility," 2004, http://nae.net/wp-content/uploads/2015/06/For-the-Health-of-the-Nation.pdf.

47. Tertullian, "To Scapula," in *Tertullian Apologetical Works and Minucius Felix Octavius*, trans. Rudolph Arbesmann, Emily Joseph Daly, and Edwin Quain (New York: Fathers of the Church, 1959), 10:152, quoted in Robert Louis Wilken, "The Christian Roots of Religious Freedom," in *Christianity and Freedom*, vol. 1, *Historical Perspectives*, ed. Timothy Samuel Shah and Allen D. Hertzke, Cambridge Studies in Law and Christianity (New York: Cambridge University Press, 2016), 82.

48. Tertullian, *Apology*, in *Tertullian Apologetical Works and Minucius Felix Octavius*, 10:76.

49. On the social context of "ius" in Roman law, see Charles Donahue, "Ius in Roman Law," in *Christianity and Human Rights: An Introduction*, ed. John Witte Jr. and Frank S. Alexander (Cambridge: Cambridge University Press, 2012), 64–80.

50. Timothy Samuel Shah, "The Roots of Religious Freedom in Early Christian Thought," in *Christianity and Freedom*, vol. 1, *Historical Perspectives*, ed. Timothy Samuel Shah and Allen D. Hertzke, Cambridge Studies in Law and Christianity (New York: Cambridge University Press, 2016), 54.

51. Robert Louis Wilken, "The Christian Roots of Religious Freedom," in Shah and Hertzke, *Historical Perspectives*, 65.

52. Wilken, "Christian Roots of Religious Freedom," 1:65.

53. Tertullian, *Adversus Marcionem*, trans. Earnest Evans (Oxford: Clarendon, 1972), 100–101. See also, Robert Louis Wilken, *Liberty in the Things of God* (New Haven: Yale University Press, 2019), 15.

54. Charles, *Natural Law and Religious Freedom*, 162.

55. Henry, *Twilight of a Great Civilization*, 148.

56. David VanDrunen, *Divine Covenants and Moral Order: A Biblical Theology of Natural Law* (Grand Rapids: Eerdmans, 2014), 506.

57. VanDrunen, *Divine Covenants and Moral Order*, 509. John Locke makes a similar argument, stating, "It appears not that God has ever given any such authority to one man over another, as to compel anyone to his religion." John Locke, *A Letter concerning Toleration*, ed. James H. Tully (Indianapolis: Hackett, 1983), 27.

58. VanDrunen, *Divine Covenants and Moral Order*, 508.

59. Jeremy Waldron, "The Image of God: Rights, Reason, and Order," in Witte and Alexander, *Christianity and Human Rights*, 229.

60. Waldron, "Image of God," 234.

61. Carrillo de Albornoz, *Basis of Religious Liberty*, 80.

62. Villa-Vicencio, "Christianity and Human Rights," 587.

63. Duke, "Christian Doctrine of Religious Liberty," 93.

64. Waldron, "Image of God," 225.

65. Carrillo de Albornoz, *Basis of Religious Liberty*, 96.

66. Waldron, "Image of God," 216.

67. Waldron, "Image of God," 222.

68. Villa-Vicencio, "Christianity and Human Rights," 587.

69. James E. Wood, "A Biblical View of Religious Liberty," *Ecumenical Review* 30, no. 1 (January 1978): 35.

70. Wood, "Biblical View of Religious Liberty," 35.

71. Wood, "Biblical View of Religious Liberty," 35.

72. See Committee of the Virginia Assembly, "A Bill for Establishing Religious Freedom, 18 June 1779," National Archives, accessed September 14, 2020, https://founders.archives.gov/documents/Jefferson/01-02-02-0132-0004-0082.

73. Matthew J. Franck, "Two Tales: Getting the Origins of Religious Liberty Right Matters," *Touchstone* 29, no. 4 (August 2016): 24.

74. Rebecca C. Mathis, "The Roots of Religious Liberty in Scripture," *Sewanee Theological Review* 55, no. 4 (2012): 397.

75. Mathis, "Roots of Religious Liberty in Scripture," 397.

76. Mathis, "Roots of Religious Liberty in Scripture," 398.

Chapter 6 Religious Liberty as Christian Mission

1. John Piper, *Let the Nations Be Glad! The Supremacy of God in Missions*, 3rd ed. (Grand Rapids: Baker Books, 2010), 15.

2. It is important to note the difference in terminology between "the mission of God" and "mission." "The mission of God" denotes God's self-revealing and saving efforts in the universe, while "mission" refers to the particular forms and practices that a commitment to God's mission manifests among his people in the world.

3. For an account of how God's mission is tied covenantally and narratively to the entire message of the Bible, see Graeme Goldsworthy, *According to Plan: The Unfolding Revelation of God in the Bible* (Downers Grove, IL: InterVarsity, 2002); and James Hamilton, *God's Glory in Salvation through Judgment: A Biblical Theology* (Wheaton: Crossway, 2010).

4. Christopher J. H. Wright, *The Mission of God: Unlocking the Bible's Grand Narrative* (Downers Grove, IL: InterVarsity, 2006), 17.

5. David J. Bosch, *Transforming Mission: Paradigm Shifts in Theology of Mission*, 20th anniv. ed. (Maryknoll, NY: Orbis Books, 2011), 9.

6. John Stott and Christopher J. H. Wright, *Christian Mission in the Modern World* (Downers Grove, IL: InterVarsity, 2015), 19.

7. For recent Christian formulations on the nature of mission, see Bosch, *Transforming Mission*; Stott and Wright, *Christian Mission in the Modern World*; Wright, *Mission of God*; Michael W. Goheen and Craig G. Bartholomew, *Living*

at the Crossroads: An Introduction to Christian Worldview (Grand Rapids: Baker Academic, 2008); Lesslie Newbigin, *The Gospel in a Pluralist Society* (Grand Rapids: Eerdmans, 1989); Kevin DeYoung and Greg Gilbert, *What Is the Mission of the Church? Making Sense of Social Justice, Shalom, and the Great Commission* (Wheaton: Crossway, 2011); Michael W. Goheen and Craig G. Bartholomew, *Introducing Christian Mission Today: Scripture, History, and Issues* (Downers Grove, IL: InterVarsity, 2014); and Lesslie Newbigin, *One Body, One Gospel, One World: The Christian Mission Today* (London: International Missionary Council, 1959).

8. For an examination of how the kingdom of Christ unlocks the grand narrative of the Bible, see Russell D. Moore, *The Kingdom of Christ: The New Evangelical Perspective* (Wheaton: Crossway, 2004).

9. Roman Catholic Church, "*Ad Gentes*: On the Missionary Activity of the Church," 1965, http://www.vatican.va/archive/hist_councils/ii_vatican_council/doc uments/vat-ii_decree_19651207_ad-gentes_en.html.

10. For representative camps between "transformationalist" approaches to missiology and a Reformed two-kingdoms view of mission, see Timothy Keller, *Center Church: Doing Balanced, Gospel-Centered Ministry in Your City* (Grand Rapids: Zondervan, 2012); and DeYoung and Gilbert, *What Is the Mission of the Church?*

11. Goheen and Bartholomew, *Living at the Crossroads*, 2.

12. Goheen and Bartholomew, *Introducing Christian Mission Today*, 2.

13. Bosch, *Transforming Mission*, 9.

14. Carl F. H. Henry, "An Ecumenical Bombshell," *Christianity Today*, September 15, 1967, 28.

15. Goheen and Bartholomew, *Living at the Crossroads*, 2.

16. T. Desmond Alexander, *From Eden to the New Jerusalem: An Introduction to Biblical Theology* (Grand Rapids: Kregel, 2009).

17. Peter Morden, *Offering Christ to the World: Andrew Fuller (1754–1815) and the Revival of Eighteenth Century Particular Baptist Life*, Studies in Baptist History and Thought 8 (Carlisle: Paternoster, 2003), 136.

18. Josh Pater, "An Interview with Oliver O'Donovan," *Chimes*, November 9, 2001, 16.

19. David C. Innes, *Christ and the Kingdoms of Men: Foundations of Political Life* (Phillipsburg, NJ: P&R, 2019), 75.

20. Stott and Wright, *Christian Mission in the Modern World*, 18.

21. Jason G. Duesing, "The End of Religious Liberty," in *First Freedom: The Beginning and End of Religious Liberty*, ed. Jason G. Duesing, Thomas White, and Malcolm B. Yarnell III, 2nd ed. (Nashville: B&H, 2016), 255.

22. Barrett Duke, "The Christian Doctrine of Religious Liberty," in *First Freedom: The Baptist Perspective on Religious Liberty*, ed. Thomas White, Jason G. Duesing, and Malcolm B. Yarnell III (Nashville: B&H, 2007), 22.

23. Duke, "Christian Doctrine of Religious Liberty," 22.

24. Michael Hanby, "The Civic Project of American Christianity," *First Things* 250 (February 2015): 36.

25. Hanby, "Civic Project of American Christianity," 36.

26. Edwin S. Gaustad, *Roger Williams* (Oxford: Oxford University Press, 2005), 41.

27. Gaustad, *Roger Williams*, 107.

28. John Locke, *A Letter concerning Toleration*, ed. James H. Tully (Indianapolis: Hackett, 1983), 27.

29. John Milton, *Areopagitica*, The Project Gutenberg EBook, http://www.gutenberg.org/files/608/608-h/608-h.htm.

30. John Leland, "The Rights of Conscience Inalienable," in *The Writings of John Leland*, ed. L. F. Greene (New York: Arno Press and the New York Times, 1969), 185.

31. A. F. Carrillo de Albornoz, *The Basis of Religious Liberty* (New York: Association Press, 1963), 63.

32. For an excellent review of Paul's evangelism strategy at Mars Hill, see J. Daryl Charles, *Retrieving the Natural Law: A Return to Moral First Things* (Grand Rapids: Eerdmans, 2008), 45–54.

33. Charles, *Retrieving the Natural Law*, 51.

34. For a helpful explanation of the concept of general revelation, see Baptist theologian and ethicist Russell D. Moore, "Natural Revelation," in *A Theology for the Church*, ed. Daniel L. Akin and Paige Patterson (Nashville: B&H, 2007), 71–117.

35. Greg Forster, *The Contested Public Square: The Crisis of Christianity and Politics* (Downers Grove, IL: InterVarsity, 2008), 29.

36. C. S. Lewis, *The Abolition of Man* (New York: HarperOne, 2015), 41.

37. Charles, *Retrieving the Natural Law*, 63.

38. Charles, *Retrieving the Natural Law*, 63.

39. Thomas Aquinas, *Summa Theologiae* I-II.90.4. I have used the translation of James V. Schall, SJ, from "Understanding Law with Thomas Aquinas," Law & Liberty, October 2, 2018, https://lawliberty.org/understanding-law-with-thomas-aquinas/.

40. James E. Wood, "A Biblical View of Religious Liberty," *Ecumenical Review* 30, no. 1 (January 1978): 39.

41. Carrillo de Albornoz, *Basis of Religious Liberty*, 115.

42. Wood, "Biblical View of Religious Liberty," 40.

43. Wood, "Biblical View of Religious Liberty," 40.

44. Jim Spivey, "Separation No Myth: Religious Liberty's Biblical and Theological Bases," *Southwestern Journal of Theology* 36, no. 3 (1994): 13.

45. Spivey, "Separation No Myth," 13.

46. For a review of the church's abuses stemming from church-state alliances, see Perez Zagorin, *How the Idea of Religious Toleration Came to the West* (Princeton: Princeton University Press, 2003).

47. Matthew J. Franck, "Two Tales: Getting the Origins of Religious Liberty Right Matters," *Touchstone* 29, no. 4 (August 2016): 23.

48. Spivey, "Separation No Myth," 14.

49. John David Hughey, "The Theological Frame of Religious Liberty," *Christian Century* 80, no. 45 (November 1963): 1367.

50. Stanley Hauerwas, *After Christendom? How the Church Is to Behave If Freedom, Justice, and a Christian Nation Are Bad Ideas* (Nashville: Abingdon, 1991), 71.

Chapter 7 Moral Ecology and Christian Mission

1. Jim Spivey, "Separation No Myth: Religious Liberty's Biblical and Theological Bases," *Southwestern Journal of Theology* 36, no. 3 (1994): 11.

2. Carl F. H. Henry, *The Christian Mindset in a Secular Society: Promoting Evangelical Renewal and National Righteousness* (Portland, OR: Multnomah, 1984), 80.

3. Roger Williams's famous quip also bears relevance: "God requireth not an uniformity of religion to be enacted and enforced in any civil state." Roger Williams, *The Bloudy Tenent of Persecution*, ed. Richard Groves (Macon, GA: Mercer University Press, 2002), 13.

4. Oliver O'Donovan, "Reflections on Pluralism," *Princeton Seminary Bulletin* 29 (2008): 55.

5. Dallas Willard, "Being a Christian in a Pluralistic Society," The Student, 1992, https://dwillard.org/articles/being-a-christian-in-a-pluralistic-society.

6. John Piper, "Making Room for Atheism," Desiring God, August 10, 2005, http://www.desiringgod.org/articles/making-room-for-atheism.

7. S. M. Hutchens, "Toleration and Divine Forbearance," *Touchstone* 29, no. 4 (August 2016): 33.

8. Richard J. Mouw, *Uncommon Decency: Christian Civility in an Uncivil World*, 2nd ed. (Downers Grove, IL: InterVarsity, 2010), 143.

9. Richard J. Mouw and Sander Griffioen, *Pluralisms and Horizons: An Essay in Christian Public Philosophy* (Grand Rapids: Eerdmans, 1993), 106.

10. Larry Siedentop, *Inventing the Individual: The Origins of Western Liberalism* (Cambridge, MA: Belknap, 2014), 360.

11. Sylvie Avakian, "Christianity and Secularisation in the West and the Middle East: A Theological Stance," *Journal of Religious History* 40, no. 3 (September 2016): 383.

12. Jacques Maritain, *On the Use of Philosophy: Three Essays*, Princeton Legacy Library (Princeton: Princeton University Press, 2015), 24.

13. Abraham Kuyper, *Our Program: A Christian Political Manifesto*, ed. Harry Van Dyke, Jordan J. Ballor, and Melvin Flikkema, Collected Works in Public Theology (Bellingham, WA: Lexham, 2015), 68.

14. Peter Somers Heslam, *Creating a Christian Worldview: Abraham Kuyper's Lectures on Calvinism* (Grand Rapids: Eerdmans, 1998), 156.

15. Heslam, *Creating a Christian Worldview*, 66.

16. Steven D. Smith, *The Rise and Decline of American Religious Freedom* (Cambridge, MA: Harvard University Press, 2014), 101.

17. S. Smith, *Rise and Decline of American Religious Freedom*, 102.

18. On the theological significance of the waxing and waning of Christianity's influence throughout various periods of history, see Robert A. Markus, *Saeculum: History and Society in the Theology of St Augustine*, 2nd ed. (Cambridge: Cambridge University Press, 1989), 54.

19. Robert A. Markus, *Christianity and the Secular* (Notre Dame, IN: University of Notre Dame Press, 2006), 56.

20. Markus, *Christianity and the Secular*, 56.

21. *Catechism of the Catholic Church*, Vatican, para. 1906, accessed September 14, 2020, http://www.vatican.va/archive/ccc_css/archive/catechism/p3s1c2a2.htm#I.

22. George Duke, "The Common Good," in *Natural Law Jurisprudence*, ed. George Duke and Robert P. George (Cambridge: Cambridge University Press, 2017), 376.

23. This list is by no means exhaustive. My thinking is informed here by the work of the New Natural Law school. For an example of this type of thinking, see John Finnis, *Natural Law and Natural Rights*, 2nd ed. (Oxford: Oxford University Press, 2011).

24. On the dangers of Christian nationalism and civil religion, see Søren Kierkegaard and Howard A. Johnson, *Kierkegaard's Attack upon "Christendom" 1854–1855*, trans. Walter Lowrie, 2nd ed. (Princeton: Princeton University Press, 1968); and Stephen Backhouse, *Kierkegaard's Critique of Christian Nationalism*, Oxford Theology and Religion Monographs (Oxford: Oxford University Press, 2011).

25. Markus, *Christianity and the Secular*, 65.

26. James Davidson Hunter and Os Guinness, eds., *Articles of Faith, Articles of Peace: The Religious Liberty Clauses and the American Public Philosophy* (Washington, DC: Brookings Institute, 1990); and John Courtney Murray, *We Hold These Truths: Catholic Reflections on the American Proposition* (Lanham, MD: Sheed & Ward, 2005).

27. For more on the theme of common grace, see Henry R. Van Til, *The Calvinistic Concept of Culture*, 2nd ed. (Grand Rapids: Baker, 1959), 117–36; and Cornelius Van Til, *Common Grace and the Gospel*, 2nd ed. (Phillipsburg, NJ: P&R, 2015). Abraham Kuyper grounds a doctrine of common grace in the Noahic covenant. For more, see Abraham Kuyper, *Common Grace: God's Gifts for a Fallen World, Volume 1*, ed. Jordan J. Ballor and Stephen Grabill, trans. Nelson D. Kloosterman and Ed M. van der Maas, Collected Works in Public Theology (Bellingham, WA: Lexham, 2016), 10–13.

28. I want to express gratitude to my friend Joe Rigney for helping me think through this insight with greater clarity.

29. This phrase is associated with Pope Pius IX's encyclical "The Syllabus of Errors." On the relationship between Roman Catholic magisterial teaching and its transformation throughout time, see Charles E. Curran, *Catholic Social Teaching, 1891–Present: A Historical, Theological, and Ethical Analysis* (Washington, DC: Georgetown University Press, 2002).

30. Peter A. Lillback, "Pluralism, Postmodernity, and Religious Liberty: The Abiding Necessity of Free Speech and Religious Convictions in the Public Square," *Journal of Ecumenical Studies* 44, no. 1 (2009): 39.

31. J. Daryl Charles, *Retrieving the Natural Law: A Return to Moral First Things* (Grand Rapids: Eerdmans, 2008), 56.

32. John David Hughey, "The Theological Frame of Religious Liberty," *Christian Century* 80, no. 45 (November 1963): 1367.

33. David French and Alexandra Desantis, "Episode 9: Robert P. George," Liberty Files (podcast), *National Review*, June 21, 2017, https://www.nationalreview.com/podcasts/ordered-liberty/liberty-files/.

34. "Nor is religious freedom simply the right of any one church to fulfill its own particular mission, while other faiths in the same state are denied that right. Espousal of religious freedom for one's own church, therefore, must also include the espousal of the right of all other churches and religious traditions. This means that freedom and human rights must be the concern of all religions everywhere." James E. Wood, "A Biblical View of Religious Liberty," *Ecumenical Review* 30, no. 1 (January 1978): 40.

35. William Penn made an argument for religious liberty on the basis of neighbor love. See Lillback, "Pluralism, Postmodernity, and Religious Liberty," 36.

36. Oliver O'Donovan, *Resurrection and Moral Order: An Outline for Evangelical Ethics* (Grand Rapids: Eerdmans, 1994), 228.

37. James K. A. Smith, *Awaiting the King: Reforming Public Theology* (Grand Rapids: Baker Academic, 2017), 163.

38. Rebecca C. Mathis, "The Roots of Religious Liberty in Scripture," *Sewanee Theological Review* 55, no. 4 (2012): 402.

39. Roger Williams, "The Ship of State Letter, ca. January 1654/55," in *The Correspondence of Roger Williams: 1654–1682*, ed. Glenn W. LaFantasie (Hanover, NH: Brown University Press, 1988), 419–25.

40. James Calvin Davis, *The Moral Theology of Roger Williams: Christian Conviction and Public Ethics* (Louisville: Westminster John Knox, 2004), 111.

41. For an explanation of Rawls's "overlapping consensus," see John Rawls, *Political Liberalism*, 2nd ed. (New York: Columbia University Press, 2005), 133–72.

42. Martha Nussbaum, *Liberty of Conscience: In Defense of America's Tradition of Religious Equality* (New York: Basic Books, 2010), 362.

43. Nussbaum, *Liberty of Conscience*, 361.

44. Williams, *Bloudy Tenent of Persecution*, 246.

45. Davis, *Moral Theology of Roger Williams*, 122.

46. "Public reason" refers to Rawls's exhortation that in liberal societies there should be a "pursuit of a common ground on which people can stand despite deep ethical and religious differences." See Charles Larmore, "Public Reason," in *The Cambridge Companion to John Rawls*, ed. Samuel Freeman (Cambridge: Cambridge University Press, 2002), 368. See also Micah Watson, "'The Late Rawls': What Is Public Reason?," in *John Rawls and Christian Social Engagement*, ed. Greg Forster and Anthony B. Bradley (Lanham, MD: Lexington Books, 2015), 29–45.

47. For a review of the impact of Rawlsian liberalism on religious discourse in society, see Johannes Van Der Ven, "The Religious Hermeneutics of Public Reasoning: From Paul to Rawls," in *Rawls and Religion*, ed. Tom Bailey and Valentina Gentile (New York: Columbia University Press, 2014), 170–94; Peter Jonkers, "A Reasonable Faith? Pope Benedict's Response to Rawls," in *Rawls and Religion*; and Robert Song, *Christianity and Liberal Society* (Oxford: Oxford University Press, 2006).

48. Harlan Beckley, "Christian Affirmation of Rawls's Idea, Part 1," *Journal of Religious Ethics* 13, no. 2 (Fall 1985): 235.

49. Matthew J. Franck, "The Unreasonableness of Secular Public Reason," *Public Discourse*, August 28, 2015, http://www.thepublicdiscourse.com/2015/08/14619/.

50. Nicholas Wolterstorff, "Why We Should Reject What Liberalism Tells Us about Speaking and Acting in Public for Religious Reasons," in *Religious and Contemporary Liberalism*, ed. Paul J. Weithman (Notre Dame, IN: Notre Dame University Press, 1997), 171.

51. See Wolterstorff, "Why We Should Reject What Liberalism Tells Us," 179.

52. J. Smith, *Awaiting the King*, 153.

53. As Richard John Neuhaus writes, "A perverse notion of disestablishment of religion leads to the establishment of the state as church." Richard John Neuhaus,

The Naked Public Square: Religion and Democracy in America, 2nd ed. (Grand Rapids: Eerdmans, 1988), 86.

54. Neuhaus, *Naked Public Square*, 66.

55. Jeffrey Stout, *Ethics after Babel: The Languages of Morals and Their Discontents* (Princeton: Princeton University Press, 2001), 233–34.

56. For more on the political relevance of Augustine's book 19, see Oliver O'Donovan, "Augustine's City of God XIX and Western Political Thought," *Dionysius* 11 (December 1987): 89–110; and Oliver O'Donovan, *Bonds of Imperfection* (Grand Rapids: Eerdmans, 2003), 48–72.

57. Augustine, *The City of God against the Pagans*, ed. R. W. Dyson, Cambridge Texts in the History of Political Thought (Cambridge: Cambridge University Press, 1998), 945–47. For more on the topic of Augustine and religious liberty, see John Rist, "Augustine and Religious Freedom," in *Christianity and Freedom*, vol. 1, *Historical Perspectives*, ed. Timothy Samuel Shah and Allen D. Hertzke, Cambridge Studies in Law and Christianity (New York: Cambridge University Press, 2016), 103–22; and Perez Zagorin, *How the Idea of Religious Toleration Came to the West* (Princeton: Princeton University Press, 2003), 45–56.

58. Augustine, *City of God*, 945.

59. Augustine, *City of God*, 946.

60. Song, *Christianity and Liberal Society*, 171.

61. Augustine, *City of God*, 946.

62. Augustine, *City of God*, 946.

63. Augustine, *City of God*, 947.

64. Augustine, *City of God*, 947.

65. Markus, *Saeculum*, 102.

66. J. Smith, *Awaiting the King*, 218.

67. Lesslie Newbigin, *Foolishness to the Greeks: The Gospel and Western Culture* (Grand Rapids: Eerdmans, 1988), 132.

68. Augustine, *City of God*, 947.

69. Franck, "Two Tales," 23.

70. Markus, *Christianity and the Secular*, 69.

Conclusion Does Religious Liberty Require Liberal Democracy?

1. Peter A. Lillback, "Pluralism, Postmodernity, and Religious Liberty: The Abiding Necessity of Free Speech and Religious Convictions in the Public Square," *Journal of Ecumenical Studies* 44, no. 1 (2009): 53.

Epilogue Liberal Democracy and Religious Liberty

1. Roger Scruton, *How to Be a Conservative* (London: Bloomsbury Continuum, 2014), 80.

2. Robert Audi and Nicholas Wolterstorff, *Religion in the Public Square: The Place of Religious Convictions in Political Debate* (Lanham, MD: Rowman & Littlefield, 1997), 109.

3. John D. Inazu, *Confident Pluralism: Surviving and Thriving through Deep Difference* (Chicago: University of Chicago Press, 2016), 6.